Utopia beyond Capitalism in Contemporary Literature

New Horizons in Contemporary Writing

In the wake of unprecedented technological and social change, contemporary literature has evolved a dazzling array of new forms that traditional modes and terms of literary criticism have struggled to keep up with. *New Horizons in Contemporary Writing* presents cutting-edge research scholarship that provides new insights into this unique period of creative and critical transformation.

Series Editors:
Martin Eve and Bryan Cheyette

Editorial Board: Siân Adiseshiah (University of Lincoln, UK), Sara Blair (University of Michigan, USA), Peter Boxall (University of Sussex, UK), Robert Eaglestone (Royal Holloway, University of London, UK), Rita Felski (University of Virginia, USA), Rachael Gilmour (Queen Mary, University of London, UK), Caroline Levine (University of Wisconsin–Madison, USA), Roger Luckhurst (Birkbeck, University of London, UK), Adam Kelly (York University, UK), Antony Rowland (Manchester Metropolitan University, UK), John Schad (Lancaster University, UK), Pamela Thurschwell (University of Sussex, UK), Ted Underwood (University of Illinois at Urbana-Champaign, USA).

Volumes in the series:
Creaturely Forms in Contemporary Literature, Dominic O'Key
Thomas Pynchon and the Digital Humanities, Erik Ketzan
Northern Irish Writing after the Troubles, Caroline Magennis
Jeanette Winterson's Narratives of Desire, Shareena Z. Hamzah-Osbourne
Transatlantic Fictions of 9/11 and the War on Terror, Susana Araújo

Life Lines: Writing Transcultural Adoption, John McLeod
South African Literature's Russian Soul, Jeanne-Marie Jackson
The Politics of Jewishness in Contemporary World Literature, Isabelle Hesse
Writing after Postcolonialism: Francophone North African Literature in Transition, Jane Hiddleston
David Mitchell's Post-Secular World, Rose Harris-Birtill
New Media and the Transformation of Postmodern American Literature, Casey Michael Henry
Postcolonialism after World Literature, Lorna Burns
Jonathan Lethem and the Galaxy of Writing, Joseph Brooker
The Contemporary Post-Apocalyptic Novel, Diletta De Cristofaro
David Foster Wallace's Toxic Sexuality, Edward Jackson
Wanderwords: Language Migration in American Literature, Maria Lauret
Contemporary Fiction, Celebrity Culture, and the Market for Modernism, Carey Mickalites

Forthcoming volumes:
Encyclopaedism and Totality in Contemporary Fiction, Kiron Ward

Utopia beyond Capitalism in Contemporary Literature

A Commons Poetics

Raphael Kabo

BLOOMSBURY ACADEMIC
LONDON • NEW YORK • OXFORD • NEW DELHI • SYDNEY

BLOOMSBURY ACADEMIC
Bloomsbury Publishing Plc
50 Bedford Square, London, WC1B 3DP, UK
1385 Broadway, New York, NY 10018, USA
29 Earlsfort Terrace, Dublin 2, Ireland

BLOOMSBURY, BLOOMSBURY ACADEMIC and the Diana logo
are trademarks of Bloomsbury Publishing Plc

First published in Great Britain 2023
Paperback edition published 2025

Copyright © Raphael Kabo, 2023, 2025

Raphael Kabo has asserted his right under the Copyright,
Designs and Patents Act, 1988, to be identified as Author of this work.

For legal purposes the Acknowledgements on pp. xi–xii constitute an
extension of this copyright page.

Series design by Eleanor Rose
Cover illustration by Annabel Hewitson

All rights reserved. No part of this publication may be reproduced or transmitted
in any form or by any means, electronic or mechanical, including photocopying,
recording, or any information storage or retrieval system, without prior
permission in writing from the publishers.

Bloomsbury Publishing Plc does not have any control over, or responsibility for,
any third-party websites referred to or in this book. All internet addresses given
in this book were correct at the time of going to press. The author and publisher
regret any inconvenience caused if addresses have changed or sites have ceased
to exist, but can accept no responsibility for any such changes.

A catalogue record for this book is available from the British Library.

A catalog record for this book is available from the Library of Congress.

ISBN:	HB:	978-1-3502-8855-3
	PB:	978-1-3502-8859-1
	ePDF:	978-1-3502-8856-0
	eBook:	978-1-3502-8857-7

Series: New Horizons in Contemporary Writing

Typeset by Integra Software Services Pvt. Ltd.

To find out more about our authors and books visit www.bloomsbury.com
and sign up for our newsletters.

For my parents Elena and Vladimir, who built their utopia.

Contents

List of figures   x
Acknowledgements   xi

Introduction   1

1   Commons beyond capitalism: *That Winter the Wolf Came*   25
2   Utopias beyond borders: *Exit West*   55
3   Utopias beyond disaster: *New York 2140*   93
4   Utopias beyond death: *Walkaway* and *The Book of Joan*   133

Epilogue   169

Bibliography   176
Index   189

Figures

1. Harry Pettit, 'The Cosmopolis of the Future' from *King's Views of New York* (New York: Moses King, 1908). Image courtesy of The Skyscraper Museum — 102
2. Front cover of *New York 2140* by Kim Stanley Robinson, copyright © 2017. Image reprinted by permission of Orbit, an imprint of Hachette Book Group, Inc — 107
3. The Hooverville in Central Park, New York City, 1930s. Image courtesy of the Everett Collection — 114

Acknowledgements

There is no better way to open a study on the commons than by evoking a commons of my own. To paraphrase Sophie Lewis, herself quoting others: all authorship is co-authorship, and all writing is shared, collective labour.[1]

I am deeply grateful to those who graciously offered their time and knowledge in reading drafts of this book and its various primordial permutations: Katie Stone, Harriet Israel, Louis Klee, Georgia Kartas, Jenna Vincent, Kira Scaife and Dominica Duckworth. I am fortunate and humbled to edit a book in such company – I do not believe it is usually meant to be so much fun. I extend my sincere gratitude to my PhD supervisor Dr Caroline Edwards for originally pointing me towards the horizon of utopian theory. Both she and co-supervisor Professor Martin Paul Eve supported me unfailingly throughout the development of my thesis and extended this support as I shaped it into a monograph. Thank you very much to the anonymous peer reviewers at Bloomsbury Academic, whose fresh eyes, wide-ranging knowledge and generous commentary helped me hone this project into a book I am proud of.

The academic communities which have surrounded me for the last five years were wonderful spaces to develop and explore many of the ideas in this book, some in practice. First and foremost, I am grateful with all my heart to my brilliant utopian comrade and co-conspirator Katie Stone: an inspiration and a joy who creates concrete utopias wherever she goes. To many others in the orbit of the academic community at Birkbeck University I am deeply grateful for your time, work and energy. In particular, thank you to my friends and academic peers Sasha Myerson, Amy Butt, Rachel Hill, Sinéad Murphy, Sing Yun Lee and Tom Dillon for times of critical utopian joy and collective close reading. Thank you to everyone who came to, shared dreams at and helped with the 2018 Utopian Acts conference. Thank you to the Beyond Gender Collective, the London Science Fiction Research Community, the Society for Utopian Studies and the Utopian Studies Society for creating accessible spaces for collective imagining, creation and reflection.

Sections of this book have appeared in earlier forms as journal articles, and I extend my gratitude to the editors, peer reviewers and proofreaders of those publications. An earlier version of Chapter 1 appeared as '"Come here, it sang, listen": Juliana Spahr's commons poetics in *That Winter the Wolf Came*', *Textual Practice* 37, no. 7 (2021): 1195–214. An earlier version of Chapter Three appeared as '"Life! Life!": The Precarious Utopianism of Kim Stanley Robinson's *New York 2140*', *Utopian Studies* 32, no. 2 (2021): 252–76.

My deepest gratitude to my mother Elena Govor for her love and her embodied and powerful understanding of utopianism. To my partner Harriet Israel, supportive and patient as only a fellow academic can be, thank you from the very bottom of my heart.

Thank you, finally, to the activists of countless anti-capitalist organizations in the UK and around the world who give me hope for better futures – if there is a shred of inspiration for you in these pages, I will be overjoyed that the collective labour of this commons has had a material impact.

Note

1   Sophie Lewis, *Full Surrogacy Now: Feminism Against Family* (London: Verso, 2019), 26–7.

Introduction

Someone once said that it is easier to imagine the end of the world than to imagine the end of capitalism.
Fredric Jameson, 'Future City'¹

We live in capitalism. Its power seems inescapable. So did the divine right of kings. Any human power can be resisted and changed by human beings. Resistance and change often begin in art, and very often in our art – the art of words.
Ursula K. Le Guin, speech at the 2014 National Book Awards[2]

Writing in 2003, cultural theorist Fredric Jameson argued that the utopian literature of the twentieth-century *fin de siècle* had changed considerably in comparison with its forebears of a century prior. The period from 1880 to 1910 had seen an explosion in utopian literature, with hundreds of works inspiring real-world political reform movements and the foundation of utopian intentional communities. The new utopian literature of the 1990s, however, was no longer involved in representing fully developed utopian worlds, nor did it seek to bring such worlds into being outside the realm of fiction. This transition could be articulated as a shift from a didactic to an exploratory mode in utopian thought; rather than helping readers imagine better concrete futures, twentieth- and early twenty-first-century utopian literature was structured by 'all the arguments about how Utopia should be constructed in the first place'.[3] Jameson argues persuasively that this change had occurred because the contemporary globalized world is located so deep within the late capitalist totality that its subjects are unable to even imagine a utopian totality in opposition, and after the 1990s, the function of utopian literature lies in revealing and analysing the 'ideological closure' of this system.[4] On the basis of these assertions, Jameson deploys his now infamous phrase: 'it is easier to imagine the end of the world than to imagine the end of capitalism'.[5] The world which Jameson imagines ending here is the world of late capitalism, but this parasitical system now figures so centrally in every social relation, every ecosystem and every human and more-than-human body on the planet that its destruction would surely necessitate an apocalypse on a planetary scale. Utopia, in this context, becomes not fundamental, but occasional; not transformative, but investigative; not constructive, but palliative.

Almost twenty years have passed since Jameson's utopian magnum opus, *Archaeologies of the Future*, decisively critiqued the possibility of genuine utopian transformation in the late capitalist present. Since that time, all three elements of this equation – utopian literature, capitalism and radical politics – have changed significantly. While it continues to be cited without a particular desire for re-evaluation, Jameson's argument is overdue for a rethink. Utopian literature and utopian critical theory of the last decade provide new insights on the question of utopia and late capitalism. This book suggests that the utopias of which Jameson wrote did not represent the end of the road, but merely signalled a necessary readjustment. Utopias of the 2010s and early 2020s have again begun to reshape and reinvigorate the possibility of profound social transformation; they do so, crucially, from within the late capitalist present.

The contemporary utopian texts analysed in this book employ the anti-capitalist concept of the 'commons', a form of social and political organization widespread in pre-capitalist Great Britain, Ireland and Europe. Despite the almost total eradication of pastoral commons in Europe by capitalist forces in the sixteenth century and their subsequent four-century-long demonization in Western liberal and neoliberal economic theory, the ideas in which they were grounded are being rehabilitated in the twenty-first century.[6] In literature, this comeback manifests in two ways. Firstly, these texts pay an invigorated attention to the simultaneously negating and productive possibilities of utopia, the no-place which is also the good-place. This manifests as a refusal of the capitalist reality of the present coupled with a committed representation of new realities which emerge from within it. Secondly, they demonstrate a newly politicized interest in the representation and production of commons, a tendency which I identify in this book as a 'commons poetics'.[7]

I use the term 'commons poetics' throughout this book to refer to the creation of commons in literature. The poetic act (*poiesis*) is a 'breach of newness', an act of creative imagination which generates a new world.[8] This act manifests on three distinct yet interrelated levels in the texts I explore in this book. At the narrative level, we witness the representation of commons and related collective formations – unions, anarchic communities, occupations and camps. At the level of language and form, commons emerge between texts and sentences through tactics including intertextuality, parataxis, polyphony and reflexivity. These techniques bring different texts, and different parts of the same texts, into discourse and interplay with one another. At the level of politics, these texts hold the utopian power to transform social life, illustrating Paul Ricoeur's claim that 'while ideology bears the stamp of rhetoric, utopia bears that of poetics to the extent that utopia is nothing other than the invention of a social fable capable, it is believed, to "change life"'.[9] By assembling commons of fellow readers, finessing and shaping their utopian imaginaries, and creating textual spaces for them to see themselves represented, these texts bring nearer the possibility of utopian worlds in the present. For this reason, I refer to the texts in this book as 'commons utopias' – poietic works which create common utopian worlds through a combination of narrative, formal technique and political commitment.

Transformations of utopia

For revolutionaries, visionaries and malcontents, utopian texts illuminate alternatives to the stultifying and suffocating realities of their present. The best of these utopian works engage in 'the persistent attempt to imagine alternatives to the present state of affairs while remaining assiduously of the world'.[10] They not only construct and envisage such alternatives, but educate their readers, showing them the ways in which alternative futures might become concrete utopian presents. In utopian philosopher Ernst Bloch's work, this core quality of utopian literature is described as *docta spes*, 'comprehended hope', while for contemporary utopian critic Tom Moylan, utopian literature forms the 'seeds for changing the present society' through 'willed transformation', serving 'to stimulate in its readers a desire for a better life and to motivate that desire toward action by conveying a sense that the world is not fixed once and for all'.[11] In each of these cases, utopian writing is understood as a transformational tool with the power to finesse the hopes and wishes of its audience into deed and action.

To function as seeds for the transformation of society, utopias must be written and rewritten from within the ongoing present moment. Jameson's critique – that it is no longer possible to imagine a world fundamentally distinct from the everyday, familiar one of late capitalism – is a response to the unmooring of utopian literature from the everyday struggles of real-world political conflicts. This diminishment of utopian literature's political acuity began as early as the 1970s, with the establishment of neoliberal late capitalism as the dominant form of economic governance worldwide. As a form of opposition, contemporary utopian texts return the depiction of concrete political transformations to the forefront of their imagined worlds.

In the five centuries since Thomas More's *Concerning the Best State of a Commonwealth, and the New Island of Utopia* (1516) neologized the term, utopian literature has undergone a set of shifts in style and subject matter. Much valuable work has been done in the field of utopian studies to periodize these shifts and place them within the social and cultural contexts of their emergence; I aim in this introduction to bring this lineage of critical work up to date with the most recent developments in the primary literature. From the second half of the twentieth century, three key tendencies have emerged in utopian literature, which I delineate as *critical* (1960s–1970s); *late* (1980s–2000s), and *commons* (2010s to the present) utopias. Commons utopias, the new periodization I offer in this book, share features with both critical and late utopias. They return to the powerfully articulated political demands of critical utopias but push back against the distance which these texts placed between the real worlds of their authors and the utopian worlds of their texts. In their refusal to escape from the precarities of our present, they are more akin to late utopias, but they lack the cynical, postmodern unease with political commitment which Jameson identified in these texts.

Commons utopias draw their political energy from ongoing oppositional movements and political eruptions, connecting in this way to the origins of the influential science fiction utopias of the 1970s, which were conceptualized *post hoc* as critical utopias by Tom Moylan in the 1980s. These texts, of which the best-known examples, by way of Moylan's historicizing work, are Ursula K. Le Guin's *The Dispossessed* (1974), Joanna Russ's *The Female Man* (1975), Marge Piercy's *Woman on the Edge of Time* (1976) and Samuel R. Delany's *Trouble on Triton* (1976), were immanent to the major oppositional movements of the 1960s and 1970s: second wave feminism, the Civil Rights Movement, the Vietnam War protests and the global student and worker demonstrations of 1968.

In line with the analytical, highly informed political energies of these movements, critical utopias returned to an 'Enlightenment sense of critique – that is expressions of oppositional thought, unveiling, debunking, of both the genre itself and the historical situation', rejecting utopia 'as blueprint' while preserving it 'as dream'.[12] Critical utopias rendered the concept of utopia provisional and porous, offering to their readers multiple competing better worlds rather than a single ideal world. In these texts, for the first time, the utopian explorer often travelled between utopias and dystopias, or between the real world and multiple alternative worlds. In the process, the utopian imaginary was rendered as increasingly plausible and achievable; for the first time, too, these texts offered a range of realistically grounded processes, strategies and tactics for oppositional action, which could be employed in the present to transition it towards a utopian imaginary. Like earlier utopian traditions, however, critical utopias continued to locate their utopian worlds in spaces or times separate from the realist present; this alterity was primarily a consequence of their emergence within the booming mid-century science fiction tradition, which offered a panoply of wildly imaginative worlds to its readers. Thus, *The Dispossessed* is set on the twin planets of hyper-capitalist Urras and anarcho-syndicalist Annares, and is an early entry in Le Guin's *Hainish Cycle* of books, in which the Earth is but one member of a developing interstellar community. *Woman on the Edge of Time* and *The Female Man* are both set closer to home but their utopian worlds are contrasted with dystopias. Connie, the protagonist of *Woman on the Edge of Time*, visits a utopian community in the year 2137, but is warned that the wrong decision in the present might instead bring to bear a vision of an equally possible future which is a hyper-capitalist dystopian hell. Similarly, while the multiple protagonists of *The Female Man* visit a utopian, lesbian-separatist future where all men have long been exterminated by a virus, they also become trapped in a technological dystopia where women fight and enslave men in an endless, literal war of the sexes.

In some ways, the anti-utopian visions of these texts were materialized in the period between the social liberation struggles of the 1960s-1970s and the 2008 Global Financial Crisis (GFC), decades 'marked by anti-utopian deprivation rather than utopian achievement' in the shape of 'globalisation, neoliberalisation, postmodernism, technocracy, and financialisation'.[13] To these processes we can add, from the early 2000s onwards, the expansion of border regimes as a consequence of the War on Terror, the rise of asymmetrical warfare, increasing precarity for global populations, and the effects of anthropogenic climate change. In this recent period 'the vision of a completely different future, based on the annihilation of the present ... was replaced by a focus on a slower but effective change of the present'.[14] I name the utopian works of this period late utopias in acknowledgement of Jameson's work in analysing these decades as the period of the emergence of late capitalism. Key utopian texts of this time are Kim Stanley Robinson's *Three Californias* trilogy (1984–90) and *Mars* trilogy (1992–6), and Octavia Butler's unfinished *Parable* trilogy (1993, 1998). In late utopian texts, the multiple competing worlds common to the critical utopias are reduced again to a single world – Mars and the very different Californias of Butler and Robinson. Rather than presenting this world as an ideal and authoritative vision of society, these works use it as the setting for a range of utopian debates and experiments, highlighting, at the same time, the political stagnation of a present which has no sense of progress and no end in sight.

Most critical histories of utopian literature end here, not only because the hold of neoliberal late capitalism over the globe remains undiminished and unshaken, even after its first major setback in the shape of the GFC, but also because Jameson's theorization of utopia, like Moylan's before him, appears so comprehensive that it initially seems there is little left to say on the topic. However, most of the essays collected in *Archaeologies of the Future* (2005) were written in the late 1990s and early 2000s. Over fifteen years have passed since then, and while in 2004 Jameson could have confidently stated that at present 'there is not the slightest prospect of reform, let alone revolution, in real life', the same could not be said of the decade which followed.[15]

The emergence of commons utopias

Commons utopias emerge in the wake of the 2008 GFC, and reflect the sense of living through a period of profound and ongoing crisis which must be reckoned with, rather than escaped from, in order to be overcome. The 2011 Occupy Movement, the 2010–12 Middle East uprisings and subsequent Syrian refugee crisis, the intensification of the climate crisis, and most recently the 2020 Covid-19 pandemic are the subsequent major historical events within which commons utopias emerge as a necessary form of directed yearning for fundamental transformation on a systemic and planetary scale. I refer to commons utopias in this study as 'post-2008 texts' because the 2008 GFC serves as the historical anchor for their understandings of utopianism and capitalism, even as it remains merely in the background of their narratives. The GFC's long-lasting effects provided greater purchase for neoliberal economic doctrines, significantly exacerbated existing social and political inequalities across the world, and engendered new forms of precarity across a wider range of subjects.[16] In the post-2008 period, 'everyone now lives capitalism in proximity to risk, threat, and ongoing anxiety at the situation that something autonomous called "life" seems to present equally, everywhere'.[17] The subjects of this precarization can no longer be distinguished nor hierarchized along traditional lines, even intersectional ones. They are increasingly all of us: the traditional working class, the managerial cadre, industrial and factory workers in the Global South, 'millennial' youth, unlucky Baby Boomers, students, academics, the unemployed, the flexibly employed, those on zero-hour contracts, those living from paycheck to paycheck, lifelong renters and mortgagers, creative freelancers, care and affective labourers, sex workers, the dispossessed, blue-collar workers, administrators and bureaucrats; in short, all those who now experience life only as a series of unfolding choices, each one opening up the heightened possibility of risk, contingency and vulnerability.

Commons utopias are distinguished from spatial, temporal and critical utopias by being set in this late capitalist totality or in imaginary worlds which are very closely related to or extrapolated from it, demonstrating Jameson's point that one of the key features of capitalism in the early twenty-first century is our newfound inability to imagine qualitatively different worlds. At the same time, they are distinguished from the late utopias by representing fully realized utopian spatialities brought to life through radical political activity. Commons utopias are thus chiefly concerned with depicting the process of creating and inhabiting utopian spaces as an opposition to the capitalist present. These spaces – commons – are of a new form, distinct from the agricultural and resource commons of the early modern period in Europe and those which still exist across the Global South. Utopian commons are embedded within capitalist worlds but separate from them. They are underpinned by sustainable relationships with the wider ecologies within which they are embedded, collective labour and processes of communal social reproduction. Gradually, through focused struggle and everyday oppositional activity, these patchwork utopias expand into larger and ever more successful social and political structures. Despite these victories, even better worlds will always lie on the horizon, because for the inhabitants of such spaces, in the words of Max Haiven, 'there will never be a common *common enough*'.[18]

A 2015 poetry collection and four novels all published in 2017 are particularly valuable examples of this emerging literary tendency: Juliana Spahr's *That Winter the Wolf Came*, Mohsin Hamid's *Exit West*, Kim Stanley Robinson's *New York 2140*, Cory Doctorow's *Walkaway* and Lidia Yuknavitch's *The Book of Joan*. Each reflects its author's interest in a specific crisis of the capitalist present, and each offers a different depiction of a commons, complete with a cast of commoners and a commonwealth of resources, which eventually surpasses the capitalist systems surrounding it. Importantly, each of these utopias is written for a key collective subject of the present, celebrating their achievements and powers, equipping them, within the world of the text, with particular technologies, and teaching their brethren outside the text specific methodologies to enact their own utopias in the present. Hamid writes of and for migrants fleeing natural and anthropogenic disasters; Robinson addresses the diverse inhabitants of the cities of the Global North, differentially exposed to profound crises across vectors including species, race, gender and age; Spahr and Doctorow's focus are the alienated, university-educated and precariously employed millennials who were the genesis of the Occupy movement; and Yuknavitch, alongside Spahr, writes for queers striving for a utopian existence beyond the strictures of heteronormative 'straight time'.[19]

These utopias have emerged from a confluence of wider tendencies in contemporary Anglophone literature, exemplifying what Raffaella Baccolini and Moylan have identified as a practice of 'genre blurring' key to contemporary utopian texts.[20] Speculation – the committed imagining of alternative worlds and different futures – remains the bedrock of utopian literature, and so all are examples of speculative literature, although in terms of their literary reception, categorization and style, they range from Booker-nominated literary fiction (*Exit West*) to pulp science fiction (*Walkaway*).[21] The variety of new literary tendencies and genres with which these novels have been associated – climate change fiction or cli-fi, critical dystopias, precarity literature and solarpunk – reflects a broader literary concern in recent decades with acknowledging and opposing the political, social and environmental crises of the capitalist present. The films *Snowpiercer* (dir. Bong Joon-ho, 2013) and *Mad Max: Fury Road* (dir. George Miller, 2015), N. K. Jemisin's *The Broken Earth* trilogy (2015–17) and the novels *The Windup Girl* (Paolo Bacigalupi, 2009), *The End We Start From* (Megan Hunter, 2017) and *All City* (Alex DiFrancesco, 2019) consider the social and cultural ramifications of destructive climate change wrought by unchecked capitalist expansion, imagining worlds which are too dry, too cold, too flooded or too tectonically precarious for sustained life, and yet where humans and non-humans continue to cling on to survival. The worlds of the novels *A Closed and Common Orbit* (Becky Chambers, 2016) and *Dear Cyborgs* (Eugene Lim, 2017) are more subtly broken, depicting far- and near-future strategies of everyday management of neoliberal precarity in what Lauren Berlant has so incisively named the 'ongoing present'.[22] The characters of these novels learn to adapt, get by and keep afloat, forming strategies, sometimes individual and sometimes collective, for mitigating neoliberal atomization and alienation.

While they are at times utopian, albeit in minor and ciphered ways, the majority of these texts do not specifically depict commons as an alternative or solution to contemporary crises. The collectives which come together in their narratives tend to be short-lived or prone to catastrophic collapse, providing only temporary respite from the dystopian or outright post-apocalyptic worlds outside their borders. In contrast, commons utopias represent and explore collective and collaborative utopian formations, in particular ones which operate alongside capitalist social relations, but are radically opposed to them. In these texts, the commons do not collapse, but find ways to sustain themselves and their specific populations. These texts are self-aware, intentional, manifestary and radically political. They engage directly with their readerships across a variety of formats, including within their own narratives, and continue to change beyond their own emergence in the smelters of online discourse and intertextual reference, reinvigorating an older mode of reading 'as a form of communication, friendship, solace, and succour', which models 'richer forms of belonging than the diluted and impoverished forms on display in the neoliberal present'.[23] Writing from the shores of a precarious present defined by ongoing crisis, they direct their readers towards a horizon of radical alterity – a world in which capitalism is absent, or its authority is greatly diminished, and where the commons are a vital socio-political structuring form.

Commons utopian temporalities

In looking towards this activist horizon, commons utopias highlight a profound distinction between two conceptions of the future active in the current moment. As has been highlighted by a swathe of Marxist critics since the late 1980s, especially Jameson, David Harvey, Mark Fisher, Lauren Berlant, Nick Srnicek and Alex Williams, and the Laboria Cuboniks collective, the future is *absent* under capitalism: the capitalist ideology which organizes and delivers the present promises only a repetitive, cyclical future practically indistinguishable from the present, offering no fundamental sense of progress, no paradigm-shifting social transformations and no genuinely alternative political possibilities.[24]

Berlant describes the period from the early 1990s to the present day as an *ongoing present* – a formless, lingering timespan within which humans continue to survive and adapt to a constant stream of changing situations never accreting into something that could be coherently understood as an 'era' or 'age', a 'stretched out "now" that is at once intimate and estranged'.[25] The social, political and affective contours of the ongoing present are derived from several interconnected historical tendencies. In brief, these are: the consolidation of post-Fordist, immaterial labour as the dominant labour form in the global economy; the replacement of liberal forms of governance via discipline and surveillance with neoliberal modes of control and self-precarization; and the collapse, particularly in the Global North, of faith in the narratives of the 'good life ... upward mobility, job security, political and social equality, and lively, durable intimacy' alongside the meritocracy which upheld it.[26] Lastly, and significantly, the effects of anthropogenic climate change are well on their way to exerting a deleterious effect on global social security, political stability and belief in better modes of life. At the individual scale, the effects of climate change take on an appearance Hunter Lovins refers to as 'global weirding' – a play on words which captures the increasingly unpredictable, untimely and alien behaviour of the planet's hitherto comprehensible climate system.[27] Taken together, these transformations reveal the ongoing present as a time dominated and conditioned by precariousness, vulnerability, endangerment and contingency, disassociated from the temporal and spatial frameworks which had historically contained its inhabitants, and exposing them instead to a radical instability which permeates all levels of life.

Living in an ongoing present, the question then becomes not how to escape into a better future – because it is no longer accessible – but how to transform and refashion the present. In part this is because the ongoing present is not an historical period – one which is determined and produced by historical actors – but an affective one, which is felt and sensed by its inhabitants. Bodies experience the ongoing present as a glitch, impasse or loop. A glitch – such as a stutter on a video tape, a momentary forgetting, or the way in which a body or political class is forced to adapt to everyday crisis – is an interruption amidst the transition of time, a felt encounter with the sense of being outside historical progression, which brings our attention to the inconsistencies and inequalities of the present. This puts paid to Jameson's contention that the value of contemporary utopian thinking and writing is restricted purely to discovering what is missing in contemporary totality, and has little to do with concrete political transformation. *Contra* Jameson, desires, hopes and manifestations of the future function as tools for socio-political transformation in a present where the very notion of the future is under threat. Commons utopias written from within this present are recuperative, transformational glitches, forcing their readers to come up hard against the realities of the ongoing present within which they flounder, atomized and alienated from each other. Such texts present an imaginary of concrete political tactics – 'plausible desirable futures' – for generating a different future, opposed to the tactics of capitalist teleology.[28]

Contemporary Marxist critics, including Joshua Clover, Endnotes and the Invisible Committee, describe the tactics of the commune as a way to refigure capitalism from within the present. For Clover, the commune is a new 'tactic of social reproduction' and 'collective action' beyond both capitalism and programmatic communism. For Endnotes, in a reading of Marx's later work, communes appear as prefigurative transitions to collective life absent of a revolutionary break: 'the point is that communes could take on capitalist innovations, without proletarianising'.[29] Elsewhere, Endnotes describe 'communisation' as 'a rejection of the view of revolution as an event where workers take power followed by a period of transition', but as a movement of 'immediate communist measures (such as the free distribution of goods) both for their own merit, and as a way of destroying the material basis of the counter-revolution', ultimately aiming to eradicate 'all capitalist categories: exchange, money, commodities, the existence of separate enterprises, the state and – most fundamentally – wage labour and the working class itself'.[30] The Invisible Committee's call for 'an insurrectional surge' against capitalism is premised on the 'multiplication of communes, their coming into contact and forming of ties', a communizing tactic which extends from relations of friendship and rejects extant organizational structures in favour of survival tactics that wait 'neither for the numbers nor the means to get organized, and even less for the "right moment" – which never arrives'.[31] Literary evocations of utopian commons, akin to communes and communizing tactics, are based on a materialist analysis of what exists to prefigure new forms of life in the present. They represent struggles which make space and then remain within it. In the words of Christian Haines, they are a 'redefinition of what is possible in the world, as the renewal of politics through the finding of another world within this world'.[32] The targets of their opposition, while generally capitalist in nature, tend to be specific, perhaps because these commons themselves emerge most readily in liminal spaces, lacunae and peripheries where capital does not exert absolute control – the migrant camps of *Exit West*, the disaster commons of *New York 2140*, and the Canadian wilderness of *Walkaway* – or where it has long bled its subjects dry, as in *That Winter the Wolf Came* and *The Book of*

Joan. Yet from these spaces of relative freedom, the utopian commons of these texts return to the centres of capital to challenge their logics and institute new forms of mass collective being.

Commons utopias are thus profoundly prefigurative. A prefigurative ethics 'challenges the claim that the reconstitution of society can only begin after the complete overthrow of existing social arrangements'. Instead, taking up Martin Buber's argument that an anarchist politics 'must create here and now the space now possible for the thing for which we are striving, so that it may come to fulfilment then', prefiguration contends that 'action in the present must embody its goals for the future'.[33] Prefigurative action combines practical tactics for the transformation of everyday conditions in the present – direct action, strike, mutual aid, solidarity, consciousness raising, occupation and squatting – with the utopian dreaming and imagining which negate the negation of the future under capitalist realism. Thus, a prefigurative politics not only strives to create a better society in the present but ensures that the future will be a welcoming space for that society.

Max Haiven and Alex Khasnabish capture this sense of temporal continuity in the term 'radical imagination', the assemblage of narratives, hopes and archives collectively produced within anti-capitalist movements:

> On the surface level, the radical imagination is the ability to imagine the world, life and social institutions not as they are but as they might otherwise be. It is the courage and the intelligence to recognize that the world can and should be changed. But the radical imagination is not just about dreaming of different futures. It's about bringing those possible futures 'back' to work on the present, to inspire action and new forms of solidarity today.[34]

Writing on the Occupy Movement, Julian Brigstocke identifies 'foreclosure; obduracy; prefiguration; and future generations' as four tactics promoting an 'attunement to forms of temporality that recover a sense of the future as unknown, incalculable, but insisting within alternative practices in the present'.[35] The processes of recovery and ongoingness highlighted by these critics is a key feature of commons utopias, which mediate between present struggles and future imaginaries, bringing them into conversation with each other. This prefigurative method takes seriously the sense of hope and desire for an alternative future inherent in the utopian impulse, making use of this impulse to create structures of social, economic and political reproduction which ensure its transformation, through constant struggle, into concrete utopian spatialities – what Bloch productively characterizes as 'concrete utopia' in opposition to the 'dreaminess' and 'immaturity' of unrealized 'abstract utopia'. Forms of everyday struggle and everyday life depicted in commons utopias embrace what Bloch names 'anticipatory consciousness' – the transformation of future-directed affects of hope, longing and desire into a concrete, realizable set of political tools and social methodologies for escaping the ontological and conceptual limitations of the present.[36] But tools and methodologies are never enough by themselves. By working to realize a concrete utopia, Bloch writes, 'quarters are arranged for the future' within the present.[37]

The quality Brigstocke identifies as 'obduracy', or endurance, is equally vital to the development of a utopian prefigurative impulse in the here and now. Haines, examining the shift from abstract oppositional modes of critique to new, concrete forms of living otherwise, writes that 'the elsewhere springs up in the midst of things, just as new forms of life often arise from residual social forms', continuing on to say that 'the immanence of utopia – its location in the here and now – implies endurance, or the ongoing practice of insisting on deviation despite the pressure of normative regimes'. Critics including Haines also describe this notion as a utopian *militancy*. These qualities are imperative because they continually return the oppositional subject to the problems and challenges of the present, never allowing them to stray into abstract utopian daydreaming. The goal of this venture is not punishment, although as any activist will agree, obdurate exposure to the instruments of capitalism is exhausting and debilitating, but the realization of concrete ways of utopian life in the present. To recognize the value of concrete utopianism, which transforms the present with ways of life borrowed from a utopian future, we must also understand the form that these 'quarters … for the future' take – the shape of utopian spaces.

Commons utopian spatialities

A broad definition of a utopia might be *a space considered by its producer(s) to be significantly better than the space within which it was produced*. Such spaces can equally be real-world spaces such as exilic utopian communities, occupations, squats and commons, or represented spaces which exist only within the pages of utopian narratives. The uniting quality is that of space – utopia must be understood as a spatial construct first and foremost. Much of contemporary utopian theory approaches its subject from angles which diminish this spatial relation, understanding it as a hermeneutic method, a form of affective relation, or a political process. Gathering together a number of these strands, Ruth Levitas argues that the 'utopian method' begins with an 'expression of the desire for a better way of being or of living', then works to explore culture for its 'utopian aspects, its expression of longing or fulfilment', before extending to concrete plans for actual transformation in 'the social and structural domain'. The utopian method in this context is an 'education of desire', a term Levitas derives from the work of Miguel Abensour: it helps subjects understand what they are missing and wanting in the real world, then provides ways to enact these desires.[38] It is not, however, a method which itself generates utopian spaces – it simply emerges within them, as the result of modes of directed social dreaming and imagining. David Harvey, in a similar fashion, warns that a 'spatiotemporal utopianism' is always limited and enclosed by the spaces within which it finds itself developing: 'to materialize a space is to engage with closure (however temporary) which is an authoritarian act'.[39]

For David M. Bell, utopianisms which refuse to create utopian places are a form of 'topophobic' escape from the ongoing spaces and times which come to define the existence of contemporary subjects. Born of a profound distrust of place, 'these escapes may reject closure and inspire attempts to create better place but are not attempts to create better place themselves'.[40] In a prefigurative mode, Bell instead charts a form of utopianism which 'creates the future as an open, yet-to-be-determined space unfolding from the here-and-now ... a process of place-making' which 'makes its flight create'.[41] This strand of theory draws both on Gilles Deleuze and Félix Guattari's sense of immanence and on the work of Henri Lefebvre. Space, much like prefigurative time, is best understood not as a limiting, static container, but an ongoing process born of social interrelations clustered at a particular nexus. This reading of space as socially produced was developed by Lefebvre in *La production de l'espace* (1974, translated into English in 1991 as *The Production of Space*), as an extension of Marx's theory of modes of production. In Lefebvre's understanding, 'the social relations of production have a social existence to the extent that they have a spatial existence; they project themselves into a space, becoming inscribed there, and in the process producing the space itself'.[42] These theories were subsequently elaborated by critics including Harvey, Doreen Massey, Edward W. Soja and Philip E. Wegner. In their work, we see the totality of space divided into *perceived space* (the everyday space of production and social reproduction), *conceived space* (the ideal space of architecture, planning and social engineering) and *social space*, which, through political action, combines perceived and conceived space to transform and reappropriate them into 'a different space (either the space of a counter-culture, or a counter-space in the sense of an initially utopian alternative to actually existing "real" space)'.[43] Harvey describes this 'third space' as *imagined space*, a particularly productive term suggesting that social/spatial transformations can safely be imagined in such spaces before being ultimately deployed upon physical space. A reformulation closer in spirit to Lefebvre's would perhaps be 'spaces of re-presentation' – the repeated, and ever-changing, presenting of spaces back to those who produce them.

While Soja and Wegner locate utopian literature generally in the realm of conceived space, commons utopias – through their imaginary of utopian spaces produced and inhabited in radical opposition to the capitalist present – are situated in social space. Commons utopias not only conceive of alternative spaces, but aim to bring them into concrete being by educating, inspiring and energizing their readers to transform their own present. Their utopian spaces are thus not only grounded, that is, necessarily spatial, but are also peopled, that is, necessarily political. Each of the texts I look at in this book has a living, complex cast of political actors with differing, albeit variously utopian, desires for social transformation on scales ranging from the intimate to the planetary. As utopian critics since the 1970s have contended, utopian space is certainly not a totalitarian blueprint for specific forms of happiness or perfection, but it is also not a constant struggle between the potentialities of a temporally oriented utopian method and the (separate, distinct) closures immanent within the more traditional notion of space. Rather, it is produced through the complex, ongoing interrelation of place-making methods that, as Bell has it, '*make place through their taking place*'.[44] Massey, a feminist critical geographer, describes place memorably as 'a simultaneity of stories-so-far ... always under construction, ... a product of relations – between, relations which are necessarily embedded material practices which have to be carried out'.[45] Commons utopias are cyclical, ongoing place-making machines: they cultivate and support political subjects who then work to transform their space in a utopian mode. Political activity of this sort remains fundamentally spatial, and such spaces remain spaces for oppositional politics – for utopian forms of transformation – to occur. Utopian commons are an example of what Jacques Rancière has described as political spaces for 'the appearance of a subject: the people, the workers, the citizens'. Their emergence 'consists in re-figuring space, that is in what is to be done, to be seen and to be named in it'.[46] In the field of commons theory, this mode of activity is categorized as *commoning*.

Contemporary commons theorists, in particular Massimo De Angelis, Max Haiven, and Stavros Stavrides, have identified the process of commoning as one of the three pillars of commons which are successful by virtue of being sustainable both ecologically and socially, for their human and non-human inhabitants alike. The other two features are a community of commoners willing to provide labour and services for each other, and a commonwealth – the sources of material and immaterial resources upon which such labour bears fruit.[47] This conception of a commons as a complex system, networked with other commons, expands significantly, and usefully, on the more traditional understanding of the commons solely as 'a territorially defined space'.[48] Moving away from a space called 'the commons' to a process or practice called 'commoning' allows for the inclusion of intangible, temporal, knowledge-based and non-anthropocentric forms under the general form of commoning. It also returns an oppositional framework to a field which has been largely seen in the twentieth century as exclusively economic. Commons have always been a threat to capitalism (as demonstrated by their centuries-long expropriation by capital), but when these systems are oriented towards a networked expansion of commoning processes across social, political and ecological fields, they can 'represent a meaningful challenge to capitalist processes and statists' neoliberal policies'.[49]

The foregrounding of commoning as a process does not, however, do away with a conception of a commons as the *site* of an iterative, spatially oriented process which could be termed 'prefigurative utopian inhabiting' or 'commoning'. This, in turn, allows the discourse on commons to turn away from an understanding of the commons as a space at constant risk of 'the spectre of its enclosure', and towards understanding them instead as an oppositional spatio-temporal system which itself challenges enclosure practices.[50] As we shall discover in the coming chapters, one of the ways in which this challenge is mounted is through the telling of prefigurative stories about utopian victories and transformations in commons spaces. Understood thus, commoning practices are a form of utopian prefiguration which prefigure further prefiguration: further commoning and further productive inhabiting of utopian space which aims for, but never attains, the commons which is common enough.

Structure

Each of the following four chapters offers a close reading of a commons utopia. Chapter 1 focuses on contemporary American poet Juliana Spahr's 2015 collection *That Winter the Wolf Came*, exploring the way in which this work makes use of different modalities of the commons – material, literary and temporal. Although Spahr's voice is often negative and cynical, it is ultimately an expression of deep yearning and longing for a utopian revolution which would transform society at its foundations. In the meantime, Spahr writes of the long, quotidian history of those struggling under capitalism to tear it apart through riot, multi-species care, lyrical erotics and allied forms of oppositional life in common. Spahr's key subjects – animals, petrocapitalism, activist movement making and futurity – return in each of the book's other chapters, making *That Winter the Wolf Came* an important touchstone for this study.

In Chapter 2, I argue that Mohsin Hamid's fabulesque 2017 migration novel *Exit West* represents the emergence of a planetary mobile commons predicated on autonomy and care. In this novel, we witness a world very similar to the contemporary present – defined by border regimes, military violence and nation-state governmentality – slowly transform into a mobile commons of free movement guided by a post-state, no-borders planetary ethics. As the novel's cast, denizens of the Global South, build a new world in the decaying shell of the old, they collectively create a *Heimat*, a term used by Ernst Bloch to evoke the experience of an unalienated, universal, utopian being-at-home-in-the-world.

In Chapter 3, I read Kim Stanley Robinson's 2017 novel *New York 2140* through and against the many genres – cli-fi, historical fiction, urban fiction and science fiction – with which it plays, arguing that the world of extreme sea level rises, social turmoil, and hyperactive capitalism he depicts is not only an analogue of our own contemporary period, but also teaches its readers tactics for building a commons generated within and moving beyond disaster. Robinson's consciously utopian disaster commons emerge out of climatological collapse, the joy of dance and the commitment to the comprehensibility and political authority of the riot. Ultimately, they look hopefully towards a world that seems almost accessible from our own, which gives Robinson's novel genuine educational and political power.

In Chapter 4, I look at two 2017 novels: *The Book of Joan* by Lidia Yuknavitch and *Walkaway* by Cory Doctorow. These texts represent utopian commons at a more metaphysical scale than their cousins, dealing with the potential of immortality beyond capitalist control. In very different ways, Yuknavitch and Doctorow's novels offer imaginaries of utopian worlds which bear similarities to our present, but within which the totalizing grasp of capitalism has waned to the extent that human lives, deaths and rebirths no longer serve the interests of capital, but become collective, communal and queer. These novels chart the hoping and dreaming of commons utopias beyond their emergence inside the capitalist system, and into visions of new worlds built on its ruins.

Notes

1   Fredric Jameson, 'Future City', *New Left Review* 21 (2003): 76.
2   Transcript and video of the speech: Parker Higgins, '"We Will Need Writers Who Can Remember Freedom": Ursula K Le Guin at the National Book Awards', Parker Higgins Dot Net, 2014, https://parkerhiggins.net/2014/11/will-need-writers-can-remember-freedom-ursula-k-le-guin-national-book-awards/.
3   Fredric Jameson, *Archaeologies of the Future: The Desire Called Utopia and Other Science Fictions* (London: Verso, 2005), 216–17.
4   Fredric Jameson, 'The Politics of Utopia', *New Left Review*, no. 25 (Jan/Feb 2004): 46.
5   Jameson, 'Future City', 76.
6   A notable example of this demonization is Garret Hardin's 1968 essay 'The Tragedy of the Commons', which claims that '[a]s the human population has increased, the commons has had to be abandoned in one aspect or another'. In a recent critical review, George Caffentzis and Silvia Federici find that '[f]or all the attacks on them, commons have not ceased to exist', remaining, instead,

powerful sites of anti-capitalist activity. See: Garrett Hardin, 'The Tragedy of the Commons', *Science* 162, no. 3859 (1968): 1248; George Caffentzis and Silvia Federici, 'Commons against and beyond Capitalism', *Community Development Journal* 49, no. S1 (2014): i95.

7   The very recent works of two notable utopian literary theorists, Tom Moylan and Phillip E. Wegner, both deal directly with the resurgence of utopian thought in contemporary criticism and culture: Phillip E. Wegner, *Invoking Hope: Theory and Utopia in Dark Times* (Minneapolis: University of Minnesota, 2020); Tom Moylan, *Becoming Utopian: The Culture and Politics of Radical Transformation* (London: Bloomsbury Academic, 2021). A detailed discussion of the concept of utopia simultaneously as a good-place and a no-place is found in David M. Bell's *Rethinking Utopia: Place, Power, Affect* (New York: Routledge, 2017).

8   Paul Ricoeur, 'Rhetoric – Poetics – Hermeneutics', in *From Metaphysics to Rhetoric*, ed. Michel Meyer (Dordrecht: Springer, 1989), 142.

9   Ricoeur, 'Rhetoric – Poetics – Hermeneutics', 143.

10 Robert T. Tally Jr., *Utopia in the Age of Globalization: Space, Representation, and the World-System* (New York: Palgrave Macmillan, 2013), xiii.

11 Ernst Bloch, *The Principle of Hope*, vol. 1 (Cambridge: MIT Press, 1986), 7, 9; Tom Moylan, *Demand the Impossible: Science Fiction and the Utopian Imagination*, ed. Raffaella Baccolini (Oxford: Peter Lang, 2014), 35.

12 Moylan, *Demand the Impossible*, 10.

13 Tom Moylan, *Scraps of the Untainted Sky: Science Fiction, Utopia, Dystopia* (Boulder: Westview Press, 2000), 3.

14 Fátima Vieira, 'The Concept of Utopia', in *The Cambridge Companion to Utopian Literature*, ed. Gregory Claeys (Cambridge: Cambridge University Press, 2010), 22.

15 Jameson, 'The Politics of Utopia', 44.

16 Craig J. Calhoun and Georgi M. Derluguian, eds., *Business as Usual: The Roots of the Global Financial Meltdown* (New York: New York University Press, 2011); United Nations, *The Global Social Crisis: Report on the World Social Situation 2011* (New York: United Nations Publications, 2011); Andrew W. Lo, 'Reading about the Financial Crisis: A Twenty-One-Book Review', *Journal of Economic Literature* 50, no. 1 (2012): 151–78; Anthony Elson, *The Global Financial Crisis in Retrospect* (New York: Palgrave Macmillan, 2017).

17 Lauren Berlant, *Cruel Optimism* (Durham: Duke University Press, 2011), 203.

18 Max Haiven, 'Are Your Children Old Enough to Learn about May '68?: Recalling the Radical Event, Refracting Utopia, and Commoning Memory', *Cultural Critique* 78, no. 1 (2011): 83.

19 On the relationship between utopia, heteronormativity and temporality, see: José Esteban Muñoz, *Cruising Utopia: The Then and There of Queer Futurity* (New York: New York University Press, 2009).

20 Tom Moylan and Raffaella Baccolini, 'Dystopia and Histories', in *Dark Horizons: Science Fiction and the Dystopian Imagination*, ed. Tom Moylan and Raffaella Baccolini (New York: Routledge, 2013), 1–12 (7).

21 Cory Doctorow has enthusiastically described *Walkaway* as a plot-driven pulp novel which challenges the classic pulp conceit of '"man vs. nature vs. man": the earthquake knocked your house over and then your neighbors came over to eat you'. *Walkaway* seeks to ask an alternative question: 'what if, after a disaster, everyone wanted to help, but no one could agree on how to do so?'. Cory Doctorow, 'Be the First One to Not Do Something That No One Else Has Ever Not Thought of Doing Before', *Locus Online*, 2017, https://locusmag.com/2017/07/cory-doctorow-be-the-first-one-to-not-do-something-that-no-one-else-has-ever-not-thought-of-doing-before/.

22 Berlant, *Cruel Optimism*.

23 Sean Austin Grattan, *Hope Isn't Stupid: Utopian Affects in Contemporary American Literature* (Iowa City: University of Iowa Press, 2017), 1.

24 Dick, Kirby, and Amy Ziering Kofman, directors. *Derrida* (Zeitgeist Films, 2002).

25 Berlant, *Cruel Optimism*, 15.

26 Berlant, *Cruel Optimism*, 3.

27 For a very early use of 'global weirding', see: Anne Raver, 'Bananas in the Backyard', *The New York Times*, 2002, https://www.nytimes.com/2002/11/07/garden/nature-bananas-in-the-backyard.html. For subsequent responses, see: John Waldman, 'With Temperatures Rising, Here Comes "Global Weirding"', Yale Environment 360, 2009, http://e360.yale.edu/features/with_temperatures_rising_here_comes_global_weirding; Thomas L. Friedman, 'Global Weirding Is Here', *The New York Times*, 2010, https://www.nytimes.com/2010/02/17/opinion/17friedman.html; John Sweeney, 'Signs of Postnormal Times', *East-West Affairs: A Quarterly Journal of North-South Relations in Postnormal Times* 1, no. 3/4 (2013): 5–12.

28 Mohsin Hamid, *Exit West* (London: Penguin Books, 2018), 216.

29 Joshua Clover, *Riot. Strike. Riot.: The New Era of Uprisings* (London: Verso, 2016), 191, 187; Endnotes, 'Afterword: The Idea of the Workers' Movement', *Endnotes* 4 (2015): 187.

30 Endnotes, 'Communisation and Value-Form Theory', *Endnotes* 2 (2010): 75.

31 The Invisible Committee, *The Coming Insurrection* (Los Angeles: Semiotext(e), 2009), 102, 117.
32 Christian P. Haines, *A Desire Called America: Biopolitics, Utopia, and the Literary Commons* (New York: Fordham University Press, 2019), 10.
33 Carissa Honeywell, 'Utopianism and Anarchism', *Journal of Political Ideologies* 12, no. 3 (2007): 242, 244.
34 Max Haiven and Alex Khasnabish, *The Radical Imagination: Social Movement Research in the Age of Austerity* (London: Zed Books, 2014), 3.
35 Julian Brigstocke, 'Occupy the Future', in *Space, Power and the Commons: The Struggle for Alternative Futures*, ed. Leila Dawney, Samuel Kirwan, and Julian Brigstocke (London: Routledge, 2016), 150.
36 Bloch, *The Principle of Hope*, 1:145, 146.
37 Ernst Bloch, *The Principle of Hope*, vol. 3 (Cambridge: MIT Press, 1986), 1368.
38 Ruth Levitas, *Utopia as Method: The Imaginary Reconstitution of Society* (New York: Palgrave Macmillan, 2013), xii, xiii, 4, 5; Miguel Abensour, 'William Morris: The Politics of Romance', in *Revolutionary Romanticism: A Drunken Boat Anthology*, ed. Max Blechman (San Francisco: City Lights Books, 1999), 145.
39 David Harvey, *Spaces of Hope* (Edinburgh: Edinburgh University Press, 2000), 183.
40 Bell, *Rethinking Utopia*, 4–5.
41 Bell, *Rethinking Utopia*, 11, 123.
42 Henri Lefebvre, *The Production of Space*, trans. Donald Nicholson-Smith (Oxford: Blackwell, 1991), 129. See: Karl Marx, *Grundrisse: Foundations of the Critique of Political Economy*, trans. Martin Nicolaus (London: Penguin Books, 1993); Gilles Deleuze and Félix Guattari, *A Thousand Plateaus: Capitalism and Schizophrenia* (Minneapolis: University of Minnesota Press, 1987).
43 Lefebvre, *The Production of Space*, 349. See: David Harvey, *The Condition of Postmodernity: An Enquiry into the Origins of Cultural Change* (Oxford: Blackwell, 1989); Doreen Massey, *For Space* (London: Sage, 2005); Edward W. Soja, *Thirdspace: Journeys to Los Angeles and Other Real-and-Imagined Places* (Cambridge: Blackwell, 1996); Phillip E. Wegner, *Imaginary Communities: Utopia, the Nation, and the Spatial Histories of Modernity* (Berkeley: University of California Press, 2002).
44 Bell, *Rethinking Utopia*, 98.
45 Massey, *For Space*, 9.
46 Jacques Rancière, *Dissensus: On Politics and Aesthetics*, trans. Steve Corcoran (London: Continuum, 2010), 37.

47 See: Massimo De Angelis, *Omnia Sunt Communia: On the Commons and the Transformation to Postcapitalism* (London: Zed Books, 2017); Max Haiven, 'Commons as Actuality, Ethos, and Horizon', in *Educational Commons in Theory and Practice: Global Pedagogy and Politics*, ed. Alexander J. Means, Derek Ford, and Graham B. Slater (New York: Palgrave Macmillan, 2017), 23–38.
48 Leila Dawney, Samuel Kirwan, and Julian Brigstocke, 'Introduction: The Promise of the Commons', in *Space, Power and the Commons: The Struggle for Alternative Futures*, ed. Leila Dawney, Samuel Kirwan, and Julian Brigstocke (London: Routledge, 2016), 19.
49 De Angelis, *Omnia Sunt Communia*, 11–12.
50 Dawney, Kirwan, and Brigstocke, 'The Promise of the Commons', 21.

1

Commons beyond capitalism:
That Winter the Wolf Came

This chapter considers what the future and poetics could look like in commons of different kinds: literary, communal, political and temporal. My guide through these different common worlds and their interrelations is the work of contemporary American poet, essayist and critic Juliana Spahr. Spahr's 2015 poetry collection *That Winter the Wolf Came* embraces a commons poetics and a politics of collectivity, beginning by drawing together isolated and precarious subjects in anti-capitalist struggle and ending with a celebration of future-directed joy in the moment of riot. Spahr is a frequently pessimistic and cautiously realist interlocutor in *That Winter the Wolf Came* – a narrative of defeats and failures as much as victories and transformations. It is precisely this cautious deployment of hope, coupled with Spahr's realist depiction of utopian commons in the historical past and her imaginative prefiguration of utopian commons from the future, that makes *That Winter the Wolf Came* an effective and compelling utopian text. Spahr's commons poetics moves deftly between the *poiesis* of commons spaces within the bounds of the page, the evocation of a history of riotous activism, and of writing about and around this activism. At each stage it reminds its readers of the compelling power of a *literary commons*, a practical utopian form 'renewing our political vocabulary through aesthetic means'.[1]

Juliana Spahr is a contemporary American writer best known for her poetry, although, like her frequent collaborators Joshua Clover and Jasper Bernes, she is equally a literary and political critic, essayist, editor and activist. Alongside Clover and Bernes, she is the co-founder of Commune Editions, a small poetry press and was involved with the activist work of Occupy Oakland. Spahr's work and political activity are therefore located at the nexus of a number of fields relevant to the project of this book – anti-capitalist politics, contemporary literary theory and poetry. Spahr's poetry collection *That Winter the Wolf Came* interfaces closely with the idea of the contemporary as a time of ongoing precarity and crisis, particularly in the period from 2008 onwards; and a reading of the spatial and social-reproductive strategies of contemporary commons as emerging from utopian processes of inhabiting and place-making.[2] This collection deliberately foregrounds the relationship between capitalism, oppositional politics and the collective subjects who enact these politics. Spahr's key subjects are the 2010 BP Deepwater Horizon oil spill disaster, the largest marine oil spill in the history of petroleum extraction and among the most damaging anthropogenic environmental disasters in history; Occupy Oakland, the Oakland, California offshoot of the global 2011–12 Occupy Movement, which was distinguished by opposition to police brutality and alliance with a general strike that shut down the Port of Oakland in November 2011, the experience of motherhood and the complexity and fragility of the planet's non-human ecosystems.

Many of these subjects, in earlier incarnations and with different inflections, have been key thematic strands of Spahr's critical and poetic work since the 1990s. At this time, Spahr emerged from under the wing of the Language school of poetry, having previously studied under poets including Susan Howe and Charles Bernstein.[3] As a member of the generation characterized by Lynn Keller as 'post-Language', Spahr uses a large repertoire of formal and performance devices in her poetry, particularly narrative, lyric, apostrophe, extensive lists, repetition, incantation and refrain. While some of these techniques embrace the linguistic and political avant-gardism of the Language school, others – such as her use of lyric and narrative – move beyond it. Spahr's work also tends away from the Language school thematically; her collections *This Connection of Everyone With Lungs* (2005) and *Well Then There Now* (2011) reveal her interest in ecopoetry, and therefore in the politics of relationality and collectivity with which this school of poetry is concerned. These tactical and thematic innovations generate a poetics Meliz Ergin characterizes as 'combining formal experimentation with the desire to *mean* ethicopolitically'.[4]

Spahr's association with ecopoetics merits particular note in view of its relation to the subject of the commons. One of the foundational sources of the term 'ecopoetics' is the eponymous journal, founded in 2001 by Jonathan

Skinner. In the inaugural issue, Skinner writes: '"Eco" here signals – no more, no less – the house we share with several million other species, our planet Earth. "Poetics" is used as *poesis* or making, not necessarily to emphasize the critical over the creative act (nor vice versa). Thus: ecopoetics, a house making'.[5] Writing in the midst of a subsequent influx of interest in this field, Kate Rigby defines ecopoetics as 'the incorporation of an environmental perspective into the study of poetics, and into the reading and writing of (mainly) literary works' – a perspective particular for its marked consideration of 'how what we make – especially, but not exclusively, with words – might in turn help sustain … other-than-human poietic practices and autopoietic processes', such as the flourishing of other species and ecological systems.[6] Both the ethical (pro-environmental) and the political (anti-capitalist) concerns of ecopoetics are clearly signposted here.

Like ecopoetics, commons poetics can be conceived of as a 'house making', albeit in a different mode and with a different distribution of subjects in its 'house'. Both are concerned with collectivity and community, including networks of human and non-human species, which are essential for the functioning of all commons. Both are notable for their production through a wide variety of frequently experimental formal techniques. Their differences lie in the greater attention given to human actors – particularly oppositional ones – within commons poetics, while ecopoetics is focused on the non-human. Furthermore, ecopoetics is primarily concerned with bringing attention to the ecological and political crises of the present, whereas commons poetics is concerned with the better systems which can be designed to escape these crises by using the imaginative potential of a prefigured future. Given this close association between the two forms, it is unsurprising that Spahr collapses the languages of the eco and the common throughout her work.

Commons in poetry

Throughout the last two decades, Spahr has continually revisited the question of which kinds of commons are generated by poetic textual practices, and the political consequences of adopting such practices. In her 2001 critical book *Everybody's Autonomy*, Spahr states that she is 'interested in works that encourage communal readings' and which look at 'the relation between reading and identity in order to comment on the nature of collectivity', including communal moments 'of partial or qualified identification; moments when one realizes and respects unlikeness; moments when one connects with other readers (instead of characters)'.[7] In her essay 'Poetry in a Time of Crisis', written shortly after the 9/11 attacks, she refashions this argument, demanding an alternative to the introspective, deeply personal poetry which was permeating the public sphere at that time:

> In this time of crisis, as in others, it is philosophies of connection that help me think things through. In this time of crisis, as in others, I need models of intimacy that are full of acquaintance and publics; that are declarations of collective culture and connective agency. And I need those models to also leave room for individuals, to respect their multiple 'onlys.'[8]

In this piece, the model of intimacy Spahr gestures towards is pain and its ability to form 'political, public communities in which no one is absent'. Her collection *This Connection of Everyone With Lungs* comprises two long poems – one written after 9/11 and the other between the end of 2002 and the beginning of the US invasion of Iraq in March 2003. In these poems, Spahr deploys precisely such political 'philosophies of connection', which are filled with pain and anguish, intimacy, individual subjectivity, 'collective culture and connective agency'. The collection ends with an uncomfortable, exacting recognition that even the most seemingly intimate and personal forms of human relations are, in this contemporary moment, penetrated by the agents and languages of military imperial capitalism:

> When I rest my head upon yours breasts, I rest upon the *USS Kitty Hawk* and the *USS Harry S. Truman* and the *USS Theodore Roosevelt*.
> Guided missile frigates, attack submarines, oilers, and amphibious transport/ dock ships follow us into bed.
> Fast combat support ships, landing crafts, air cushioned, all of us with all of that.[9]

Writing in response to these lines, Heather Milne has argued that Spahr's work can be read as a critical examination of the 'affects and complicities of global intimacy in the context of war, mediatization, and advanced capitalism', which shows 'how even the most intimate spaces we share with our beloveds are inflected with global politics and how, in turn, global politics can function as complicated sites of intimacy'.[10] In *That Winter the Wolf Came*, as we shall see, Spahr's focus shifts away from the uneasy commons which exist as a result of the military-industrial complex and towards the equally uneasy commons which exist as a result of contemporary petrocapitalism. In both collections, the reminder is the same: we do not always choose the exact shapes of the commons we form, and we must create an oppositional politics in spite of them.

In a 2009 piece titled 'The 90s', Spahr turns to the corpus of poetry, incorporating languages other than English, written and published in the United States during the 1990s. Spahr describes these literatures as forming a multilingual 'literary commons, one complicated in interesting ways by an awareness of imperialism's shared and yet unequal histories', whose writers aimed towards a 'universalism with room for particularity' in their use of language and languages.[11] Spahr indexes many of these poetic and political concerns in the poetry of Korean American poet Myung Mi Kim, particularly her 2002 collection *Commons*, where Kim writes: 'What is English now, in the face of mass global migrations, ecological degradations, shifts and upheavals in identifications of gender and labor?'[12] After 9/11, Spahr contends, this multilingual commons and its implication that 'we need, at moments, the languages of others', begin to disintegrate under the effects of 'a wilful attempt to reclaim the poetic commons in the name of a nationalist literature in standard English'.[13] Where this piece, and Spahr's 2001 collection *Fuck You-Aloha-I Love You*, deal with the oppositional possibilities and colonial complicities of using the languages of other people, *That Winter the Wolf Came* broadens these concerns, examining what it might mean to incorporate the behaviour and existence of non-human species into poetry – and the anthropocentric complicities which permeate this undertaking.

The corpus of multilingual 1990s poetry Spahr identifies in 'The 90s' receives expanded treatment in her 2018 book *Du Bois's Telegram*, where it is situated within a larger historical context alongside avant-garde modernism and movement poetry. Here, Spahr appears increasingly ambivalent about the potential for oppositional political poetry to effect or seriously relate to real-world political change. Perhaps unsurprisingly, it is also here that Spahr expresses with great clarity both the political possibilities of poetry, and the realities of the processes which suppress and deny these possibilities. Political literatures exist, she argues, 'because there are writers who want to fulfil Lorde's claim that poetry "forms the quality of the light within which we predicate our hopes and dreams towards survival and change, first made into language, then into idea, then into more tangible action"'. But despite these literatures' 'utopian and revolutionary hopes', she chronicles the invariable ways in which they atrophy 'into something that makes good Adorno's claim that "this is not a time for political works of art"'.[14] Returning to this argument in her conclusion, she writes:

> It is unclear to me how literature might be reclaimed from these institutions short of revolution. [...] Revolution though. There is some historical precedence that it is revolution that frees cultural production from the institutions that constantly work to contain it. [...] We are for sure not there, yet. But one can always hope.[15]

Spahr carries this seed of hope quietly through her critical work, but in her poetry it sprouts up into a larger assembly of organisms. It is through and within this deferred and often intangible hope that Spahr, alongside Clover and Bernes, writes in a recent interview that their poetry 'might play a role something like the riot dogs of Athens, a companion to struggles and manifestations whose contribution is ultimately minor, providing inspiration, maybe distracting the enemy now and then but unable to do much to alter the balance of forces'.[16] In another interview, they express this metaphor as 'describing our own modesty with regard to political effects but also our sense that we imagine the press [Commune Editions, which published *That Winter the Wolf Came*] as a part of something larger, something that can be truly transformative'.[17] It is the 'truly transformative' element in Spahr's poetry which my reading below sets out to explore – an element which is plural, collective, common.

What is a commons poetics?

That Winter the Wolf Came generates an oppositional poetics which recuperates and assembles a collective political subject for the purposes of anti-capitalist struggle. I call this poetics a commons poetics because of three features which define Spahr's recent poetic work and appear, to lesser and greater extents, in each of the texts I write on in this book. Firstly, 'commons' refers back to Spahr's use of the word to index literatures which 'think about what it means to have the words of others in one's own mouth'.[18] In this sense, 'commons poetics' refers to a linguistic and literary commons, the intertextual coexistence of multiple literatures and languages. In *That Winter the Wolf Came* the 'words' Spahr takes into her mouth are the modes of being of non-human others, alongside the histories of past resistances. Secondly, commons refers to the ways Spahr's work is extensively involved in questions of collectivity and community; representations of spatial, social, economic and ecological commons allow Spahr to express novel ways of collective being.

The activist poet and critic Stephen Collis hones in on these first two aspects of commons poetics in his essay 'Of Blackberries and the Poetic Commons', describing 'poetry's compositional practice' as 'at its essence … a commoning of linguistic and creative resources'. Collis reminds us, in particular, that the 'stories of poetry's common practice' – from multiple authorship to collaborative writing to Percy Shelley's evocation of 'that great poem, which all poets, like the co-operating thoughts of one great mind, have built up since the beginning of the world' – are as old as records of poetry itself. Collis further highlights the resistance of poetic practice to the concept of the singular author and inimitable style, despite capital's attempts to 'force it to stand only for the personal and the subjective' rather than the common and the collective. Collis argues that when it escapes the demands of capital, the 'putative commons' of poetry exists 'along the margins of productive life where it fruits seemingly without purpose or exchange value'.[19] For these reasons, commons-focused poetry is an ideal home for an oppositional utopian politics. It combines a collective compositional practice, defiant intertextuality and quotation, and the convincing representation of ways of feeling and existing outside capital. Haines comes to a similar conclusion in his exploration of an American literary commons, arguing that this utopian institute 'expresses itself as literature' not only because of 'the difficulty of translating the energies of social movements into enduring institutions', but also because of 'literature's capacity for experimenting with form, for testing out new arrangements of existence, for developing new kinds of knowledge and intelligence'.[20] Not just inimical to capital, a commons poetics actively troubles capital's political hegemony.

These two readings of commons have been taken up widely in critical responses to Spahr's poetry. Critics have variously figured Spahr's poetics as an 'ecopoetics', a 'posthumanist poetics', or an 'anthropogenic poetics'.[21] These definitions share a recognition of Spahr's concern with politically charged questions of connection, collectivity and community – that is, of commons and commoning – across disparate ontological domains and ecological boundaries. Kimberly Lamm unites a number of these strands, writing that Spahr's poetry is 'full of outward, inclusive turns', always containing 'a call to collectivities that are resistant and responsible, open to the alterity of the planet and the ethical impossibilities it demands', which act as a corrective and a form of resistance to 'globalization's violently enforced homogenization'.[22] Lamm and other critics ultimately highlight the ways in which intimate and public collectivities can no longer be conceived of as distinct in a contemporary moment conditioned by neoliberal capitalism.

The third sense in which I refer to Spahr's commons poetics is drawn directly from oppositional political theory. Commons draw energy from, and prefigure, an anti-capitalist future. This argument has been given new impetus by anti-capitalist philosophy over the last decades. In *Multitude* (2004), Michael Hardt and Antonio Negri describe 'the common' as the underlying sense of collective power which allows the subject of the multitude to 'communicate and act together', arguing that 'communication, collaboration, and cooperation' are 'not only based on the common, but they in turn produce the common in an expanding spiral relationship'.[23] The multitude, a term introduced by Hardt and Negri and taken up as a rallying term by anti-precarity movements, describes the acting subject of anti-capitalist politics in the landscape of post-Fordist capitalism and neoliberal economic strategy. Born of late capitalist processes, in particular globalization, the hollowing out of class identity and the growth of the information economy, the multitude is a collective subject situated beyond class and other identitarian categories. Hardt and Negri conceive of it as 'composed of innumerable internal differences that can never be reduced to a unity or a single identity – different cultures, races, ethnicities, genders and sexual orientations; different forms of labor; different ways of living; different views of the world; and different desires … a multiplicity of all these singular differences'.[24] It is unlikely that Hardt and Negri knew how closely Spahr had prefigured their words only a few years earlier with 'Poetry in a Time of

Crisis', wherein she had called for connective models which 'leave room for individuals'.

More recently, De Angelis has argued that the process of commoning – of producing commons – 'is flow-like in its praxis: like a bike chain it continues to rotate, to iterate, to start anew a new cycle … (re)producing resources and commoners, and in turn (re)producing the commons at new levels and in new forms'.[25] Collis adds, of the relationship between the blackberry thicket – a classical commons – and the imagination: '[i]t holds forth a possible world, and thus opens the door for the vision of other possible worlds'.[26] To talk of commons is to talk simultaneously of the futures that commons produce through their prefigurative (re)production. Picking up on the same wellspring of prefigurative utopian energy, Levitas has read Occupy Wall Street as a utopian 'prefiguration of the good society'.[27] The poetics, or modes of making, of real-world commons – and the texts which represent them – demand to be understood as utopian; they seek to imagine and prefiguratively make a future which is more common than the present within which they operate.

Spahr's commons emerge over and over again in the nine linked pieces of *That Winter the Wolf Came*, (re)producing themselves through formal techniques of intertwined collectivity. Chief among these techniques and thematics is lyric. While the long tradition of lyric has been seen as the enemy of Language poetry's political avant-gardism, Spahr's politics and her allegiances to Language poetry allow her to 'engage strategically with lyric', revitalizing its 'ancient ability to affirm communal values as she stages her resistance to destructive global politics'.[28] The lyricism of *That Winter the Wolf Came* is encoded not only in structure and form, but in compositional practices and content matter. Almost every poem in the collection alludes to, intertextually borrows from or is thematically built upon a song. Spahr's concern for lyric at a fundamental and frequently literal level – for musicians, for lyrics, for the structures and the performances of songs, for the ways in which we listen to them – goes to the heart of her text. Spahr has been singled out for the way she uses chant and repetition in her performance of her poetry and, in this light, her preoccupation with lyric and its performance is unsurprising.[29] The connections which link Spahr's investment in lyric with her concern for collectivity run even deeper. In a prefacing note to 'Poem written from

November 30 2002 to March 27 2003' in *This Connection of Everyone With Lungs*, she writes:

> September 11 shifted my thinking in this way. […] I felt I had to think about what I was connected with, and what I was complicit with, as I lived off the fat of the military-industrial complex on a small island. […] This feeling made lyric – with its attention to connection, with its dwelling on the beloved and on the afar – suddenly somewhat poignant, somewhat apt, even somewhat more useful than I usually find it.[30]

Spahr's focus on lyric in *That Winter the Wolf Came* tackles the same desire for 'dwelling on the beloved and on the afar', in terms of physical distance across the planet as well as the irreconcilable distance from the perceptual and epistemological worlds of non-human beings. To understand Spahr's commons poetics, it is imperative that we understand the use of the lyric within and across the pieces of *That Winter the Wolf Came* – the ways in which, as form and subject, it unites and collects, assembles and organizes.

'If You Were a Bluebird': multi-species commons

The poem 'If You Were a Bluebird' takes its title from a 1989 Emmylou Harris cover of a 1977 song by Butch Hancock and Joe Ely.[31] The song is a sentimental lyric, whose narrator describes the subject of their love as a series of creatures and objects: a crying bluebird, a raindrop calling home, a train stop, a hotel. Spahr writes: '[d]oes it matter if it doesn't entirely make sense and yet is still entirely a love song, one about being there for someone no matter what they are and no matter what they might do?'[32] The poem interrogates this question further, employing a commons poetics to strip back the song's sentimentality and hone in on the question of what it means to love someone 'no matter what they are and no matter what they might do' – not by forgiving someone for their bad behaviour, but in a more fundamental, ecological sense of foregrounding care and responsibility for a plurality of non-human subjects. As Siobhan Phillips writes: '[i]n her poems, love does not resist the world beyond; love lets it in. Politics demands feeling rather than denuding it'.[33]

Bringing her readers' attention to her frequent use of lists, Spahr begins the poem with the words: 'Began with a list'. This list, and the two following, are each set out on the bottom half of a page, demarcated from the surrounding text by white space. The first list, like the two that follow, consists of three animals: 'A bird. Reed cormorant. | Added a fish and a monkey. Hingemouth. White throated monkey'. These animals are described in exacting anatomical detail; then they are linked to each other, not through any specific behaviour, but with the lines 'Added the phrase the principle of relation | Because it was with the principle of relation that the Niger Delta came to teem'. Here, we discover that these animals all live in one complex ecosystem – the next lines focus on the ways in which their behaviours relate them to each other and their larger ecosystem. The hingemouth 'swims'; the 'silvery wings, longish tail, and short head crest of the reed cormorant dives down to considerable depths in the Delta … bringing slow-moving mormyrids and chiclids to the surface'; the white-throated monkey 'bangs objects against the ground, throws sticks'. Surely, these lines seem to say, the 'principle of relation' is the recognition that nothing is not related – that relation permeates all subjects and spaces. The 'principle of relation' returns in the next two lists, uniting a Eurasian spoonbill, a crab and a fish in the Kuwait Bay, and a pelican, a dolphin and a rednose snapper in the Gulf of Mexico. In these opening sections, however, the three ecosystems are visually separated through their layout on their respective pages – the only 'relation' between them is assumed through Spahr's repetition of an identical formal structure. Beyond these uses of repetition and location, Spahr makes the formal features of her commons poetics plainly visible, even formulaic ('Began with a list', 'Added because'), bringing her readers' attention to her construction of poetic meaning not by argument and inference, but by the formal techniques of the 'new sentence', parataxis and free association common in Language poetry.[34] It is no large leap to draw a connection between these formal techniques of relation, and the subjective and symbolic parataxis which allows Spahr to assemble, in a single poem, something of the unconveyable complexity of a planetary multi-species commons.

The next section of the poem also begins halfway down a page, but is continuous until the poem's end. Here, a human narrator is introduced, along with the concept of speech which appears to distinguish this subject from those which came before: 'I am waiting. | Said this out loud'. But this subject rapidly becomes a 'we': 'Said we are waiting. | Some of us are waiting'. The 'we', in turn, becomes something more organized and less diffuse: 'Waiting to be infiltrating the land. | And waiting for the assembly of animals. | Waiting to be complete'. In these short, repetitive lines, the individuated webs of relation which open the poem become more general – figured now as assemblies of fish, animals, and birds – but also become weaponized against an as-of-yet undefined threat. The threat is revealed in these lines, each of which recontextualizes the word 'gathering':

> Wanting to be coming to be possibility gathering.
> As it happened with blood cockle gathering when the women went to gather blood cockles and the cockles were covered in oil.
> And then began another sort of gathering.
> Gathering so as to be seizing.
> Seizing a boat.
> Dividing into groups.
> Occupying airstrips, helicopter pads, oil storage areas, docks.

The meaning of 'gathering' here is transformed from a symbolic gathering of possibility into a form of labour practised by women who are, like the animals, integrated closely with the ecologies within which they exist. Then, in response to an oil spill, begins an oppositional, activist gathering and occupation. The commons poetics threaded through this poem allow Spahr to intermingle, in language and narrative, a plural diversity of different assemblies – of animals, fish, birds and humans.

Traditional economic commons have been characterized as containers for 'common-pool resources', that is, 'spatially delimited natural resources that may be appropriated for use by different communities and incorporated into different economic logics'.[35] Although the relationship between the blood cockle gatherers and the seafront is precisely such an economic relationship, the commons Spahr evokes is a commons at the level of structure and poetic form. The separated lists with which 'If You Were a Bluebird' opens are united by its rolling, unstoppable, chant-like conclusion, which reveals a similar 'universalism with room for particularity' to the one Spahr had indexed in 1990s multilingual poetry. Here, rather than holding the words of others on her tongue, Spahr holds the histories and behaviours of others, including '[t]he women and the women-identified of 1789 and 1871 and 1917 and 1918 and 1929 and 1969', who assemble '[f]rom four hundred one day to four thousand the next', but unites them also with 'the white-throated monkey', an animal which likewise assembles in groups for collective survival: 'five or six at the beginnings, then more gathering up to thirty'. Only the poet's innovative use of language is able to assemble these diverse multitudes as a single 'possibility gathering', looking beyond the constraints of an anthropocentric focus which distinguishes the survival of animals from the survival of humans in the face of petrocapitalist disaster.

'If You Were a Bluebird' ends, as it began, with a list:

> But not stopping then.
> Gathering like the silt too.
> Traveling through the circuits that already exist.
> Traveling with the ease of oil tankers.
> From Banias in Syria, Tripoli, Ceyhan in Turkey.
> Through the Neutral Zone to the terminals at Mena Saud and Ras Al
>   Khafji.
> Through Umm Said.
> Through Das Island and Jebel dhanna.
> Arjuna, Balongan, and Cinta, and Widuri.

By listing some of the oil ports, fields and refineries which underpin contemporary petroculture, Spahr underscores our understanding of oil as hidden and, simultaneously, inseparable from the ways in which we live and relate to the ecosystems around us. Ross Barrett and Daniel Worden refer to this dichotomy when they write that '[o]il is not entirely visible to us as a commodity, a fuel, a resource, or a political and economic agent, yet it is also not invisible … it is foundational and ever present, yet it is also secreted away'.[36] These names are unfamiliar outside the professional vocabulary of the petroleum industry and the local cultures of the nations where this industry has established its foothold. At the same time, the economies of developed and developing nations rely wholesale on the labour and extraction which occurs in these places. Following the section of the poem which assembles human and non-human beings in a history of anti-petrocapitalist resistance, this section suggests that oil, too, must be reckoned with as part of this history – and as part of its future. The 'possibility gathering' does not stop once it reaches the circuits of oil production, but gathers and travels, staking an oppositional claim on an expanding global sphere indexed by these place names. In these concluding lines, Spahr draws our attention to the circuits of petrocapitalist production and circulation, which, like the US military-industrial complex in her earlier work, penetrate and envelop even the most radical and transformative forms of anti-capitalist opposition. The lists which begin and end the poem underscore this message when we realize that the ecosystems with which Spahr begins – the Niger Delta, Kuwait Bay and the Gulf of Mexico – are home to some of the world's largest active oil fields and have been the sites of the world's worst oil disasters.

The utopian hope glimmering in this poem lies in the final, surprising relation Spahr makes between the 'ten thousands' of 'women and women-identified' who rise to challenge capitalism, and the networks of petrocapitalist circulation. Revolutionary subjects, in these lines, are seen 'Traveling through the circuits that already exist. | Traveling with the ease of oil tankers'. The anti-capitalist challenge here is double. Firstly, Spahr suggests that contemporary forms of anti-capitalist resistance must, like capitalism itself, involve movement and circulation across increasingly complex networks; as the Invisible Committee write, 'it's not about possessing territory … it's a matter of increasing the density of the communes, of circulation, and of solidarities to the point that the territory becomes unreadable, opaque to all authority'.[37] As the list of oil ports suggests, these solidarities must be anti-border and anti-colonial at the same time as they are anti-capitalist. The second aspect of Spahr's anti-capitalist challenge draws on Marxist tactics of communization which move away from the desire for a totalizing historical break and embrace forms of revolutionary life within the capitalist present. This final list suggests, then, that there is an opportunity for revolution within the totality of capitalism – that the master's tools, *contra* Lorde, might yet have a role in dismantling the master's house, if only out of necessity. Beyond this, the poem's commons poetics speak to a sense of care and responsibility immanent and implicit in the notion of being common, evoked through the desire of a plurality of subjects who are all 'Wanting the principle of relation. … Wanting to be together'. However, 'If You Were a Bluebird', which is more apostrophic than narrative in structure, does not extend past our petrocapitalist present to fully prefigure a utopian future. To explore how Spahr creates such futures we must turn to other poems in *That Winter the Wolf Came*.

'Transitory, Momentary' and 'It's All Good, It's All Fucked': (anti-)capitalist assemblages

In 'Transitory, Momentary', the opening poem of *That Winter the Wolf Came*, Spahr creates a symbolic common space for a number of concerns which are threaded through the rest of the collection. A narrative prose poem filling up four pages with an unbroken column of text, 'Transitory, Momentary' defies the sense of sequentially ordered time, common to narrative poetry, by moving through a disordered collection of subjects, histories and futures.[38] The formal tactics on display here are similar to those of 'If You Were a Bluebird': using parataxis and association at the level of 'new sentences', Spahr collects and unites individuated subjects into a common subject. Her sentences travel through a variety of locations, subjects and times, and move fluidly between distinct, specialized, seemingly irreconcilable vocabularies: explications of animal ethology and the economics of the global oil trade sit alongside the narrative of a protest occupation being taken over by the police, the formal analysis of an unnamed pop song, and a lyrical, sentimental reflection on the life of the song's singer. The poem's conclusion offers us an account of the kinds of political tactics which could be used by a plural subject in opposition to planetary capitalism – but it is also a partial account, hopeful yet cautious, uncertain of its own possibilities.

The poem opens with the lyrical, ecopoetic line 'The Brent geese fly in long low wavering lines on their migrations', before proleptically introducing Spahr's own voice: 'What I have to offer here is nothing revolutionary'. Indeed, the migration patterns of Brent geese, while impressive, are not revolutionary, but Spahr prefigures the political content of the poem, and the way that the Brent geese link to it, by continuing: 'It is just an observation, just a small observation, that sometimes art can hold the oil wars and all that they mean and might yet mean within.' With the phrase 'oil wars', Spahr captures the unbroken line which links her earlier work on the US military complex with her current focus on petrocapitalism – these are two aspects of the same global capitalist hegemony. This moment of ironic meiosis ('just a small observation'), pivoting on the vast understatement of 'just', signals to the reader that *That Winter the Wolf Came* attempts to rise to the challenge of capturing the totality ('all they mean') of late neoliberal petrocapitalism – its present as well as all its possible futures ('might yet mean') – while foregrounding the absolute impossibility of this task. It is a task made easier, however, through the generation of a collective subject which includes the Brent geese; they are one of many paths towards oil, one of the key symbols which fuel this collection. As the poem's narrative continues, Spahr offers one of her tonally neutral, and for this reason, all the more affecting observations: 'When this oil company named their oil fields off the coast of Scotland, they chose the names of water birds in alphabetical order: Auk, Brent, Cormorant, Dunlin, Eider, Fulmar and so on.' In this she exemplifies the strategies by which capitalism generates a simulacrum of the natural world it destroys – here, in the epistemic sense of naming its production facilities after the wild seabirds who die in their millions after oil spill disasters.[39]

Also of importance here are the subjects Spahr names in their particularity, as well as those she leaves unnamed. While the seabirds killed by oil disasters are named, the oil company, in this poem and elsewhere in the collection, is nameless. Naming is an expression of power – both power over the thing named, and the extension of power to the named thing to act in a particular way indexed by the name. Both power and the reader's attention are transferred, by Spahr's tactics and politics of naming, to non-human lives which are frequently disregarded in part due to their anonymity; in her memoir *The Transformation* (2007), she reminds us that '[f]lora and fauna grow next to and around each other without names. Humans add the annotation.'[40] At the same time, in losing their names, specific companies, and later specific parks, protest actions, occupied buildings and instances of police violence become general and anonymous, which allows them to stand in for universal processes of precarization, opposition and violence in the ongoing present. Spahr employs the same tactic in one of her best-known poems, 'Unnamed Dragonfly Species', where the names of specific endangered species, melting glaciers and islands at risk of being submerged by rising sea waters are contrasted with an anonymized narrative, in which the protagonists live on 'an island in the Pacific and … an island in the Atlantic':

> **Least Bittern** One had a smallish city and one had one of the largest cities in the world. **Least Tern** One was six hundred square miles and one was twenty-six square miles. **Leatherback Sea Turtle** Both were likely to feel

the effects of the rising ocean although many of the residents of both were pretending that what was happening to the nations of Tuvalu, Kiribati, Marshall Islands, and Tokelau Islands did not really foretell anything relevant to them at all.[41]

Oil's semiotic and epistemic fluidity has long been noted by petrocultural critics; Barrett and Worden describe it as simultaneously 'material, mystical, historical, geological, and agential'.[42] In 'Transitory, Momentary', this anonymous, generalizing agent unites not only the geese, but also the oil company building which will be built in the occupied park; the singer of the pop song travelling through a landscape of Californian oil fields; and thus his song, which 'reflects and refracts the oil in ways both relevant and trivial'. Ultimately, oil links to this plural subject a symbolic assembly of 'the many that are pulled from intimacies by oil's circulations', a group of people sharing few ties of traditional political solidarity, united only by their shared experience of the aforementioned 'epiphanic song' which spills 'out and over them':

> The truckers, the sailors and deckhands, the assembly line workers, those who maintain the pipelines, those who drive support in the caravans that escort the tankers, the fertilizers, the thousands of interlocking plastic parts, the workers who move two hundred miles and live in a dorm near a factory, alone, those on the ships who spend fifty weeks circulating with the oil unable to talk to each other because of no shared language […].

The subject of the clause 'thousands of interlocking plastic parts' is ambiguous – it is unclear whether the workers are simply 'escorting' the parts along with 'the tankers, the fertilizers', or whether this classic image of the factory machine has become metonymic for 'the workers who move two hundred miles and live in a dorm near a factory, alone'. The workers, like the plastic parts, are immanent within the circuits of capital. They are both produced by, and help produce, the commodity of oil. In this way, and perhaps only in this way, can they be understood as an assemblage – an assemblage which, in this poem, atomizes, anonymizes and alienates them even as they become part of it. Rather than indexing a moment of resistance to petrocapitalism, Spahr's purpose here is to heighten and sharpen an awareness of subjects at the mercy of its logics.

The 'epiphany' Spahr offers us in this poem is as diminished as the range of oppositional actions offered to this group: 'It might be that there is nothing to epiphany if it does not hint at the moment of sweaty relation larger than the intimate'. What kind of epiphany can emerge from uniting these workers with nothing more than a 'song about minor loss', worlds apart from the focused, dangerous '[c]hanting of threatening songs' by the 'women and women-identified' in 'If You Were a Bluebird'? Margaret Ronda incisively writes that Spahr's work deals in 'thematics of collective intimacy', challenging 'the logics of neoliberal privatization that divert attention from collective commitments towards individual interests and private encounters', but here, Spahr demands a 'moment of sweaty relation' beyond the intimate.[43] Perhaps she gestures with these lines at the physical labour the workers perform. Perhaps the answer lies in the lines which follow, paratactically, immediately on from them:

> Before the police come, before the building, in the middle of one night, a group of people form a line leading to the entrance of the park. [...] All pass bricks, one by one, down the line so as to make a pile. [...] The pile gets bigger and bigger. It is waist high. Then chest high. Some get out of the line and climb on the pile, hold both their hands in the air because they know now is the transitory, momentary triumph and it should be felt. Others continue passing brick after brick, from one hand to another hand, arms extended, torsos at moments also going back and forth with the bricks.

What kind of time does Spahr evoke in this narrative? With the twice repeated 'before', the latter instance of which refers to a building which we already know 'right now, [...] is not there', and the ahistorical 'in the middle of one night', we sense that this occupation is happening outside time, neither quite in the past nor the present. The use of 'before' in combination with the historical present tense, in particular, creates a space of analepsis where the past becomes unmoored and extends into the now of the rest of the poem. In the poem's 'right now' – perhaps the 2011 of Occupy Oakland which, like the rest of the Occupy movement, was ultimately policed out of material existence – the police 'know [...] that they will win'. In the 'moment of sweaty relation', however, the occupiers build a barricade which might keep the flow of history itself out. The barricade is material, physical, reckoned in terms of the bodies that are making it ('waist high', 'chest high') and built also from the movements and physical articulations of its builders ('arms extended, torsos […] going back and forth with the bricks').

Even here, Spahr diminishes the revolutionary potential of oppositional action: this act of barricade building is only a 'transitory, momentary triumph'. As witnesses to a long history of rebellion, Spahr and her readers know that most anti-capitalist 'moments' do not result in victory for the activists; the physical labour and materiality of barricade building merely hint at victory, stopping short of opening out beyond these specific subjects. Instead, by way of conclusion, Spahr offers us the following lines:

> Then they gather behind it, waiting. Back there, someone might possibly be singing to a child, singing the epiphanic song that alludes to losing the moment of tongue on clit or cock over and over because the child cannot be comforted, because the singer knows only loss. […] they had agreed to be with shadows when they had the child. They had gambled in a sense on a question of sustaining. They had agreed to exist from now on with a shadow. A shadow of love and a shadow of the burning of the oil fields that has already happened and is yet to come and yet must come and a million other shadows that might possibly disappear in the light at that moment.

Physically, erotically, intimately, these lines return us to a difficult and unceasing present, turning away from minor 'epiphany' and towards a 'question of sustaining', perhaps a question to which 'the principle of relation' could serve as one answer. At the same time, these lyrical lines, which could be an inward turn from Spahr herself (the thematics of motherhood are another fruitful aspect of *That Winter the Wolf Came* which I do not have space to examine in this book) are revolutionary in a way that the rest of the poem cannot be. Here, the singer/parent looks out from a shadowy present into a temporal slippage. The phrase 'has already happened and is yet to come and yet must come' offers us the possibility of a recuperative utopian future. It also captures the sense of events being out of the subject's control, reminiscent of modes of life in the ongoing present. But within this fuzzy temporality, Spahr's subject sees the truly revolutionary, albeit terrible, 'burning of the oil fields', paratactically situated next to 'love' – which recalls the immanent love Spahr writes of in 'If You Were a Bluebird'. That oil fields have burnt before in nations targeted by US neo-imperialism does not mean that petrocapitalist systems as a whole cannot burn away in a revolutionary moment ('the light') which moves the planet beyond that particular economic relation. 'Transitory, Momentary' ultimately offers a lyrical hope that the 'sweaty relation' of real-world, communal, oppositional action, occurring not in a generalized future, but in 'that moment', might yet be able to oppose the petrocapitalist present and its bleak non-futures.

The phrase 'transitory, momentary' returns as a haunting in a later poem in the collection, 'It's All Good, It's All Fucked', as does the hopeful, fearful, anticipatory longing for revolution which comes at the end of 'Transitory, Momentary'. Another long prose poem, 'It's All Good, It's All Fucked' brings the reader into a confessional, erotic retelling of the narrator's symbolic love affair and breakup with the 'cloudy and confused meme' of 'Non-Revolution'. Using this term, Spahr codes the riots, occupations, protests and actions of the Occupy movement and its brethren in late 2011 – anti-capitalist oppositional activity which never spills into the full-scale revolution Spahr wishes for in *Du Bois's Telegram* ('We are for sure not there, yet. But one can always hope'). The second half of the poem forms a reflection – part essay, part memoir – on the Occupy movement's collapse, especially among its most passionate supporters, and its transformation from 'Non-Revolution with its minor insurrections to social center', signalling a defanging of the movement's riotous energy by its absorption into the sphere of local government and community services. Spahr recognizes that, had the movement continued to grow and Non-Revolution 'became Revolution, I knew that would be hard. That was an entirely different lover, one I was not sure I was ready for and yet longed for so much'.

In the midst of her reflection, Spahr turns to the long history of riot for succour and, in doing so, highlights the surpluses – of bodies, emotion, danger and power, but also of creative energy, concrete tactics and transformational utopian anticipation – which go hand-in-hand with riot and protest:

> The moment in realist painting of the riot when the perspective switches from the soldiers' point of view to that of the crowd and the people in the crowd are individuals flowing over and out of the space in the painting and the dog is barking causing a horse to rear up and the soldiers in the crowd are at risk, isolated from the rest of the soldiers who are off there far in the distance, and one of the rioters in the crowd has a spy glass trained on these soldiers so they are far off and the crowd seems to be having fun, even the

dog joining in, things tumbling. The crowd in this moment. Complicated, but still joyous, transitory, momentary, experiencing this one moment of freedom [...].

Spahr's long sentence here, which breaks only to condense into the even larger image of '[t]he crowd in this moment', works to present the material presence of the riot as a surplus, pushing at the limits of the language, and as an embodiment of multitude. In these lines, a felt recognition of the crowd's 'one moment of freedom' – an affective surplus – is significant despite the general failure of their revolutionary project in this particular temporal context. Clover, in his work on riot, similarly characterizes riot as surplus, refusing the traditional argument which understands riot as animalistic, apolitical chaos and characterizing it more in line with an evocation of political autonomy at the limits of representation:

> Surplus danger, surplus information, surplus military gear. Surplus emotion. [...] The moment when the partisans of riot exceed the police capacity for management, when the cops make their first retreat, is the moment when the riot becomes fully itself, slides loose from the grim continuity of daily life. The ceaseless social regulation that had seemed ideological and ambient and abstract is in this moment of surplus disclosed as a practical matter, open to social contest.[44]

Haines, after Clover, pushes this sense of riot as an eruption of oppositional power to its ultimate conclusion: 'The riot doesn't simply recover unenclosed time, it reinvents it as the basis for another kind of collective life. The riot is on the time of the commons'.[45]

Much as Spahr identifies the people comprising the multitude as a bodily excess, as 'individuals flowing over and out the space in the painting', Hardt and Negri write of the 'flesh of the multitude' as 'an elemental power that continuously expands social being, producing in excess of every traditional political-economic measure of value' – a reading which incorporates an autonomist sense of late capitalist labouring subject(s) as always in the process of revolutionary labour. In Hardt and Negri's Marxist corporeal poetics, this multitudinous flesh is ultimately 'maddeningly elusive, since it cannot be entirely corralled into the hierarchical organs of a political body'.[46] Indeed, as Sylvère Lotringer incisively notes in a critique of Hardt and Virno's theories of the multitude, programmatic theories of anti-capitalist action are destined to continue failing in the face of an increasingly fluid capitalism, and thus revolutionary forces must seek a communalist combat, 'meant to strengthen some forces present in capital, and join them with other forces in order to form a new communist ensemble'. As Lotringer evocatively demands we discover, after Spinoza: 'What is a body *capable of*?'[47]

In Spahr's work, then, the focus remains on corporeal capability – 'sweaty relation' – and the desire for new forms of temporal collectivity, for 'the time of the commons'. The return of the words 'transitory, momentary' stretches history by linking the crowd of 'the space in the painting' to the crowd of the contemporary occupation – creating a commons of protest across the gulf of time – even as the occupation is already known to have failed, subtly putting the lie to the idea that the consequences of oppositional activity are limited to the activity's own present. Rather, these two 'transitory, momentary' events are situated in a long tradition of anti-capitalist resistance, and this, in turn, offers the possibility of a future where the same transitory, momentary utopian energy will again be put to work. Max Haiven has described this relationship between the past, present and future of activism as 'commoning memory', a process that sees the past as a commons:

> A radical approach to memory, one that both recalls the utopian flash of the past and yearns for its impossible future, can instigate a relentless optimism toward the labor of social justice. Commoning memory is a form of co-memorialization that takes as its challenge not the accurate representation of previous events but the rekindling of the spark of past utopianisms in the present.[48]

The final poem of *That Winter the Wolf Came* takes the anticipatory illumination of these two poems and extends it concretely into such an 'impossible future'.

'Turnt': temporal commons

The last piece in *That Winter the Wolf Came* 'Turnt', is a love poem. Its loose, free verse structure of jumbled long and short lines and fragmentary sentences suggests that the first-person narrator is turning back towards the reader, telling them the story of how 'it' – Occupy Oakland's protests, riots and parties in the autumn and winter of 2011 – went down. Spahr's ebullient, confiding tone is reinforced by occasional second-person asides – '[y]ou can hear it sometimes. It often has a soundtrack. Sometimes it has drum and bass. Sometimes just joy' – which welcome the reader into this recuperated activist history. Thomas Pynchon, in an essay on the 1965 Watts riots, renders them in a similar mode of creative, dangerous jouissance: 'a coordinated and graceful drawing of cops away from the center of the action … Others remember it in terms of music; through much of the rioting seemed to run, they say, a remarkable empathy … everybody knowing what to do and when to do it.'[49] Beyond the reference to drum and bass, 'Turnt' does not appear to have a close connection to song. However, the African-American English term 'turnt' which gives the poem its title originates in late 2000s hip-hop, where it refers to a state of excitement, wildness or intoxication, often in a collective, united mode, as in Snoop Dogg's 2009 song '1800'. Brittney C. Cooper reads 'turnt' in Black American culture as a maximal state of excess and power, an oppositional refusal to 'turn down': 'Crunk Feminism is feminism all the way turnt up! Feminism that is off the charts. Feminism that is lived out loud. Feminism that demands to be heard.'[50] As an oppositional politics, turning up – becoming turnt – is a collective activity which produces forms of common expression. In language which echoes Bloch's utopianism, Cooper writes:

> Turn up is both a moment and a call, both a verb and a noun. It is both anticipatory and complete. It is thricely incantation, invitation, and inculcation. To Live. To Move. To Have – as in to possess – one's being. […] It points to an alternative register of expression, that turns out up to be the most authentic register, because it is who we be, when we are being for ourselves and for us, and not for nobody else, especially them.[51]

For Spahr, becoming 'turnt' blurs the lines between individual and collective oppositional activity, in her case against the Oakland police: 'At first we didn't mask up. We were poets. | Then slowly one by one we did. | As we got turnt. | As I got turnt I mean'. As 'Turnt' progresses, the 'we' broadens to encompass 'everyone I have ever texted I love you to' – a plural subject united, again, by the lyrical, yet radically open quality of love and political expression in the contemporary moment.

Throughout 'Turnt', Occupy Oakland's commons of protest, riot, music and the feelings of joy and defiance they engender become a source of collective power and agency which extends beyond the space and time of oppositional action itself. This sense of ongoing oppositional possibility is reinforced in the poem's opening and closing stanzas. Spahr begins: 'Sometimes it feels like it's over and it's not. Sometimes it feels like it has just begun and it's over'. Spahr never specifies the 'it' of these lines or those following; contextually, it is clear that she is referring to night-time protests but, in their position at the start of the poem, the lines could also refer to something far more general: the idea of collective oppositional action as a whole, generating radical temporal slippages between the past and the future. The final lines of the poem offer an even more profound sense of revolutionary temporal slippage:

> I took all the names of this poem and never wrote them in.
> There is no electronic record of them.
> I found a list of the most popular baby names for various countries in 2015, the year in which I am writing this poem. I made a list, one male and one female from each list. Then I alphabetized it. And I put these names in this poem one by one. I got to O.
> But Olivia, Saanvi, Santiago, Seoyeon, Sofia, Yui, and Zeynep, I love you too.

The remixing of primarily non-Anglophone baby names into the subjects of a revolutionary collective is a delightful subversion of the bourgeois subjectivity which upholds the individual child at the cost of the social and political systems of frequently unpaid neo-colonial labour which provide it with care; likewise, the fact that there is 'no electronic record' of Spahr's radical collaborators protects them, as do their masks, from the powers of the surveillance state. This list is also reminiscent of the many such lists which fill Spahr's poetry, reminding us of the listing of endangered species in 'Unnamed Dragonfly Species'. Spahr has said of her listing tactics:

> I like the list. I like lists because they are inclusive. You can keep sticking things into them. And they don't require categorization. So each item in the list can be as important as the others. I especially like the list as lament. As a sort of recognizing or call out of what is becoming lost. In these poems with lists of plants and animals in them I am thinking of poetry as a place

for storing information. I am thinking of the age old uses of the list poem as a way of keeping knowledge that needs to be kept.

It could therefore be tempting to claim that in 'Turnt', Spahr is writing a utopian, decolonial paean – a lyrical lament – for the future children of the world who, like the non-human beings in 'Unnamed Dragonfly Species', intervene in the organic flow of her narrative to remind us of their own existence and the danger of their 'becoming lost' to the strategies of capitalism. However, the linear fashion in which her readers encounter this poem complicates this reading. Rather than front-loading these apostrophic lines to set the tone for the rest of the poem, Spahr essentially tricks us by revealing her hand only at the end. Unlike in 'Unnamed Dragonfly Species', the names are not set in bold face or otherwise distinguished from the rest of the story; in fact, Spahr goes out of her way to merge them seamlessly into her narrative, repeating certain names when the narrative refers to the same person, pseudonymizing her subjects, but refusing to fully anonymize them.

The real power of these lines, then, is that they function as a time machine: although we originally read this poem as describing the events of 2011, our discovery that none of the subjects Spahr names were even born in 2011 prompts a moment of cognitive estrangement.[52] Containing only the names of children born in 2015, this poem narrates the events of a resistance occupation which will happen at some point in the years to come – a corrective and recuperatory (de)colonization of a hopeless future with alternative possibilities for political opposition. As Cooper indicates, being turnt up is 'both a present and future state of being', both 'anticipatory and complete'.[53] When we re-read the poem with a new awareness of Spahr's estranging strategy, the process works in reverse, suggesting that work to oppose capitalism in the present is always a defiant prefiguration of futures which contain the material conditions, and the love, necessary to contain this turnt collective of revolutionary names.

Writing alongside Bernes and Clover, Spahr notes that, in their poetic and critical work, they have to consider the subjects of 'poetry and concrete social or political struggle … together at every turn, because they are entangled whether we want them to be or not'. To write such poetry, the collective argue, is to write poetry which is oppositional, responsive and mutable, which 'might change in the future, even slip out of its current shell' as a result of the 'unfolding of social antagonisms'.[54] On one hand, Spahr, Clover and Bernes voice an understandable hope for formally experimental and politically challenging poetry to move beyond the outskirts of literary culture where it currently resides – the post-capitalist poetic commons Stephen Collis associates with the blackberry thicket, energetic and unruly yet largely absent from the centre of public discourse. On the other hand, these words also gesture powerfully and longingly at another kind of commons – a utopian future where all the precarious and damaging relations formed under late capitalism can be challenged, rearticulated and transformed.

That Winter the Wolf Came is a powerful example of this form of textual anticipation and temporal recuperation. Commons poetics hold out the possibility – however occasionally faint and minor it may seem – that the ongoing present of late capitalism is not just escapable, but can be transformed into a world of common flourishing. In the sense that capitalism can be conceived of as telic – that it can have an end – the future of commons utopias is the time in which that end will ultimately take place.

The texts I explore in the following three chapters pick up this sense of the future as not already written, and of certain activity in the present as engaged in a conversation with oppositional pasts and imaginative futures; they are concerned primarily with change, process and transformation – with a multitude of journeys, both literal and social-structural, out of the precarious impasse of the here and now and towards a sense of common possibility, a multitude of commons utopias. In various ways, these texts respond to the demands of an anonymous collective of activists associated with Occupy Oakland, who write, in a reflection on their movement:

> Another wave of struggle and unrest will undoubtedly explode in our streets and plazas sooner or later. Our task in the meantime is to cultivate fierce and creative forms of cooperating, caring for each other, and fighting together that can help us smash through the fundamental limits of contemporary revolt when the time is right.[55]

Like Spahr, the authors in the following chapters use a diverse field of textual tactics and depict, defend and occasionally destroy commons and collectives in a variety of timespaces which blur the distinctions between the precarious present and the many futures which are ready to emerge from it. In doing so, they work to create a time which is 'right' to smash through the fundamental limits of contemporary capitalism.

Notes

1. Haines, *A Desire Called America*, 21.
2. Juliana Spahr, *That Winter the Wolf Came* (Oakland: Commune Editions, 2015). All quotations are from this edition.
3. Juliana Spahr, *Du Bois's Telegram: Literary Resistance and State Containment* (Cambridge: Harvard University Press, 2018), 7.
4. Lynn Keller, '"Post-Language Lyric": The Example of Juliana Spahr', *Chicago Review* 55, no. 3/4 (2010): 74–83; Meliz Ergin, 'Intimate Multitudes: Juliana Spahr's Ecopoetics', in *The Ecopoetics of Entanglement in Contemporary Turkish and American Literatures* (New York: Palgrave Macmillan, 2017), 85–125 (95).
5. Jonathan Skinner, 'Editor's Statement', *Ecopoetics* 1 (2001): 5–8 (7). See also: Juliana Spahr, *Well Then There Now* (Boston: David R. Godine, 2011), 71.
6. Kate Rigby, 'Ecopoetics', in *Keywords for Environmental Studies*, ed. Joni Adamson, William A. Gleason, and David N. Pellow (New York: New York University Press, 2016), 79.
7. Juliana Spahr, *Everybody's Autonomy: Connective Reading and Collective Identity* (Tuscaloosa: University of Alabama Press, 2001), 5.
8. Juliana Spahr, 'Poetry in a Time of Crisis', *Poetry Project Newsletter* 189 (2002).
9. Juliana Spahr, *This Connection of Everyone with Lungs* (Berkeley: University of California Press, 2005), 74–5.
10. Heather Milne, 'Dearly Beloveds: The Politics of Intimacy in Juliana Spahr's *This Connection of Everyone with Lungs*', *Mosaic: A Journal for the Interdisciplinary Study of Literature* 47, no. 2 (2014): 216, 217.
11. Juliana Spahr, 'The '90s', *Boundary 2* 36, no. 3 (2009): 179, 173.
12. Myung Mi Kim, *Commons* (Berkeley: University of California Press, 2002), 110.
13. Spahr, 'The '90s', 178, 179.
14. Spahr, *Du Bois's Telegram*, 15.
15. Spahr, *Du Bois's Telegram*, 188–94.
16. Jasper Bernes, Joshua Clover, and Juliana Spahr, 'Self-Abolition of the Poet (Part 3)', *Jacket2* (2014), http://jacket2.org/commentary/self-abolition-poet-part-3.

17 Stephen Voyce, '"Poetry and Other Antagonisms": An Interview with Commune Editions', *The Iowa Review* 47, no. 1 (2017): 177–87.
18 Spahr, 'The '90s', 181.
19 Stephen Collis, 'Of Blackberries and the Poetic Commons', Forum on Public Domain (2014), https://www.yumpu.com/s/GaMgC9QgHE9Qvofj. For an alternative, published version of this text, with certain differences from the one available exclusively online, see: Stephen Collis, 'Of Blackberries and the Poetic Commons', in *The Commons* (Vancouver: Talonbooks, 2014), 127–36. See also: Percy Bysshe Shelley, 'A Defence of Poetry', in *Essays, Letters from Abroad, Translations and Fragments*, ed. Mary Shelley (London: Edward Moxon, 1840), 28.
20 Haines, *A Desire Called America*, 22.
21 Dianne Chisholm, 'Juliana Spahr's Ecopoetics: Ecologies and Politics of the Refrain', *Contemporary Literature* 55, no. 1 (2014): 118–47; Ergin, 'Intimate Multitudes'; Margaret Ronda, 'Anthropogenic Poetics', *The Minnesota Review* 83 (2014): 102–11; Tana Jean Welch, 'Entangled Species: The Inclusive Posthumanist Ecopoetics of Juliana Spahr', *The Journal of Ecocriticism* 6, no. 1 (2014): 1–25.
22 Kimberly Lamm, 'All Together/Now: Writing the Space of Collectivities in the Poetry of Juliana Spahr', in *American Poets in the 21st Century: The New Poetics*, ed. Claudia Rankine and Lisa Sewell (Middletown: Wesleyan University Press, 2007), 134, 136.
23 Michael Hardt and Antonio Negri, *Multitude: War and Democracy in the Age of Empire* (New York: Penguin, 2004), xv.
24 Hardt and Negri, *Multitude*, xiv.
25 De Angelis, *Omnia Sunt Communia*, 203–4.
26 Collis, 'Of Blackberries and the Poetic Commons.'
27 Levitas, *Utopia as Method*, 205.
28 Keller, '"Post-Language Lyric"', 83.
29 Ergin, 'Intimate Multitudes', 103–5.
30 Spahr, *This Connection of Everyone with Lungs*, 13.
31 Jasper Bernes, Joshua Clover, and Juliana Spahr, 'Book Notes – Joshua Clover, Jasper Bernes, and Juliana Spahr (Commune Editions)', *Largehearted Boy*, 2015, http://www.largeheartedboy.com/blog/archive/2015/09/book_notes_josh_28.html.
32 Bernes, Clover, and Spahr, 'Book Notes.'
33 Siobhan Phillips, 'A Catalogue of Us with All: Juliana Spahr's "Well Then There Now"', *Los Angeles Review of Books*, 2011, https://lareviewofbooks.org/article/a-catalogue-of-us-with-all-juliana-spahrs-well-then-there-now/.

34 Bob Perelman writes of the 'new sentence' of Language poetry: 'a new sentence is more or less ordinary but gains its effect by being placed next to another sentence to which it has tangential relevance. New sentences are not subordinated to a larger narrative frame nor are they thrown together at random. Parataxis is crucial: the internal, autonomous meaning of a new sentence is heightened, questioned, and changed by the degree of separation or connection that the reader perceives with regard to the surrounding sentences'. See: Bob Perelman, 'Parataxis and Narrative: The New Sentence in Theory and Practice', *American Literature* 65, no. 2 (1993): 313.

35 Elinor Ostrom, *Governing the Commons* (Cambridge: Cambridge University Press, 2015); Dawney, Kirwan, and Brigstocke, 'The Promise of the Commons', 6.

36 Ross Barrett and Daniel Worden, eds., *Oil Culture* (Minneapolis: University of Minnesota Press, 2014), xvii.

37 The Invisible Committee, *The Coming Insurrection*, 108.

38 As Seymour Chatman notes, it is not sequentiality *per se* which defines narrative, but contingency, of which there is plenty in 'Transitory, Momentary.' See: Seymour Chatman, *Story and Discourse: Narrative Structure in Fiction and Film* (Ithaca: Cornell University Press, 1993), 45–8.

39 On capitalism's generation of simulacra of the world it plunders for raw materials, see: Karl Marx, *Economic and Philosophic Manuscripts of 1844*, trans. Martin Milligan (Amherst: Prometheus Books, 1988), 69–84.

40 Juliana Spahr, *The Transformation* (Berkeley: Atelos, 2007), 13.

41 Spahr, *Well Then There Now*, 84.

42 Barrett and Worden, *Oil Culture*, 84.

43 Margaret Ronda, 'Mourning and Melancholia in the Anthropocene', *Post45*, 2013, http://post45.research.yale.edu/2013/06/mourning-and-melancholia-in-the-anthropocene/.

44 Clover, *Riot. Strike. Riot.*, 1.

45 Haines, *A Desire Called America*, 185.

46 Hardt and Negri, *Multitude*, 192.

47 Sylvère Lotringer, 'Foreword: We, the Multitude', in Paolo Virno, *A Grammar of the Multitude* (Los Angeles: Semiotext(e), 2004), 16–17.

48 Haiven, 'Are Your Children Old Enough to Learn about May '68?' 83.

49 Thomas Pynchon, 'A Journey into the Mind of Watts', *New York Times*, 1966, https://archive.nytimes.com/www.nytimes.com/books/97/05/18/reviews/pynchon-watts.html. For more on Pynchon's exploration of the riot, the commune and common time, see: Haines, *A Desire Called America*.

50 Brittney C. Cooper, 'An Ontology of CRUNK: Theorizing (the) Turn Up', *Crunk Feminist Collective*, 2014, http://www.crunkfeministcollective.com/2014/04/29/an-ontology-of-crunk-theorizing-the-turn-up/.
51 Cooper, 'An Ontology of CRUNK'; see also: Regina Duthely, 'Black Feminist Hip-Hop Rhetorics and the Digital Public Sphere', *Changing English* 24, no. 2 (2017): 202–12.
52 The term 'cognitive estrangement', originally developed in the work of Bertold Brecht and brought into utopian studies by Darko Suvin and Lucy Sargisson, refers to the estranging effect that a text, particularly a science fiction text, has on its readers – a glitch which forces realization and discovery through discomfort or surprise. Estrangement, for Sargisson, is an 'integral part of utopianism … disrupting it, stretching it and creating something new from its remains'. See: Lucy Sargisson, *Fool's Gold?: Utopianism in the Twenty-First Century* (London: Palgrave Macmillan, 2012), 18; Darko Suvin, *Metamorphoses of Science Fiction: On the Poetics and History of a Literary Genre*, ed. Gerry Canavan (Oxford: Peter Lang, 2016), 3–10.
53 Cooper, 'An Ontology of CRUNK.'
54 Jasper Bernes, Joshua Clover, and Juliana Spahr, 'Spring and All, Farewell to Jackets', *Jacket2*, 2014, http://jacket2.org/commentary/spring-and-all-farewell-jackets.
55 Some Oakland Antagonists, 'The Rise and Fall of the Oakland Commune', *CrimethInc.*, 2013, https://crimethinc.com/2013/09/10/after-the-crest-part-ii-the-rise-and-fall-of-the-oakland-commune.

2

Utopias beyond borders:
Exit West

British Pakistani novelist Mohsin Hamid's 2017 novel *Exit West* has been described by Viet Thanh Nguyen as motivated by a 'gentle optimism' and a 'refusal to descend into dystopia' despite the often bleak and precarious world it depicts. For Thanh-Nguyen, it elicits 'empathy and identification to imagine a better world' which is also, crucially, a 'possible world' – a prefiguration of a utopia.[1] *Exit West* emerges within the historical context of a decade of refugee crises and hard-line border regimes, and as a response to these anxieties, the novel depicts a gradual transition from a realistic near-present to a planetary utopia-in-progress which redefines the concepts of migrancy, homeland and belonging. With fabulesque tone and in long, winding narrative sentences, *Exit West* tells the story of two young people who fall in love and escape their city through a series of mysterious black doorways which have begun to open up around the world. By collapsing the gruelling migrant journey into a brief and fantastical process of teleportation, the black doors lead the populations of the Global South into the old empires of the Global North from which they had hitherto been prohibited. As the young lovers travel from Greece to London to America, the old world order collapses around them, ushering in a worldwide commons predicated in no-borders politics and the absolute right for populations to move and live anywhere they please.

The concept of the 'mobile commons', with which Hamid's vision is allied, has been given a great deal of attention in recent critical work emerging in the wake of the worldwide mobility crises of the last decades. Discourses which oppose the border regime tend to understand migrancy not as a desperate, last-ditch response to precarity and destruction, but as an (albeit gruelling) exercise in autonomy, by recognizing its 'capacity to develop its own logics, its own motivation, its own trajectories'.[2] Such migrant autonomy discourses avoid forming generalizations about all those who migrate and refuse to romanticize nomadism – forms of life predicated on movement; instead they study particular narratives of movement. Fundamentally, migrant autonomy discourses see migrancy as an ongoing attempt at creating an autonomous, non-alienated everyday existence without recourse to a stable home or homeland.

As a depiction of mobile commons, *Exit West* is written *contra* the border regime and the Western liberal conception of the sovereign nation state, but it is also written, albeit less explicitly, *contra* capitalism. The basis for migration crises can often be found in the demands of the capitalist labour market, or in its destructive collapse. As Hannah Cross argues, capitalism, migration and the border regime must be considered and opposed together: 'the character of global capitalism and the persistence of capital accumulation ... binds the causes and consequences of migration with the process of working across borders'.[3] Sandro Mezzadra declares even more forcefully: 'there is no capitalism without migration ... with the regime that attempts to control or tame the mobility of labour playing a strategic role in the constitution of capitalism and class relations'.[4] *Exit West* is – as befits its title – a repudiation of the governmental, cultural and political project of the West and its reliance on capitalist economies, neoliberal governmentality and necropolitical border regimes to uphold its sovereignty. Nadia and Saeed, the novel's central protagonists, first appear employed in prototypical post-Fordist workplaces: an advertising agency and an insurance agency. They abandon these jobs when they flee their country, but *Exit West* ultimately presents a far broader social and political imaginary than can be encompassed solely in the rejection of the labour relations of late capitalism. *Exit West* is a utopian novel concerned with migrancy, exodus and the desire and refusal to return home; it is therefore particularly inviting to read its mobile commons through the lens of Bloch's concept of *Heimat*, a utopian reimagining of the idea of homeland as a radically anti-nationalist and anti-capitalist 'place on earth of arrived-at Being, of world as homeness, homeness as world'.[5] In his novel, Hamid uses the subject of the migrant and a narrative model developed through the crossing and destruction of borders to depict a utopian spatiality whose inhabitants are unalienated and at home in 'the world as homeness' – the world reimagined as a utopian mobile commons of resources, socialities and mobilities.

Although Hamid is at pains throughout his novel and in subsequent public commentary to avoid identifying the city where his narrative begins, it is associated readily in the reader's mind with Damascus or with Hamid's native Lahore – where he moved in 2009 after many years living in London – by virtue of its Islamic culture, the civil war narrative, and the novel's focus on migration.[6] Among the reasons for this ready identification is the fact that the Syrian refugee crisis – visually immortalized by the 2015 photograph of the body of the child Alan Kurdi lying on a Turkish beach – has been widely recognized as one of the defining crises of the previous decade. Although the flow of refugees from Syria is on the wane, new refugee crises have emerged since 2015, and the same factors – militarized border regimes, dangerous sea routes, badly equipped human traffickers and a lack of resources in (often unwilling) host nations – continue to play a part in exacerbating their effects. In 2018, approximately 140,000 refugees made their way to Europe across the Mediterranean, with 27 per cent of those coming from Guinea, Morocco, Mali and Syria; another 2277 died in the attempt.[7] In 2019, the Mexico-US border became the site of a new migrant crisis generated by the hard-line border policies of the Trump administration and by changes in the demographic makeup of the refugees: from a majority of single men looking for work to a surge of families seeking asylum. As a result, numerous children were separated from their families and subjected to unsanitary, traumatic and at times life-threatening conditions in detention centres In June 2019, a photograph of a dead asylum seeker and his twenty-three-month-old daughter drowned in the Rio Grande river, eerily reminiscent of the image of Alan Kurdi, circulated online and in international press.[8]

Two significant features emerge in analyses of these refugee crises: their exceptional deadliness and their relationship to capitalist economic systems. In a recent study of migrant movement into Europe, Óscar García Agustín and Martin Bak Jørgensen argue that, while such refugee crises emerge from 'economic inequalities, low income, structural unemployment, and protracted conflicts' in their countries of origin, their deadliness is the result of European border policies which they accurately describe as 'necropolitical': 'at least since the 1990s the illegalization of Mediterranean migration has made that space one of the most lethal zones of the world – in terms of irregular border crossing – and has claimed scores of lives … The illegalization of the migrants and their insistence on crossing have turned the Mediterranean into a maritime graveyard.'⁹ The concept of necropolitics, articulated by Achille Mbembe, indexes the state's exercise of sovereignty specifically through killing, bringing close to death and letting die. One of Mbembe's examples of necropolitics in the 'age of global mobility' highlights the mobility not of populations, but of sovereign state borders, which increasingly appear not as monolithic entities but as patchworks of 'overlapping and incomplete rights to rule … in which different *de facto* juridical instances are geographically interwoven and plural allegiances, asymmetrical suzerainties, and enclaves abound'. Applying Mbembe's considerations to the Mediterranean situation, where war is waged not against state armies but against the racialized threat of the migrant-cum-terrorist, we can argue that 'the new technologies of destruction' – here recast as the EU refusal to rescue migrants at sea – 'are less concerned with inscribing bodies within disciplinary apparatuses as inscribing them, when the time comes, within the order of the maximal economy now represented by the "massacre"'.¹⁰

Exit West's commons poetics

Exit West is Mohsin Hamid's fourth novel, and like his previous novels *The Reluctant Fundamentalist* (2007) and *How to Get Filthy Rich in Rising Asia* (2013), it is impelled by what Paul Gilroy describes as 'planetary humanism'. This term describes an ethics 'capable of comprehending the universality of our elemental vulnerability to the wrongs we visit upon each other', and so, as Mai Al-Nakib extrapolates, 'the speculative component of Hamid's otherwise realistic narrative reveals the connectivity of global life – economic, social, cultural, and environmental – delimited and obfuscated by national boundaries, armies, police, passports, walls, and so on'.¹¹ The narrative begins in a plausibly realist near-present where fantastic doors start to appear around the globe – reality-defying black portals 'that could take you elsewhere, often to places far away, well removed from this death trap of a country' without the need for transport, border controls, passports, visas or any of the other instruments and technologies associated with mobility in the contemporary world.¹² These doors allow the young lovers Nadia and Saeed, along with millions of others, to escape their unnamed country for the nations of the Global North, hence the novel's title can reference an exit *to* the West. However, as Nadia and Saeed make their way in search of better and less precarious lives, the Global North, and in the end the whole planet, changes with them – revealing the title's other implication, an exit *of* the West from its position of neo-colonial planetary dominance. This decolonial imaginary, which has featured in all of Hamid's novels to date, is complemented by techniques of formal and narrative experimentation which compel his readers, like his characters, to adopt new positions and locations from which to make sense of these new planetary formations.[13] *The Reluctant Fundamentalist* takes the form of a dramatic monologue delivered by the Pakistani-born character Changez to an American listener who never speaks. *How to Get Filthy Rich in Rising Asia* is also narrated in the second person, encouraging the reader either to take on the perspective of the anonymous South Asian protagonist or to absorb the advice of the pulp self-help literature which stylistically influences the novel. Furthermore, the novel's occasional perspectival shifts to the distant, all-seeing position of a drone or satellite help reveal 'the systems above the systems, and [show] that the self is just a tiny node within a vast constellation of networks'.[14]

Exit West is formally inventive in ways which distinguish it from Hamid's previous work. Rather than playing with narrative perspective, the key experiment in this novel – the mysterious doors – plays with narrative structure and form. The style of the text is flowing and lyrical, characterized by parataxis and very long sentences, and is interspersed with occasional authorial comments and asides, as if the doors are creating passages not only between nations, but between individual sentences and between the author and his world. These winding sentences produce a commons poetics at a formal level – like Spahr's use of parataxis, the unusual length of Hamid's sentences, each one comprising a series of paratactically located clauses, suggests a refusal to give up on the utopian desires of the novel's characters, capturing not only their movement from space to space, but also their sense of the contemporary moment as a prefiguration of a utopian future. For instance, early in the novel we read this sentence:

> As they hurried home, Saeed and Nadia looked at the night sky, at the forcefulness of the stars and the moon's pockmarked brightness in the

absence of electric lighting and in the reduced pollution from fuel-starved and hence sparse traffic, and wondered where the door to which they had purchased access might take them, someplace in the mountains or on the plains or by the seaside, and they saw an emaciated man lying on the street who had recently expired, either from hunger or illness, for he did not appear wounded, and in their apartment they told Saeed's father the potential good news but he was oddly silent in response, and they waited for him to say something, and in the end all he said was, 'Let us hope.'[15]

In this sentence, Hamid switches from the human subjects of Saeed and Nadia to the 'forcefulness of the stars and the moon's pockmarked brightness', a world which is inaccessible and thus somewhat alien and frightening in its alterity, before returning to the city in which the characters live, which is disintegrating around them, and in danger of becoming unfamiliar by merging with the silence ('sparse traffic') and darkness ('absence of electric lighting') of the night sky. Next, via the contrivance of the door, Hamid rushes us from the city to imagined far-away worlds, before returning us to the city, this time highlighting the disintegration not only of its infrastructure but its social elements through the image of the 'recently expired' man, whose death is so removed from the escapist imaginings of Nadia and Saeed that he barely registers in their consciousness. Lastly, however, Hamid reflects on the universality of human beings, a theme to which he devotes much of *Exit West*, through the introduction of Saeed's father and the network of interpersonal relations he embodies. The final utopian words, 'Let us hope', extend not only to the three characters, but because of the scope of the sentence which precedes them, also include the dead man, the city, the planet beyond and even the universe within which this universal 'us' exists. Saeed's father's hope is common and inclusive, even in the darkest of times, because it extends beyond the limitations of their situation.

The core narrative of *Exit West* is that of Nadia and Saeed, the novel's only named characters. With their names, as Claire Chambers incisively notes, Hamid 'engages in onomastic play', with Nadia signifying North and Saeed South, while the novel's title supplies East ('Exit') alongside the West. Nadia is an independent atheist and feminist, who listens to Western music and wears a 'virtually all-concealing black robe' only to avoid the unwanted attentions of men, while Saeed is more reserved, traditionalist, community-minded and broadly adherent to his (implicitly Islamic) faith; their association with the cardinal directions therefore aligns to some extent 'with generalizations about the global north and ... south'.[16] The two meet and fall in love in a purposefully unidentified city in the opening weeks of a civil war; as the war worsens and begins to tear apart their city, claiming the life of Saeed's mother, the young couple decide to flee their city through one of the recently manifested doors.

The *dispositif* of the doors connects *Exit West* to the sub-genre of portal fantasy, notable examples of which include *The Lion, The Witch and the Wardrobe* (C. S. Lewis, 1950) and *The Subtle Knife* (Philip Pullman, 1997). Farah Mendlesohn indicates that the portal fantasy is a genre of 'entry, transition, and negotiation' which is closest in form to the 'classic utopian' tale; such fantasies see the protagonist enter a mysterious world and 'lead us gradually to the point where the protagonist knows his or her world enough to change it and to enter into that world's destiny'.[17] As in portal fantasies, which Hamid deliberately evokes in *Exit West* ('the nearby blackness [of the door] unsettled him, and reminded him of something, of a feeling, of a feeling he associated with children's books'), the migrants' travels through the doors ultimately changes their world; in an important departure from these stories, the world into which they travel is not a fantastic world separate from ours, but the real world itself, captured in a lengthy, turbulent, apocalyptic but ultimately utopian period of transition and transformation.[18]

Buying passage through one such fantastic door and out of their city, Nadia and Saeed leave what remains of their families behind and become migrants, emerging in a refugee camp on the Mediterranean island of Mykonos. They continue hopping through doors, living for a time in a migrant squat in Kensington, London, from where they are eventually resettled to a ring of new migrant settlements around the city; they finally end up in a vast migrant town in Marin County, overlooking San Francisco. With their relationship beginning to disintegrate not long after it began, here they decide to go their separate ways, meeting again only years later in the novel's final chapter. Nadia and Saeed's narrative is intercut throughout the novel with vignettes which highlight the global reach of the doors and, by extension, the universal desire of the planet's population to be mobile. Among these stories, a black man emerges in a bedroom in Sydney; two Filipina women appear in Tokyo; a woman in Vienna standing in solidarity with the migrants is attacked by an anti-migrant mob; a man in Amsterdam begins a relationship with a Brazilian man who appears in his gardening shed; and a Tamil family appearing on a beach in Dubai are swiftly taken in by the authorities. In the penultimate vignette, an elderly woman in Palo Alto reflects that 'now all these doors from who knows where were opening, and all sorts of strange people were around, people who looked more at home than she was, even the homeless ones who spoke no English', suggesting that the novel's modality of radical mobility has become planetary, totalizing and habitual.[19]

The structure of *Exit West* reflects the gradual transformation of planetary life we see taking place in this narrative. Hamid divides the slim novel into twelve chapters, but the plot naturally falls into three sections of five, three and four chapters respectively. Each section is defined by a journey Nadia and Saeed undertake through a portal and introduces new spatialities, mobilities, subjectivities and relationships. The first section takes Nadia and Saeed from their homeland to Mykonos. Here, spatiality is constricted and entrapping; the central form of movement is escape; Nadia and Saeed are defined by their families and their old lives in their country; and love seems to be a source of utopian possibilities. In the second section, Nadia and Saeed travel from Mykonos to London. This section is defined by liminality, moving between various spaces, but never settling in any one; Nadia and Saeed's relationship and subjectivities also become transitional and fluid. In the final section, set in Marin, a form of *Heimat* is realized. The spaces in this section open out and become liberating, secure and full of radical possibilities; Nadia and Saeed separate and find new people with whom they create rewarding relationships beyond their original comfort zones; and battles over movement recede in importance as the entire planet embraces the reality of limitless mobility and the end of borders and states that it implies.

Furthermore, each section of the novel is defined by a particular relationship with, spatial imaginary of and aesthetics relating to home. This focus on the necessity of creating home wherever one chooses to settle, however temporarily, defines *Exit West* as a novel with a particularly contemporary understanding of utopia. As in utopian texts from More onwards, utopian spaces in *Exit West* have to be reached by travel; unlike in earlier texts, they are neither spatially nor temporally separated, but exist within the present and are produced through movement. Therefore, unlike in earlier utopian literary texts, utopia here is not a space for temporary visitation, but a process – a utopian method – of utopian inhabiting. Nadia and Saeed's home(s) are created and recreated multiple times in the novel, each time reflecting particular socio-spatial structures and modalities which define the site-specific activity of inhabiting a space. Not only is each new home which Nadia and Saeed make different from those which came before, but each of these homes is more common, more heterogeneous and more open to the influences and imaginaries of a multitude of others. By the conclusion of *Exit West*, home – and thus utopia – becomes not a container for the incubation and safeguarding of a particular form of social structure, but a reactive and reflexive space, generated by a variety of social forms.

The City to Mykonos: Enclosure and escape

The first section of *Exit West* is the most stylistically consistent of the three. The narrative largely plays with the frameworks of two well-worn literary forms: the love story and postcolonial migrant literature, described by Rosemary Marangoly George as 'contemporary literary writing in which the politics and experience of location (or rather of "dislocation") are the central narratives', and more recently articulated by Rosemarie Buikema as 'a sub-genre within postmodern writing and postmodern times in which the theme of dislocation and homelessness is articulated in a variety of forms'.[20] The novel makes its claim to these two forms – and marks out its unsettled commitment to both – in its opening sentence: 'In a city swollen by refugees but still mostly at peace, or at least not yet openly at war, a young man met a young woman in a classroom and did not speak to her'.[21] The multiple diversions from absolute truth and complete surety in this sentence – indexed by the syntactical glitching of 'but still … or at least not yet … and did not' – carry through the rest of the novel, which tells its story cautiously, leaving plenty of space for alternative decisions and multiple coexisting realities. Chambers describes this distinctive style as comprising 'textual doublings … part of [Hamid's] creation of ontological undecidability'.[22]

This possibility-multiplying discursive style emerges from the 'anything is possible' first blush of love narrative, as well as from the appearance of the doors, to which oblique references appear from the first chapter. At the same time, the style is challenged by numerous narrative and textual tactics which work to create a sense of entrapment, desperation and constriction. The first mention of the doors, for example, is a vignette set in a flat in a gentrified suburb of Sydney, where a closet door in the bedroom of a sleeping white woman has become a portal:

> The door to her closet was open. Her room was bathed in the glow of her computer charger and wireless router, but the closet doorway was dark, darker than night, a rectangle of complete darkness – the heart of darkness. And out of this darkness, a man was emerging.
>
> He too was dark, with dark skin and dark, woolly hair. He wriggled with great effort, his hands gripping either side of the doorway as though pulling himself up against gravity, or against the rush of a monstrous tide. His neck followed his head, tendons straining, and then his chest, his half-unbuttoned, sweaty, gray-and-brown shirt. Suddenly he paused in his exertions. He looked around the room. He looked at the sleeping woman, the shut bedroom door, the open window. He rallied himself again, fighting mightily to come in, but in desperate silence, the silence of a man struggling in an alley, on the ground, late at night, to free himself of hands clenched around his throat. But there were no hands around this man's throat. He wished only not to be heard.[23]

This introduction to the logics and narrative tactics of the doors is interesting for a number of reasons. Firstly, it plays with racialized preconceptions of the predatory or aggressive black man – both the migrant and the door through which he climbs are 'dark, darker than night', and the door itself is, in ironic reference to Joseph Conrad, 'the heart of darkness'. The white woman is subtly implied to be a willing participant in the structural racism which would locate a black man in this 'heart', particularly in her arrival in this house only after 'the gentrification of this neighborhood had run as far as it had now run'. Later in this vignette, which repeatedly draws the reader's attention to the woman's bare skin and sleeping vulnerability, Hamid again writes back to the racialized, colonial image of the 'native', using the self-reflexive and vacillating style noted above: 'His eyes rolled terribly. Yes: terribly. Or perhaps not so terribly.'[24]

The concept of the racialized Other as threat is further complicated by the focus on this particular man's fear and vulnerability, highlighted by language of constriction and entrapment. His actions are those of a person in danger ('wriggled', 'gripping', 'straining', 'rallied', 'fighting', 'struggling') but these are contrasted with deadly forces far more powerful than the human: 'gravity', 'the rush of a monstrous tide', 'hands clenched around his throat'. This introduction to the doors does as much to highlight the endangerment, entrapment and precarity common to the migrant condition as it does to represent the limitless spatial possibilities evinced by the mysterious portals. As we find out in later vignettes, and in Nadia and Saeed's story, simply travelling through a door by no means guarantees an escape from the numerous threats the migrant faces. In deploying the doors, Hamid makes clear that fluidity, decentralization and multiplicity are hallmarks not only of the dislocated, homeless and ontologically uncertain migrant, but also of the border regime and the forms of Western governmentality which promulgate it.

At the same time as the doors begin to open new possibilities for people in peril around the globe, generating a groundswell of migrancy and, for 'world leaders', a 'major global crisis', Hamid refutes and subverts conceptions of the migrant condition as liberating or desirable for those without resources and options.[25] Before the doors begin to open, the refugees who fill Nadia and Saeed's country are described as looking out at the city 'with what looked like anger, or surprise, or supplication, or envy. Others didn't move at all: stunned, maybe, or resting. Possibly dying'.[26] Migrancy here is presented not as mobility but as a foreclosure of options – what Berlant describes as the 'glitch' or 'impasse'.[27] This position subverts the romanticized concept of the migrant (or 'nomad') frequently adopted in contemporary Western culture, which is susceptible, as Caren Kaplan contends:

> to intensive theoretical appropriation because of a close fit between the mythologized elements of migration (independence, alternative organisation to nation-states, lack of opportunity to accumulate much surplus, etc.) and Euro-American modernist privileging of solitude and the celebration of the specific locations associated with nomads: deserts and open spaces far from industrialisation and metropolitan cultural influences.[28]

Indeed, as Natasha King warns us from within the context of her research and experience of contemporary anti-border and migrant rights movements, '[e]scape from the state is in most cases an unintended, unpleasant and temporary side effect of/for people on the move and rarely seen as valuable … the excluded don't value their exclusion. Why should they? They're no one's idea of "making it"'.[29] Hamid's nuanced politics of subjectivity force his readers, along with Nadia, Saeed and his planetary imaginary as a whole, to remain ontologically uncertain, restless and open to the profound changes which will define the narrative to come.

Saeed and Nadia's differing attitudes to nation and family in the first section of *Exit West* are reflected in their attitudes to their homes. For Saeed, who lives with his parents, home is a safe and comforting space of family, domesticity, ritual, memory and routine; for Nadia, who lives alone, home is a space of freedom, escape and independence from her family's strict religious life and the country's society more broadly. The two also differ in the ways they see their homes as receptacles and generators of history and memory. The description of Saeed's house not only evokes the narrative of his parents' own love, but connects to global histories of colonization and empire: '[t]heir small flat was in a once handsome building, with an ornate though now crumbling facade that dated back to the colonial era'.[30] Saeed's family, their house and the force of memory more generally are captured in the telescope which stands in their living room: 'given to Saeed's father by his father, and Saeed's father had given it in turn to Saeed, but since Saeed still lived at home, this meant the telescope continued to sit where it always sat', underneath a clipper ship in a bottle which again links the house to the city's colonial history, while also foreshadowing Nadia and Saeed's migrancy.[31] Looking through the telescope at the stars on clear nights, the family engage in what Saeed's father calls 'time travel', seeing objects 'whose light, often, had been emitted before any of these three viewers had been born'.[32]

Nadia's apartment, on the other hand, is historically polyvalent, looking both into the past and towards a technologized future. It sits in the middle of a market which had 'grown past and around it', with a shop on the ground floor selling electrical generators; her living room is bathed 'in the soft and shimmying glow of a large, animated neon sign that towered nearby in the service of a zero-calorie carbonated beverage'. The noir-esque aesthetics of this space, developed through the bustling and anonymizing market and the neon sign, are accentuated by Nadia and Saeed's various schemes and disguises to hide Saeed's presence from Nadia's religious landlady, by their experimentation with drugs, and especially by Nadia's collection of soul, jazz and bossa nova records. Like the telescope, her record player is a time machine, but where the telescope takes its family of viewers to a universal pre-human past, free from political affiliations, Nadia's selection of a record 'by a long-dead woman who was once an icon of a style that in her American homeland was quite justifiably called soul' haunts her apartment with a far more recent history of racial struggle and oppositional politics. Ultimately, where Saeed relies on prior histories – of his parents' lives, of his city and of the universe – to construct his sense of home, Nadia's sense of home is more oppositional and self-directed.

These first two homes in the novel are insulated and insular: intimate minor utopias which seem initially to provide their inhabitants with everything they need to live their lives as they wish to – security, comfort, memory and social and romantic ties.[33] However, as the novel's first section vacillates uncertainly between constriction and openness, these homes become porous and mutable, although not in the ways their inhabitants wish. While rumours of the doors make people 'gaze at their own doors a little differently', the city's inhabitants' relationship to windows also changes: they become sites of danger through which bullets can pass, or which can become shrapnel in a bomb blast, and so they are boarded up, removed or sealed. The security, surety and comfort of the home are thus warped and transformed, with normal doors becoming objects 'with a subtle power to mock' their viewers for dreaming of escape, while windows transform into dark and threatening portals of death.[34] Given the rapid evolution of Nadia and Saeed's relationship, which occurs in inverse proportion to the enclosing and entrapping deterioration of their city (from a relatively liberal metropolis complete with mobile internet access, drug dealers, post-Fordist capitalist workplaces and anonymous gay sex in parks to a dystopian zone of curfews, bombings, terror, civil war and gruesome public executions), their desire to escape their country and their homes quickly becomes an all-consuming need. As they plan to leave through a door to which they have bought access, Saeed, 'in whom the impulse of nostalgia was stronger', sees their exodus as 'deeply sad, as amounting to the loss of a home, no less, of his home', while the more independent and restless Nadia is afraid only of becoming dependent in their flight, 'at the mercy of strangers, subsistent on handouts, caged in pens like vermin'.[35] In the second section of the novel, we quickly learn that both of these fears are justified.

Mykonos to London: Liminality

The second section of *Exit West* sees Nadia and Saeed follow the common route of migrants travelling to Europe from the Middle East, arriving in a refugee camp on the Greek island of Mykonos, before escaping again to a near-future, apocalyptic vision of London on the brink of mass anti-migrant violence. The section concludes with their relocation to a new ring of migrant settlements beyond the city's suburbs, and is suffused with the gradual deterioration of their relationship and Saeed's discovery that his father has died. Where *Exit West* opened with a sense of possibility opposed to violence and enclosure, the Mykonos-London section draws the divides between possibility and its denial more sharply. The boundary is literalized in the depiction of a near-future London split – by the disconnection of electricity in the area given over to the migrants – into a 'light London' where 'people dined in elegant restaurants and rode in shiny black cabs, or at least went to work in offices and shops and were free to journey about as they pleased' and a 'dark London' where 'rubbish accrued, uncollected, and underground stations were sealed'.[36] The two Londons are separated by a heavily militarized and technologized border which succeeds in preventing the movement of migrants where national borders have not. Nadia's fears of rodent-like entrapment are confirmed by the presence of military robots and drones along this border, which frighten her 'because they suggested an unstoppable efficiency, an inhuman power, and evoked the kind of dread that a small mammal feels before a predator of an altogether different order, like a rodent before a snake'.[37]

At the same time as this new border encloses the migrants and curtails their abilities to find new and better lives, this middle section of the novel is liminal. It functions not only as a structural, textual threshold between the minor utopias of the opening chapters and the common, planetary utopia of the final chapters, but also as a narrative threshold for Hamid's characters' understanding of themselves, each other and the world around them. This section establishes the transformation of the concept of home as we see it in the first section – a zone of structure, stability, immobility, rigidity, history and memorialization, bitterly contested by warring factions prepared to almost completely destroy it for a chance to shape its future according to particular sets of beliefs – into a mutable *Heimat* in the Blochian sense, which emerges out of the radical mobility and fluidity of structures, beliefs and systems. The liminality in this chapter emerges in two distinct modes – a networked commons of liminal spaces, and the emergence of liminal subjects who inhabit these spaces.

The social and cultural significance of liminality has been analysed by the anthropologist Victor Turner. Turner's work is far-reaching, encompassing liminal structures among groups including kinship-based tribes in Ghana, Franciscan monasteries and 1960s hippie happenings. Among many such groups, Turner argues, liminal spaces and times are occasional and fleeting, and exist in the midst of more typical, ordered spaces and times during periods of social transformation, such as the ascension of a new chieftain, an initiation ceremony or a music festival. During such periods, social structures and the hierarchies and differences they engender disappear, forcing the lowly and the powerful to occupy undifferentiated positions before normality is once again restored to the social system: 'social life is a type of dialectical process that involves successive experience of high and low, communitas and structure, homogeneity and differentiation, equality and inequality'. Turner calls this moment of social integration and equality of status 'communitas' (in preference to, but analogous with, the term 'community', which he defines as 'an area of common living'): 'a recognition … of a generalized social bond that has ceased to be and has simultaneously yet to be fragmented into a multiplicity of structural ties'. To be in a state of communitas is to embrace a 'homogenous, unstructured' model of society 'whose boundaries are ideally coterminous with those of the human species'.[38]

Since space is socially produced, relationships of communitas produce common and liminal spaces: commons, thresholds, passages, bridges, doorways, the impossible spaces of dreams and open spaces of equality such as public squares. Some of those examined by Turner include the open, tent-strewn fields of the music festival, the cloisters of the Franciscan monastery and the cave or common house of the initiation rite. Beyond their role as portals mediating movement, in the novel's second section the doors also generate and define interstitial, liminal spaces. Every step through one such portal is, after all, a literal step across a threshold. Subha Mukherji reminds us that '[t]he idea of the threshold is politically eloquent, and has had immediate and urgent application in our times in the sphere of geopolitical boundaries, their intransigencies as well as fluidities'.[39] Thresholds, such as those of state borders and the doors, can be controlled by dominant state powers, subjected to strategies of ordering, enclosure and normalization, or alternatively, occupied and refigured by oppositional forces. Hence, on Mykonos, Nadia and Saeed soon discover that 'the doors out, which is to say the doors to richer destinations, were heavily guarded, but the doors in, the doors from poorer places, were mostly left unsecured'.[40] Such control of the doors is reminiscent of the control which states currently wield over their borders, but the sheer quantity of doors in *Exit West* makes them impossible to regulate, and soon the stakes of the issue shift from the possibility of controlling these thresholds to the possibility of inhabiting thresholds, existing in the liminal spaces the doors create without committing to either of the worlds into which they lead: '[w]ithout borders nations appeared to be becoming somewhat illusory … the nation was like … a person whose skin appeared to be dissolving as they swam in a soup full of other people whose skins were likewise dissolving'.[41]

Stavros Stavrides sees porous threshold spaces in cities – such as public squares and parks – as sites of '[e]mergent new forms of resistance' which can 'shape urban space in order to create new social bonds and build forms of collective struggle and survival'.[42] As the social movements of 2010–11 have shown, squares, large roundabouts and parks – in their physical characteristics such as openness, accessibility and brightness, and in the multitude of uses, forms of inhabiting and passages which take place in them – are natural locations for utopian, anti-capitalist forms of life premised upon sharing, equality, accessibility, collectivity and heterogeneity. Such 'spaces-as-thresholds' have the potential to transform an enclosed and privatized city into a distributed network of commons. Drawing on research into occupation protests in Greece in the last decade, Stavrides argues that urban spaces can only remain thresholds, without becoming enclosed or themselves enclosing other spaces, by 'always being open to "newcomers"', by becoming '"infectious", osmotic and capable of expanding egalitarian values and practices outside their boundaries'.[43] This form of threshold inhabiting not only ensures that the threshold remains as open as possible to new ideas and imaginaries, but expands the threshold space further into the zones around it.

In *Exit West*, the doors, and the powerful and radical possibilities for the transformation of movement that their existence implies, exert a utopian potential to transform contemporary urban spaces from an archipelago of privatized enclaves into a connected network, allowing the sharing of reciprocal social and affective flows and relations. Thus, in London 'houses and parks and disused lots ... unoccupied mansions in the borough of Kensington and Chelsea ... and similarly the great expanses of Hyde Park and Kensington Gardens' fill with a million migrants.[44] Although these areas are described by newspapers – in another racialized metaphorical use of darkness – as 'the worst of the black holes in the fabric of the nation', for the migrants themselves they become spaces of solidarity and collective power, albeit enclosed and threatened ones: 'Outside the house much was random and chaotic, but inside, perhaps, a degree of order could be built. Maybe even a community'.[45]

Liminality is not only a spatial process, but generates 'liminal personae' or 'threshold people' – subjects who exist, however briefly, within a social and often physical space of transition, marginality and collectivity. Turner observes, on the basis of anthropological studies, that such people are frequently represented as 'possessing nothing', have 'no status, property, insignia, secular clothing indicating rank or role', are 'passive or humble ... and accept arbitrary punishment without complaint', exhibit 'bisexuality' and 'tend to develop an intense comradeship and egalitarianism' among themselves as long as they remain in the liminal space. The liminal spaces they inhabit are 'frequently likened to death, to being in the womb, to invisibility, to darkness', among other metamorphic and transitional states.[46] The doors in Hamid's novel are liminal spaces, and the migrants are threshold people, in modes which run powerfully with the grain of this theorization of liminality and its subject positions. When Nadia first steps through a door, the moment of passage is described as 'both like dying and like being born, and indeed Nadia experienced a kind of extinguishing as she entered the blackness and a gasping struggle as she fought to exit it'.[47] Other examples of liminal subjectivity in the novel connect dreams and sexual identity. One of the novel's narrative strands focuses on the development of Nadia's bisexuality; in a dream she has in London she returns 'back through the door to the Greek isle' and again sees 'the girl from Mykonos'; when she wakes, she 'felt her body alive, or alarmed, regardless changed'.[48] As Turner indicates, dreams and the subconscious desires they often seem to reveal are profoundly liminal states, and a dreamed return back into the threshold zone of the doors opens a space for Nadia's identity to embrace the positive, subversive possibilities of liminal subjectivity.

The migrants' experiences moving through the doors are, furthermore, liminal in a more profound and all-consuming way, becoming the key to creating an entirely new set of ways for relating to the rapidly changing world around them. This liminality is a kind of 'staying with the trouble', Donna Haraway's phrase for the learning of the necessary capabilities for survival and resilience in a time which threatens to overwhelm our ability to respond to unpredictable crises. Haraway calls for those caught in a time of Anthropocene crisis – which she calls the 'Capitalocene' to redirect blame at the most significant cause of human impact on the planet – to 'make kin in lines of inventive connection', a 'material semiotics' which is 'always situated' in the interlinked spaces of the present, yet demands liminal modes of being with others 'in unexpected collaborations and combinations'.[49] Although Haraway's focus is on the creation of multi-species, more-than-human worlds for becoming responsive and responsible, and Hamid writes mostly of human crises and practices of survival, they share an interest in liminality. Nadia and Saeed's time in London, waiting for the nativist forces to stage an attack on the migrant encampments, is profoundly liminal:

> a resignation shot through with moments of tension, with tension ebbing and flowing, and when the tension receded there was calm, the calm that is called the calm before the storm, but is in reality the foundation of a human life, waiting there for us between the steps of our march to our mortality, when we are compelled to pause and not act but be.[50]

Or, as Haraway puts it: 'staying with the trouble requires learning to be truly present, not as a vanishing pivot between awful or edenic pasts and apocalyptic or salvific futures, but as moral critters entwined in myriad unfinished configurations of places, times, matters, meanings'.[51]

The liminal space of 'dark London' is composed of squats and small communities, some racially and culturally diverse and others replicating the divisions of nation-states; food banks and volunteer medical centres; calls for prayer and blasts of pop music; and moments of communion and understanding between human and more-than-human worlds, such as when

Nadia and Saeed are inspired to mend their relationship by the strange vision of an urban fox. The migrants feel in control of their present circumstances and future possibilities because these spaces are liminal, forcing new strategies for being and becoming which are precarious but nevertheless rewarding in the connections they help make. Nadia captures this mood when she reflects that 'a new time was here', comparing this time to the feeling of 'the wind in her face on a hot day when she rode her motorcycle and lifted the visor of her helmet and embraced the dust and the pollution and the little bugs that sometimes went into your mouth and made you recoil and even spit, but after spitting grin, and grin with a wildness'.[52] Passages like these refuse to describe the radical mobility evoked in *Exit West* as an escape towards a distant future existence disconnected from the present, but keep it grounded and tied to the 'dust and pollution and the little bugs that sometimes went into your mouth': the relationships, spaces and affects of a troubled present.

The nature of the home and of domestic spaces more generally also undergoes a transformation in the Mykonos-London section of the novel. As George indicates, the genre of (im)migrant literature is defined, on the one hand, by an antipathy to nostalgia, nationalism, homesickness and other forms of desire for home, and on the other hand by 'excessive use of the metaphor of luggage, both spiritual and material'. As a material object, luggage (or its marked absence) in such novels can be either a toolkit for survival or an unwanted hindrance which slows the migrant down. Spiritually, luggage denotes the memory of past lives and cultural and national histories, which can either empower the migrant as a constantly recreated 'bag of tricks that tells the textured tale of who the immigrant is and where s/he belongs', or signify an impossible 'yearning for the authentic home' lost to the past or inaccessible in the future.[53] Nadia and Saeed's luggage when they leave their city is generic and efficiently packed, yet carries a sense of their desire for home in their attempt not to abandon every vestige of the small domestic utopias they had constructed: 'smallish backpacks ... each full to bursting, like a turtle imprisoned in too tight a shell'. A turtle's shell, of course, is the only home it will ever know, but the mode of migrancy demands that the original home be transformed and reconfigured – as Susheila Nasta elegantly puts it, '[h]ome, it has been said, is not necessarily where one belongs but the place where one starts from'. Migration is often motivated, Nasta adds, by 'a desire to reinvent and rewrite home as much as a desire to come to terms with an exile from it'.[54] While Nadia takes nothing sentimental with her, Saeed doubles down on the domestic metaphor by bringing along with him an even more compressed sense of home: a single physical photograph of his parents and 'a memory stick containing his family album'. Upon arrival in Mykonos, the couple swap parts of their homely luggage for the necessary items of migrant life: 'some water, food, a blanket, a larger backpack, a little tent that folded away into a light, easily portable pouch, and electric power and local numbers for their phones'. Setting up their 'temporary home' for their first night as migrants, Nadia feels as if she is 'playing house, as she had with her sister as a child'.[55] In this initial period of transition, Nadia and Saeed – and their ideas of home – appear to hover, temporary and evanescent, on the threshold between their old world and a new and uncertain future.

Upon their arrival in London, Nadia and Saeed begin to build a more solid concept of home, initially helped by the fact that, for the first time in months, they find themselves in a solid structure, a formerly empty mansion in the borough of Kensington and Chelsea squatted by over fifty migrants:

> To have a room to themselves – four walls, a window, a door with a lock – seemed incredible good fortune, and Nadia was tempted to unpack, but she knew they needed to be ready to leave at any moment, and so she took out of their backpack only items that were absolutely required. For his part Saeed removed the photo of his parents that he kept hidden in his clothing and placed it on a bookshelf, where it stood, creased, gazing upon them and transforming this narrow bedroom, at least partially, temporarily, into a home.[56]

While their London room is, materially speaking, far more solid than the tent on Mykonos, the temporary and partial nature of this space as home is testament to the liminal conditions in which the couple find themselves. The mutable, threshold nature of their home is reflected on a larger scale in the changing nature of the British homeland. With millions of migrants suddenly on the move across the world, subverting the dispositif of the border regime and the Global North's neo-imperial conception of itself as the centre of rational liberal governmentality, the news on the television is apocalyptic and full of liminal spatialities: 'full of war and migrants and nativists, and it was full of fracturing too, of regions pulling away from nations, and cities pulling away from hinterlands, and it seemed that as everyone was coming together everyone was also moving apart'.[57]

The notion of 'home', as Susheila Nasta writes, 'with all the political, ideological and symbolic baggage that it still implies, was one which formed an integral part of the naturalized rhetoric of Britain as Empire and has lingered on in the nationalistic grammar of Britain as post-imperial nation'; in the plausibly realistic world of *Exit West* this monolithic assurance of 'authority over and ... means of authority within' the British nation begins to transform into a threshold zone of compromise, negotiation and openness.[58] The protagonists thus contemplate that the retreat of 'native' British forces from a planned assault on dark London is because 'they had grasped that the doors could not be closed, and new doors would continue to open, and they had understood that the denial of coexistence would have required one party to cease to exist, and the extinguishing party too would have been transformed in the process' – an evocation of Hamid's planetary ethics.[59] Another implied reason is the death of 200 migrants squatting in a cinema which burns down during the first wave of attacks. *Exit West* came out only months after the June 2017 destruction by fire of the Grenfell Tower council estate in the same borough of Kensington and Chelsea where Nadia and Saeed make their temporary home. The government response to the deaths in Grenfell of seventy-two people, most from Black and minority ethnic backgrounds, contrasts tellingly with the positioning, in *Exit West*, of the cinema fire as the impetus for a profound and utopian shift in official attitudes towards the migrants. As of late 2019, some families from Grenfell and the surrounding estates who were forced to move out of their homes remain in temporary accommodation.[60] In *Exit West*, the UK begins to resettle the migrants and integrate them into the evolving 'fabric of the nation' within months, commissioning a vast project of public works and construction and promising each family a small amount of land.[61]

In *Exit West*, when it is not conflict which transforms the shape of Britain, it is the migrants themselves. A foreman on Saeed's work team becomes 'the key to understanding their new home, its people and manners and ways and habits ... though of course their very presence here meant that its people and manners and ways and habits were undergoing considerable change'.[62] Hamid's decolonial, planetary revisioning of the British nation and its people works not from the periphery of Empire, but enters its very heart. However, the traditional anxiety Nasia Anam indexes in colonial texts, where the imperial 'metropole' becomes a 'potential site of conquest and thus colonization' in reverse, does not come to pass.[63] When Nadia and Saeed move into a literal threshold settlement built in London's edgelands, they find that while 'conflict did not vanish overnight ... overall, for most people, in Britain at least, existence went on in tolerable safety'.[64] This section, set in the 'London Halo', is suffused with a sense of perseverance, patience and mutual discovery as the migrants begin to become friends with the 'natives' of Britain.

At the same time, and seemingly paradoxically, the planet's political and social systems are completely and irreparably transformed. Hamid's ontologically indecisive style allows for multiple types of change to coexist in the same world and at the same scale – the changes in Nadia and Saeed's relationship as they fall out of love; the emergence of camaraderie and solidarity between different migrants as well as migrants and natives; and large-scale political changes, such as the institution of a 'time tax', beneficial for all in the long term, which ensures that 'a portion of the income and toil of those who had recently arrived on the island would go to those who had been there for decades'.[65] As Anam writes, in these and the following chapters, the apocalyptic in *Exit West* 'becomes quotidian, arbitrary, manageable'; this inversion occurs because the novel is written from the perspective of migrants 'who have already witnessed an apocalyptic civilizational transformation in the homelands from which they escaped'. The migrants are used to crisis as an ongoing and everyday part of life, making them exemplary subjects of the ongoing present. The critical transformation in the world order, therefore, 'amounts to no more than another trial to withstand'.[66] In this section, *Exit West* emerges as a novel not of apocalypse and its consequences, but of everyday precarity and the tactics which can be learned and shared to survive it; unlike the texts I investigate in further chapters, particularly *New York 2140* and *The Book of Joan*, *Exit West* features no moment of apocalyptic break which distinguishes the present from the future. Anam concludes that the 'distinct advantage of inhabiting the subject-position of the migrant in a time of enormous societal transformation' lies in the fact that, in *Exit West*, 'the subjectivity of the migrant becomes one of infinite elasticity and adaptability in a time of global tumult – a truly utopian idea indeed'.[67] This emergent utopianism, based on a humanist planetary ethics and on the appearance of common spaces of solidarity, support and mutual understanding – squats, migrant housing, work crews and welfare centres – is only made possible by the liminal spatialities and subjectivities which structure the Mykonos-London section of the novel.

London to Marin: *Heimat*

The final section of *Exit West* sees the development of an oppositional political subjectivity emerging from the liminal foundations laid down in the preceding chapters. Nadia and Saeed's final destination, Marin, is itself liminal, built in the urban edgeland between Sausalito and the Californian countryside, and comprises cooperatives, temporary structures and open spaces for dancing and performance.[68] The population of Marin is likewise liminal, comprising thousands of migrants from all around the world. It is here – with the size of Marin finally providing the distance that Nadia and Saeed need to uncouple from their dying relationship – that Nadia feels able to fully explore her attraction to women, while Saeed, as I shall argue below, is able to articulate an unorthodox position in regard to faith which incorporates his Muslim heritage with the Christian teachings of an African American preacher.

Marin's liminality is further evidenced by the ways in which the city's residents employ technology. Because of its proximity to the high-tech Bay Area, Marin is interwoven with a tightly integrated mesh of technology which, in its modalities and uses, is oppositional to the technologies of bordering and control which Nadia and Saeed saw employed in Britain. The technological developments in Marin do not come from the late capitalist technological companies which dominate the Bay Area, but are innovated by Marin residents and oppose the consumerist drive of Silicon Valley. Much of this technology is geared towards attenuating the basic precariousness of daily life so that it would be 'not quite as rough, nor quite as cut off, as otherwise it might have been': upon arriving Nadia and Saeed find strong 'wireless data signals', and obtain 'a solar panel and battery set with a universal outlet, which accepted plugs from all around the world, and a rainwater collector fashioned from synthetic fabric and a bucket, and dew collectors that fit inside plastic bottles'.[69]

A more profound social transformation comes in the shape of a slightly futuristic biometric voting key which some of the residents of Marin are hoping will be the first step in the foundation of a new, directly democratic political system, 'a regional assembly for the Bay Area, with members elected on the principle of one person one vote, regardless of where one came from'. This device is described as looking 'like a thimble', and its power lies in its simplicity:

> She was so happy, and he asked her why, and she said that this could be the key to the plebiscite, that it made it possible to tell one person from another and ensure they could vote only once, and it was being manufactured in vast numbers, at a cost so small as to be almost nothing, and he held it on his palm and discovered to his surprise that it was no heavier than a feather.[70]

The science fictional thimble's lightness stands in for the avowed simplicity of the regional assembly, which would be an open commons by design: a system always accessible to newcomers, incapable of denying any of its members a say in their own future. It is also a local prefiguration of the bottom-up, distributed, anti-borders socio-political formation which the doors are creating across the world. To Saeed, who has lived his whole life under the control of authoritarian systems, mass surveillance and ideological violence, technology appears understandably a weighty thing, used to crush people rather than empower them, and the lightness of the thimble in his eyes also stands for the freedoms it implies. This thimble is the first clear sign that the global adoption of migration, and the newly developing technologies which can provide security, identity and purpose to this migration, signals the end of borders, and thus of nation-states and the subject position of the citizen. This new, distributed, directly democratic politics individuates people ('it made it possible to tell one person from another'), but does so with the goal of creating 'greater justice', rather than alienation for the purpose of capitalist exploitation.

Politically, the concept of the 'regional assembly' fought for by the residents of Marin is reminiscent of anarchist theorist Murray Bookchin's concept of confederal autonomous municipalities, in which the state is replaced 'by a confederal network of municipal assemblies; the corporate economy reduced to a truly political economy in which municipalities, interacting with each other economically as well as politically, will resolve their material problems as citizen bodies in open assemblies'.[71] The utopian use of technology here also goes some way towards solving the problem identified by Harvey in Bookchin's concept – that inequality would nevertheless exist at a material level between different regions. For Harvey, the only way to solve problems of the necessary 'redistribution of wealth between municipalities … is either by democratic consensus (which, we know from historical experience, is unlikely to be voluntarily and informally arrived at) or by citizens as democratic subjects with powers of decision at different levels within a structure of hierarchical governance'.[72] The biometric voting key may resolve problems of inertia and complexity encountered in the actual enactment, 'voluntarily and informally', of democratic decision making.

The doors are crucial to the success of systems such as these, because the freedom of movement they offer allows subjects to travel from a region to one which better suits them, or to travel permanently around the world, making a home in movement. As Iain Chambers writes, while 'travel implies movement between fixed positions, a site of departure, a point of arrival, the knowledge of an itinerary', and 'intimates an eventual return, a potential homecoming', the subject identity evoked in the experience of migrancy is very different:

> Migrancy, on the contrary, involves a movement in which neither the points of departure nor those of arrival are immutable or certain. It calls for a dwelling in language, in histories, in identities that are constantly subject to mutation. Always in transit, the promise of a homecoming – completing the story, domesticating the detour – becomes an impossibility.[73]

The new social and political subjectivities which are slowly and experimentally being worked out in Marin – subjectivities which embrace the doors not as a form of transport alone, nor even as a necessary way to flee a host of precarious presents, but as a way to expand and continue expanding a 'mobile commons' of eternal transit and mutability – foster precisely this deferral of completion and domestication.

In the final months of the novel's narrative, the movements of the protagonists change from globe-spanning traversals in search of safety from violence and repression to far more minor, localized adjustments to a new and increasingly secure and liberated life. Nadia's feelings when she is invited to move into the cooperative are telling on this point: 'the possibility struck Nadia with a shock of recognition, as though a door was opening up, a door in this case shaped like a room'. For the first time since fleeing their country, Nadia is 'reminded of her apartment in the city of her birth, which she had loved, reminded of what it was like to live there alone … this room came to feel to her like home'.[74] Nadia's desire for a space in 'the city' where she can be 'alone' is a desire for unalienated wholeness – the sense of being complete as a person integrated into, yet individuated within, a community. The community which surrounds, protects and supports Nadia in her search for a new home is represented most obviously by the cooperative, whose workers become friendly with her after she fearlessly stands up to an armed robber: 'several people on her shifts began chatting with her a lot more after that. She felt she was beginning to belong.'[75] Nadia's community also includes the entire city of Marin which, in the next paragraph, is synecdochally invoked to represent Nadia's growing contentment and security:

> The locality around Marin seemed to be rousing itself from a profound and collective low in those days. It has been said that depression is a failure to imagine a plausible desirable future for oneself, and, not just in Marin, but in the whole region, in the Bay Area, and in many other places too, places both near and far, the apocalypse appeared to have arrived and yet it was not apocalyptic, which is to say that while the changes were jarring they were not the end, and life went on, and people found things to do and ways to be and people to be with, and plausible desirable futures began to emerge, unimaginable previously, but not unimaginable now, and the result was something not unlike relief.[76]

In these especially utopian paragraphs and those preceding them, *Exit West* makes use of an imaginary which I argue is closely linked with Bloch's concept of *Heimat*.

Bloch deploys the term *Heimat* as a counter to the complex network of associations with which this term is loaded in German culture, particularly after the rise of Nationalist Socialism in the 1930s. Anton Kaes reads the concept of *Heimat* in Germany in the twentieth century as a nostalgic imaginary of an Arcadian homeland, one which is both lost and comfortingly familiar: 'the site of one's lost childhood, of family, of identity … the possibility of secure human relations, unalienated, precapitalist labour, and the romantic harmony between country dweller and nature ... everything that is not distant and foreign'.[77] In a wide-ranging study on *Heimat*, Friederike Eigler describes the term as 'a manifestation of the loss of metaphysical rootedness', which emerged in the late eighteenth century as an 'affective attachment', but became steadily more ideologically weighted over the course of the twentieth century.[78] Jamie Owen Daniel notes that the sense of a 'familiar and "homey" past' with which *Heimat* was supposed to reconcile the German nation was, as such pasts often are, 'mostly imagined'.[79] Nazi ideology made great use of this simultaneous unreality and familiarity to rationalize ethnic cleansing and the expansion of the German state across Europe; as a kind of 'moveable home', the imaginary of *Heimat* meant that it was possible for ethnic Germans to feel themselves in Germany wherever they were – and thus both justified and necessitated the existence of the German nation everywhere.

Bloch's use of *Heimat* adopts the term's associations with a lost world; its fluidity, mutability and mobility; its affective and metaphysical nature; and its specific connections with childhood. Rather than looking backwards to a past which never existed, however, Bloch connects *Heimat* with the future horizon of a process of concrete utopian realization. Although his use of the term in *The Principle of Hope* is typically non-systematic, this sense is especially apparent in the closing lines of the final volume of *Principle*:

> But the root of history is the working, creating human being who reshapes and overhauls the given facts. Once he has grasped himself and established what is his, without expropriation and alienation, in real democracy, there arises in the world something which shines into the childhood of all and in which no-one has yet been: *Heimat*.[80]

Crucial to this argument is the sense that *Heimat* can be achieved as a form of concrete utopianism in the here and now, not in an abstract future or past, even as this utopia 'shines into' hitherto unexplored realms of human connection and political empowerment. Where Nazi ideology used the conceptual flexibility of *Heimat* to promote a reign of conquest and genocide in pursuit of the creation of a German homeland across Europe, Bloch sees *Heimat* as a spatially fluid homeland for every individual which can satisfy the core human desires for community, safety, non-alienation and joy anywhere humans find themselves. Bloch connects alienation in the Marxist sense – the separation of individuals from the products of their labour, their communities and ultimately their species being – with a metaphysical form of homelessness and unrootedness, suggesting that humanity's eventual homecoming will also figure as a refusal of alienated being. As Levitas puts it, '*Heimat* is the expression of a desire for a settled resolution of this alienated condition … It is a quest for wholeness, for being at home in the world'.[81]

For the inhabitants of Marin, the creation of 'plausible desirable futures' – spaces of comfort, stability, self-expression and belonging, is originally made possible by the doors and the radical mobility they introduce into the world. However, once the doors have receded into the background of the new planetary order – after Nadia and Saeed's final trip from the London Halo to Marin, they are only mentioned again once, in a vignette where an old woman chooses not to follow her daughter through them – it is not the doors themselves which continue changing the way humans relate to each other and themselves, but the realization of a kind of *Heimat* in the present: 'people found things to do and ways to be and people to be with'.[82] For Nadia, this *Heimat* comes in the literal shape of a room, but also in a romantic relationship with a woman who works at her cooperative; for Saeed, it emerges through a romance with the daughter of a preacher, alongside a more nuanced and complex development of his relationship with religion. In Saeed's homeland, prayer was a way to express himself as 'a particular sort of man, a gentleman, a gentle man, a man who stood for community and faith and kindness and decency, a man, in other words, like his father' – a connection with the traditions and memories of his family and nation as much as a wider sense of traditional masculinity.[83] In Marin, however, in the newly emerging *Heimat*, Saeed prays to connect to a planetary, universal, radical sense of non-alienated being, which Hamid describes in another particularly extended, paratactical sentence:

> Now, though, in Marin, Saeed prayed even more, several times a day, and he prayed fundamentally as a gesture of love for what had gone and would go and could be loved in no other way. When he prayed he touched his parents, who could not otherwise be touched, and he touched a feeling that we are all children who lose our parents, all of us, every man and woman and boy and girl, and we too will all be lost by those who come after us and love us, and this loss unites humanity, unites every human being, the temporary nature

of our being-ness, and our shared sorrow, the heartache we each carry and yet too often refuse to acknowledge in one another, and out of this Saeed felt it might be possible, in the face of death, to believe in humanity's potential for building a better world, and so he prayed as a lament, as a consolation, and as a hope […].[84]

Although it is implicit in *Exit West* that Nadia and Saeed's religion is Islam, Hamid's conscious choice in not naming it as such allows the novel's readers to read Saeed's prayer as a universal, utopian hope for the realization of a new world which can unite 'every human being'. This key passage most clearly highlights the connection, which threads its way through *Exit West*, of homeland and parenthood. By the end of the novel, Nadia and Saeed are both orphans, but beyond the literal loss of their families, their travels have fundamentally orphaned them from a traditional, national sense of homeland and the desire to return to it. In a sense, every inhabitant of the novel's new *Heimat* is a child who has lost the parent of their original homeland, and is now, sorrowfully yet hopefully, moving towards the horizon of a 'better world'.

Marin: An emergent mobile commons

As I have suggested in the opening of this chapter, the mobile commons is a form of shared world-building and a set of demands for greater justice by those on the move 'which creates new forms of life that sustain migrants' ordinary movements', in particular 'daily social relations, connections and conditions that evade the control of mobility' such as border regimes and citizenship infrastructures. For Papadopoulos and Tsianos, the five features of everyday life which distinguish the mobile commons are:

1. a 'knowledge of mobility', which Nadia and Saeed access during their time on Mykonos: 'the news, the tumult in the world, the state of their country, the various routes and destinations migrants were taking and recommending to each other, the tricks one could gainfully employ, the dangers one needed at all costs to avoid';
2. an 'infrastructure of connectivity', which in *Exit West* frequently appears in the shape of mobile phones, whose antennas 'sniffed out an invisible

world, as if by magic, a world that was all around them, and also nowhere, transporting them to places distant and near';
3. a 'multiplicity of informal economies' which appear throughout the novel, from agents who sell access to secret doors to black markets where one could buy or barter anything 'from sweaters to mobile phones to antibiotics to, quietly, sex and drugs';
4. 'communities of justice', extra-governmental organizations which protect the rights of migrants, represented in *Exit West* by people who wear the 'migrant compassion badge, the black door within a red heart';
5. 'the politics of care', which suffuse Hamid's novel, incorporating all of Papadopoulos and Tsianos' examples of 'mutual cooperation, friendships, favours that you never return, affective support, trust, care for other people's relatives and children, transnational relations of care, the gift economy between mobile people'.[85]

The mobile commons has much in common with commons we have seen previously in this book (Spahr's barricades and riots) and those which will be discussed in the next two chapters: they create networks of care, support and solidarity; they are oppositional to neoliberal alienation and precarization; they are based on economies of sharing and collectivity; and they have the potential to prefigure new, utopian ways of life.

For Papadopoulos and Tsianos, mobile commons are an empowering yet also temporary arrangement of social and political networks, only operating while their 'inhabitants' are in the process of movement. This reading does not open out onto the idea of a mobile commons as a more permanent and expanding social system. Natasha King and Mimi Sheller offer separate expansions on this theorization which more powerfully anchor the mobile commons' potential of support and care in the greater mobility justice movement, and thus in the creation of lasting, mobile, commons-oriented political subjects. King reads the autonomy of migration as an escape from the sovereign power of the state, and argues that greater justice for those fleeing the power of border regimes can only be won through 'collaborative community-building' occurring when 'different kinds of people participate together in the mobile commons', including people in positions of comparative privilege and power like those activists and organizers who can cross borders without threat of incarceration. Key to such participation is 'taking action, collaboratively and meaningfully, with people who experience oppressions that we do not'.[86] In this way, the tactics and knowledges acquired by migrants can be brought into already existing commons of activist networks, squats and community support organizations on both sides of borders. These wider commons become a site from which to oppose and circumvent border regimes and state power through forms of ongoing struggle and solidarity.

Mimi Sheller distinguishes between mobility commons and mobile commons, two faces of the same struggle linked through the concept of mobility justice. The mobility commons is oppositional to border regimes, and through this oppositionality, remains liminal: it 'allows for people to exercise ... productive forms of autonomous social cooperation outside of capitalism, and beyond or beneath the limits of national borders, existing in the interstices'. The key resource shared within the mobility commons is 'access to the cooperative social territories and shared infrastructures of movement (both material and immaterial) – i.e., the pathways, ways, and means of moving, sharing, and communicating'.[87] The mobile commons, for Sheller, is *a form of movement* ethically practised in mobility commons:

> A mobile commons is enacted within shared practices of movement, momentary gatherings, and fleeting assembly, for a time, in a place, without owning it, so long as one does not ruin it, lay waste to it, degrade it, or take it away from the use of others. This implies upholding principles of deliberative justice, procedural justice, reparative justice, and epistemic justice. It is a kind of mindful movement, shared with others, and based upon forms of solidarity, reciprocity, caring, trust, generosity, and stewardship. It is temporally oriented toward maintaining the intergenerational connections between past, present, and future in terms of how we move over the Earth – lightly, carefully, with concern for others, and especially through difficult efforts of translation and accompaniment across difference.[88]

Sheller's expansive theorization, coupled with the work of King on the value of activist movements to mobility justice, develops mobile commons as a utopian instrument for effecting socio-political change on a planetary scale. As Sheller argues, the anchoring of human mobility in a politics of caring common existence allows activists to 'move beyond the city street and to take on larger planetary mobility politics', and ultimately to challenge the potential 'de-politicization of humanity, and the dystopian ending of communality' – the hallmarks and effects of unconstrained contemporary capitalism.[89] Texts such as *Exit West* have an important part to play in this oppositional movement: through the transmission of poetics, tactics, ethics and politics of mobility justice and mobile commons, they can educate readers to move beyond capitalism and its border regimes.

By the end of *Exit West*, the novel's imagined world has been transformed irreversibly – rather than comprising nation-states insulated by border regimes and linked by tightly controlled flows of labour and capital, it is diffuse, mutable and diverse. States and borders become increasingly irrelevant; cities expand out from their centres to incorporate halos of new towns; and small localities and regions come under the management of directly democratic local assemblies. However, this fundamental change in global society is described not as an apocalyptic or catastrophic break with what came before, but through a commons poetics of collectivity and adjustment. The novel rejects any sense that this mobility commons will at any point disintegrate and be incorporated into a more structured social order. Rather, anti-capitalist and decolonial modes of 'solidarity, reciprocity, caring, trust, generosity, and stewardship' become the imagined world's dominant form of social organization. *Exit West* calls for a new planetary ethics built on commons, mobility, and care for humans and non-humans – a system of justice which will neither tether the Global South closer to capitalism, nor exact violent revenge on the Global North for its colonial histories, but surpass both of these short-term solutions to create a planetary commons, moving beyond borders and geographical inequalities and towards a utopian world of limitless and ethical movement, endlessly under construction and revision.

Notes

1 Viet Thanh Nguyen, 'March's Book Club Pick: "Exit West," by Mohsin Hamid', *The New York Times*, 2017, https://www.nytimes.com/2017/03/10/books/review/exit-west-mohsin-hamid.html.

2 Dimitris Papadopoulos and Vassilis S. Tsianos, 'After Citizenship: Autonomy of Migration, Organisational Ontology and Mobile Commons', *Citizenship Studies* 17,

no. 2 (2013): 178–96 (184). This discourse is based in part on the Italian Marxist Autonomism movement of the 1960s, which understood class struggle as a willing choice by workers, rather than as a *post hoc* response to oppression. See: Mario Tronti, 'A New Type of Political Experiment: Lenin in England', in *Workers and Capital* (London: Verso, 2019), 65–72.

3   Hannah Cross, *Migrants, Borders and Global Capitalism: West African Labour Mobility and EU Borders* (London: Routledge, 2013), 16.

4   Sandro Mezzadra, 'The Gaze of Autonomy: Capitalism, Migration and Social Struggles', in *The Contested Politics of Mobility: Borderzones and Irregularity*, ed. Vicki Squire (London: Routledge, 2010), 125.

5   Bloch, *Principle of Hope*, 3:1311.

6   See: Cressida Leyshon, 'Mohsin Hamid on the Migrants in All of Us', *The New Yorker*, 2016, https://www.newyorker.com/books/page-turner/this-week-in-fiction-mohsin-hamid-2016-11-14.

7   UNHCR, *Refugees & Migrants Arrivals to Europe in 2018 (Mediterranean)* (Geneva: UNHCR, 2018), https://data2.unhcr.org/en/documents/download/68006. David Miller defines a border regime as 'the set of rules and procedures that apply to those who are trying to enter the state's territory, encompassing a number of questions such as who is given legal permission to enter, what procedures are applied to those whose admission status is as yet undetermined, and what happens to people who are present in the territory without having rights of residence – for instance asylum-seekers and illegal migrants'. See: David Miller, 'Border Regimes and Human Rights', *The Law & Ethics of Human Rights* 7, no. 1 (2013): 1–23.

8   Reis Thebault, Luis Velarde, and Abigail Hauslochner, 'The Father and Daughter Who Drowned at the Border Were Desperate for a Better Life, Family Says', *Washington Post*, 2019, https://www.washingtonpost.com/world/2019/06/26/father-daughter-who-drowned-border-dove-into-river-desperation/.

9   Óscar García Agustín and Martin Bak Jørgensen, *Solidarity and the 'Refugee Crisis' in Europe* (Cham: Springer, 2019), 6–7.

10 Achille Mbembe, 'Necropolitics', *Public Culture* 15, no. 1 (2003): 14, 31, 34.

11 Paul Gilroy, *Postcolonial Melancholia* (New York: Columbia University Press, 2004), 4; Mai Al-Nakib, 'Finding Common Cause: A Planetary Ethics of "What Could Happen If"', *Interventions*, 2019: 10.

12 Hamid, *Exit West*, 69.

13 Decoloniality is a praxis for unlinking power, knowledge and progress from colonial and neocolonial logics of globalization, neoliberalism, Eurocentricity

and modernity, originating as a theoretical form in the twenty-first century within Latin American contexts. See: Walter Mignolo and Catherine E. Walsh, *On Decoloniality: Concepts, Analytics, Praxis* (Durham: Duke University Press, 2018).

14 Claire Chambers, *Making Sense of Contemporary British Muslim Novels* (New York: Palgrave Macmillan, 2019), 218.
15 Hamid, *Exit West*, 85.
16 Chambers, *Making Sense of Contemporary British Muslim Novels*, 216.
17 Farah Mendlesohn, *Rhetorics of Fantasy* (Middletown: Wesleyan University Press, 2008).
18 Hamid, *Exit West*, 127.
19 Hamid, *Exit West*, 209.
20 Rosemary Marangoly George, *The Politics of Home: Postcolonial Relocations and Twentieth-Century Fiction* (Berkeley: University of California Press, 1999), 171; Rosemarie Buikema, 'A Poetics of Home: On Narrative Voice and the Deconstruction of Home in Migrant Literature', in *Migrant Cartographies: New Cultural and Literary Spaces in Post-Colonial Europe*, ed. Sandra Ponzanesi and Daniela Merolla (Oxford: Lexington Books, 2005), 177.
21 Hamid, *Exit West*, 1.
22 Chambers, *Making Sense of Contemporary British Muslim Novels*, 228.
23 Hamid, *Exit West*, 6–7.
24 Hamid, *Exit West*, 7; cf. *Heart of Darkness*: 'He held his head rigid, face forward; but his eyes rolled, he kept on lifting and setting down his feet gently, his mouth foamed a little'; Chambers connects this reference with similar representations of the dangerous and desperate black man in 'Raj fiction' of the British Imperial presence on the Indian subcontinent. See: Joseph Conrad, *Heart of Darkness* (London: Penguin Books, 2007), 55; Chambers, *Making Sense of Contemporary British Muslim Novels*, 241.
25 Hamid, *Exit West*, 83.
26 Hamid, *Exit West*, 23.
27 Berlant, *Cruel Optimism*, 198.
28 Caren Kaplan, *Questions of Travel: Postmodern Discourses of Displacement, Post-Contemporary Interventions* (Durham: Duke University Press, 1996), 90.
29 Natasha King, *No Borders: The Politics of Immigration Control and Resistance* (London: Zed Books, 2016), 131.
30 Hamid, *Exit West*, 9.
31 Hamid, *Exit West*, 13.

32 Hamid, *Exit West*, 14.
33 These intimate utopias are allied with Davina Cooper's concept of everyday utopias – minor, local spaces for experimentation with new forms of sociality. See: Davina Cooper, *Everyday Utopias: The Conceptual Life of Promising Spaces* (Durham: Duke University Press, 2014), 167–72.
34 Hamid, *Exit West*, 70.
35 Hamid, *Exit West*, 90.
36 Hamid, *Exit West*, 142.
37 Hamid, *Exit West*, 151.
38 Victor Turner, *The Ritual Process: Structure and Anti-Structure* (Ithaca: Cornell University Press, 1977), 97, 96, 132.
39 Subha Mukherji, 'Introduction', in *Thinking on Thresholds: The Poetics of Transitive Spaces*, ed. Subha Mukherji (London: Anthem Press, 2011), xxiii.
40 Hamid, *Exit West*, 101.
41 Hamid, *Exit West*, 155–6. Spahr uses the same metaphor of skin as a porous boundary in *This Connection of Everyone with Lungs*.
42 Stavros Stavrides, 'Common Space as Threshold Space: Urban Commoning in Struggles to Re-Appropriate Public Space', *Footprint*, 2015, 10.
43 Stavrides, 'Common Space as Threshold Space', 13.
44 Hamid, *Exit West*, 126.
45 Hamid, *Exit West*, 126, 129.
46 Turner, *The Ritual Process*, 95, 98.
47 Hamid, *Exit West*, 98.
48 Hamid, *Exit West*, 169–70.
49 Donna J. Haraway, *Staying with the Trouble: Making Kin in the Chthulucene* (Durham: Duke University Press, 2016), 47, 2, 4.
50 Hamid, *Exit West*, 136.
51 Haraway, *Staying with the Trouble*, 1.
52 Hamid, *Exit West*, 156–7.
53 George, *The Politics of Home*, 171, 174–6.
54 Susheila Nasta, *Home Truths: Fictions of the South Asian Diaspora in Britain* (Basingstoke: Palgrave, 2002), 1, 7.
55 Hamid, *Exit West*, 102.
56 Hamid, *Exit West*, 120.
57 Hamid, *Exit West*, 155.
58 Nasta, *Home Truths*, 1.
59 Hamid, *Exit West*, 164.

60 Julia Gregory, '8 Grenfell Families Are Still Living in Temporary Homes 27 Months On', *My London*, 2019, https://www.mylondon.news/news/west-london-news/8-grenfell-families-still-living-17131649.

61 However, see Chambers' connection of the '40 square metres and a pipe' each migrant family is promised with the '40 acres and a mule' promised to African-American slaves after abolition; in comparison with the fate of the freed slaves, the space given to the migrants is truly paltry. The reality of post-Civil War land redistribution, however, was far more piecemeal than the '40 acres and a mule' fiction. See: Chambers, *Making Sense of Contemporary British Muslim Novels*, 239.

62 Hamid, *Exit West*, 74.

63 Nasia Anam, 'The Migrant as Colonist: Dystopia and Apocalypse in the Literature of Mass Migration', *ASAP/Journal* 3, no. 3 (2018): 673.

64 Hamid, *Exit West*, 168.

65 Hamid, *Exit West*, 168.

66 Anam, 'The Migrant as Colonist', 674.

67 Anam, 'The Migrant as Colonist', 675–6.

68 On the use of edgelands as zones for the development of oppositional subjectivities in contemporary literature, see: Raphael Kabo, 'Towards a Taxonomy of Edgelands Literature', *Alluvium*, 2015, https://www.alluvium-journal.org/2015/06/26/towards-a-taxonomy-of-edgelands-literature/.

69 Hamid, *Exit West*, 191.

70 Hamid, *Exit West*, 219–20.

71 Murray Bookchin, *Urbanization without Cities: The Rise and Decline of Citizenship* (Montreal: Black Rose Books, 1992), 286.

72 David Harvey, 'From Space to Place and Back Again: Reflections on the Condition of Postmodernity', in *Mapping the Futures: Local Cultures, Global Change*, ed. John Bird et al. (Hoboken: Taylor and Francis, 2012), 152.

73 Iain Chambers, *Migrancy, Culture, Identity* (London: Routledge, 1994), 5.

74 Hamid, *Exit West*, 87.

75 Hamid, *Exit West*, 214.

76 Hamid, *Exit West*, 215–16.

77 Anton Kaes, *From Hitler to Heimat: The Return of History as Film* (Cambridge: Harvard University Press, 1989), 165.

78 Friederike Eigler, *Heimat, Space, Narrative: Toward a Transnational Approach to Flight and Expulsion* (Rochester: Camden House, 2014), 2, 13.

79 Jamie Owen Daniel, 'Reclaiming the "Terrain of Fantasy": Speculations on Ernst Bloch, Memory, and the Resurgence of Nationalism', in *Not Yet: Reconsidering Ernst Bloch*, ed. Jamie Owen Daniel and Tom Moylan (London: Verso, 1997), 59.
80 Bloch, *Principle of Hope*, 3:1376; translation by: Ruth Levitas, *Utopia as Method: The Imaginary Reconstitution of Society* (New York: Palgrave Macmillan, 2013), 7.
81 Levitas, *Utopia as Method*, 17. On Marx's concepts of alienation and species being, see: Karl Marx, *Economic and Philosophic Manuscripts of 1844*, 70–84.
82 Hamid, *Exit West*, 215–16.
83 Hamid, *Exit West*, 200–1.
84 Hamid, *Exit West*, 201–2.
85 Papadopoulos and Tsianos, 'After Citizenship', 191–2; Hamid, *Exit West*, 103, 35, 101, 105.
86 King, *No Borders*, 36, 132.
87 Mimi Sheller, *Mobility Justice: The Politics of Movement in the Age of Extremes* (London: Verso, 2018), 168–9.
88 Sheller, *Mobility Justice*, 169–70.
89 Sheller, *Mobility Justice*, 167, 170.

3

Utopias beyond disaster: *New York 2140*

The New York City of Kim Stanley Robinson's 2017 novel *New York 2140* is a near future metropolis defined, much as it is today, by runaway global warming, unregulated finance, economic inequality, sensationalized mass media, widespread precarity and desperate refugees fleeing ongoing disaster. A fifty-foot rise in the sea level has transformed lower Manhattan, once the capital of global finance, into an 'intertidal zone' of canals, partially drowned buildings and skybridges. In one of the novel's repeated returns to the history and aesthetics of nineteenth-century New York, life in this liminal urban zone now resembles 'earlier centuries of cheap squalid tenement reality, moldier than ever, the occupants risking their lives by the hour. Same as ever, but wetter'.[1] Despite the novel's committed representation of the precarity, trauma and destruction wrought by the capitalist profit motive's drive to irreversibly alter the planetary climatological and ecological balance, *New York 2140* has been widely described as 'surprisingly utopian', 'genuinely utopian' and 'decidedly utopian'.[2] Indeed, like all self-aware contemporary utopias, *New York 2140* is a blend of warning and hope, a novel about unevenly distributed capitalist disaster and the utopian commons which can emerge to oppose and attenuate it – commons formed of concrete spatial tactics, collective relations and environmental engagements. This chapter will argue that, in a deliberate and direct engagement with contemporary utopian theory, *New York 2140* employs a commons poetics, inspired by the events of the GFC and contemporary anti-capitalist politics, not only to promote the idea of utopia as contingent, open and diverse, but to challenge the idea that it must occur outside of or beyond our current world. Instead, like Spahr in *That Winter the Wolf Came* and Hamid in *Exit West*, Robinson offers a prefigurative vision of the future as working upon the present in utopian ways.

Kim Stanley Robinson has been described as America's most committed (and perhaps, as he himself ironically remarks, last) utopian writer.[3] Robinson wrote his doctorate on science fiction author Philip K. Dick under the supervision of Jameson in the 1980s, and Jameson's writings on utopianism have influenced Robinson's development of an analytical, rationalist, dialectic and reflexive project of passionate and hopeful utopian imagining over the following three decades. Each of the books of his *Three Californias* trilogy (1984, 1988, 1990) reimagines Robinson's home state, in turn, as a survivalist frontier in the aftermath of a nuclear war, a near future high-tech dystopia, and an ecological utopia, exhibiting Robinson's ability to manipulate genre and laying the groundwork for his interest in a process-oriented, dialogic, piecemeal utopianism which manifests even in the least utopian of worlds. Robinson takes this rejection of straightforward generic categories further in the sprawling *Mars* trilogy (1992, 1993, 1996), which chronicles the colonization, terraforming and revolutionary struggle for power on Mars over a period of almost 200 years. The trilogy's ambitious temporal scope allows Robinson to fictionally bring to life multiple competing utopian imaginaries, but particularly the utopia of reasoned debate itself: 'a kind of utopian community, cozy and bright and protected', where people 'gave talks, asked questions, debated details of fact, discussed implications'.[4]

Jameson has returned the favour of his utopian politics being realized, in fiction, by writing at length on Robinson's work in a number of the essays collected in *Archaeologies of the Future*, where, with specific reference to Robinson's *Mars* trilogy, he describes the utopian literature of the late twentieth century as 'not the representation of Utopia, but rather the conflict of all possible Utopias'.[5] In Jameson's extensive critiques of late twentieth-century utopian literature, including Robinson's work, he concludes that although such utopias hold a vital social, cultural and aesthetic role in highlighting and critiquing the many contradictions of the late capitalist world system, they fail to exert the political function of opposing it or developing concrete proposals for transformation and escape. The real work of utopian representation thus becomes 'to think the break itself', to meditate 'on the impossible, on the unrealizable in its own right' – to ceaselessly debate, like the Martian settlers, about what utopia might include and exclude.[6] Jameson's argument that utopian thinking is a kind of dream which will always fade away as the revolutionary body wakes from its slumber and brings its attention to the real, non-utopian work of escaping the late capitalist totality likewise draws on Robinson's writing. At the end of an essay on the *Mars* trilogy, he writes: 'utopia as a form is not the representation of radical alternatives; it is rather simply the imperative to imagine them'. Of the utopia of *Blue Mars*, the concluding volume of the trilogy, he claims: 'we do not ever witness its evolution as a narrative event; perhaps indeed we could not do so'.[7]

New York 2140 is best understood as a gentle yet assured critique and corrective of Jameson's theory of utopia, a paradigmatic utopian text for a post-GFC, post-Occupy contemporary moment which is distinct from the late twentieth-century totality. It is a leading example of a new 'formal tendency' in utopian fiction, emerging within and moving beyond those tendencies centred by Jameson. At least in terms of its deliberately and self-consciously utopian form, its didacticism and its anti-capitalist politics, *New York 2140* may be the clearest example we yet have of a commons utopia. At the same time, Robinson's project is not perfect: while it is a political and economic utopia, it is oddly traditional in its portrayal of gender roles, and only briefly touches on the Indigenous Lenape histories and resistance practices which are crucial to understanding the spaces of Manhattan in which it is set. Where *New York 2140* proves most effective is in deploying a ruthless economic and political critique of late capitalist totality, while at the same time retaining a steely-eyed commitment to representing the possibility of utopian commons-building. Robinson's project works not in spaces and times far removed from our present, but in the very world we currently inhabit, educating and inspiring its readers with the hope that capitalism can be overthrown today.

The genres of *New York 2140*

New York 2140 represents a utopia which feels reassuringly realist and familiar, yet is politically and economically aligned beyond the capitalist relations which condition the contemporary world system – a contemporary space inhabited in a prefigurative mode. The novel's on-the-nose title echoes numerous science fiction texts including *Nineteen Eighty-Four* (George Orwell, 1949), *2012* (dir. Roland Emmerich, 2009), *2001: A Space Odyssey* (dir. Stanley Kubrick,

1968) and, indeed, Robinson's own *2312* (2012), which both anticipates and futuristically extends many of the themes of *New York 2140*. The title, alongside its glitzy, futuristic cover, suggests to the reader that *New York 2140* is a science fiction novel. However, the novel plays with the conventions and styles of a variety of genres, exploiting the verisimilitude of the historical novel, the aesthetics of twentieth-century science fiction, and the dystopian and utopian tensions of twenty-first-century cli-fi.

Understanding *New York 2140* as a text working between and within the genres of the historical novel, science fiction, cli-fi and utopia allows us to explore the generic and formal strategies Robinson implements in his commons poetics. The commons evoked in *New York 2140* are not limited to the level of narrative. The novel is also a textual, literary commons in the mode evoked by Spahr and Collis – produced by a multitude of authors, constantly contending with the idea of 'what it means to have the words of others in one's own mouth', and among those 'appropriation-heavy literatures of the turn of the twenty-first century [which] insist that the words of others are in our mouths all the time'.[8] Robinson's characters continually have the nineteenth and twentieth centuries on their tongues, not only because this helps us relate to their drowned world, but also because they cannot help but return, in their imaginings, to ours. As Gerry Canavan generously and powerfully argues:

> I came to understand that this was not simply as-you-know-Bob overexposition; it was also a token of the immense trauma they and everyone in Future New York is still living through. What else would you think about, as you flew through a strange web of skybridges and ziplines crisscrossing the ruins of what used to be the greatest city in the world? Of course they talk and think often about how things used to be, back when the world was normal. They live with that temporal confusion every day.[9]

For Robinson's New Yorkers, the simultaneous nearness and inaccessibility of the past force them to contend with centuries of trauma – both that of their own time, and that of past times eerily similar to theirs. As a result, the novel is also a temporal commons, a combination of pasts and futures into one continuous, reflexive, emergent narrative. Max Haiven describes the collision of the past with the present and future in a shared, radical archive as 'commoning memory … a form of co-memorialization that takes as its challenge not the accurate representation of previous events but the rekindling of the spark of past utopianisms in the present … in order to provoke future radical events'.[10]

David Sergeant contends that *New York 2140* 'seems in many ways so close to our historical moment as to be almost indistinguishable from it'. In its proliferation of intertextual reference and callback, of which very little refers to the period of time between 2017 and 2140, the novel 'thereby builds the impression of a thickly textured historical past feeding into a present that is not so much 2140 as 2017'.[11] As Gerry Canavan drily notes: 'the people of 2140 seem awfully well informed about nuts-and-bolts details of the 2008 financial crisis'.[12] Indeed, beyond brief references to 'the two that followed' the 2008 crisis, for which the latter in any case 'served as the model', the economic ontology of *New York 2140*, alongside its cultural and social history, is located squarely in the twentieth and early twenty-first centuries.[13] As an example, in the novel's opening pages, the itinerant hackers Mutt and Jeff (named after the comedy duo of the eponymous twentieth-century American newspaper cartoon) argue about the failures of the financial system and the market, with one didactically announcing to the other: 'We're in a mass extinction event, sea level rise, climate change, food panics … the problem is capitalism'.[14] In short order, Mutt and Jeff reference the WTO (World Trade Organization), the G20, the SEC (Securities and Exchange Commission), the computer scientist Ken Thompson, the mid-century fictional detective Nero Wolfe and American poet Walt Whitman. Only when the text locates them in 'the open-walled farm floor of the old Met Life tower, from which vantage point lower Manhattan lies flooded below them like a super-Venice' does the future come colliding back into the contemporary neoliberal present from which they appear to be talking.[15]

Robinson not only describes, but politically critiques this real-world history. *New York 2140* characterizes the late capitalist present as ongoing, repetitive and futureless. The apocalyptic urban spatiality of New York in 2140 is thus also a representation of the most likely future which stems *from* our present. Sergeant quite clearly captures the parameters of this political and temporal conceit:

> By telling the story of the present in the further future, the novel gives the former a dual nature. It is static, as is reflected in its continuation over a

century into the future, and it is charged with forward motion, as is reflected in the novel's account of societal change prior to and then through an economic crash. And in imbricating present and future, the novel prevents a paradigm-altering Event – technological or apocalyptic – from slipping in between them to offer a more convenient transition into a radically different future.[16]

Instead, *New York 2140* shows the next century painfully, precariously and disastrously being lived through by populations familiarly trapped under the 'stupid laws' of capitalism – namely the growth imperative, the 'shock doctrine' and the demand for competition.[17]

As part of its haunting by the pasts of our own present, *New York 2140* bears numerous hallmarks of urban novels, social novels and historical novels from the eighteenth, nineteenth and twentieth centuries, particularly in its intertextual returns to authors including John Dos Passos, Herman Melville, Walt Whitman and Henry James; its flaneuresque interest in the social history of particular streets and buildings; its large ensemble cast of characters gathered from various social classes and occupying various political and social positions; its pointed critiques of consumerist excess and inequality; its adulations of urban community and the social character of New Yorkers; and its grand, sweeping narrative scope. Three authors whose influence emerges with particular force here are Charles Dickens, Dos Passos and Henry Fielding.

Dickens's literary world of colourful urban types and improbable occurrences, and keen eye for injustice, inequality, suffering and sickness in the city haunt much of *New York 2140*; his spirit is particularly evident in the characters of Stefan and Roberto, the orphaned 'water rats' who are taken in by the Met Life co-operative. In a memorable scene, Stefan announces that, in the absence of parents, guardians or foster parents, the boys are 'free citizens of the intertidal'. While Stefan's parents died 'of the cholera' after they emigrated to New York from Russia – a melodramatic sequence of events which could have been lifted directly from a Dickens novel – Roberto dramatically claims that he 'brought himself up', subsisting on food fallen through the slats of the Skyline Marina from the tender age of nine months.[18] Almost unthinkably for a reader situated in a neoliberal world system of omniscient biopolitical governmentality, Stefan and Roberto have also fallen through the metaphorical cracks of New York: there is 'no record for them' in the city. Far from depicting a new stage in an ongoing chain of historical progress, Robinson's future world is a regression into Dickensian capriciousness, injustice and disorder.

The legacies of Dos Passos and Fielding appear in the character of 'the Citizen', the opinionated, trenchant, didactic and loquacious narrator of a number of chapters spaced through the novel. Like the 'overt narrators' of *Joseph Andrews* (1742) and *Tom Jones* (1749), and with reference to Dos Passos's 'Camera Eye' in the *U.S.A.* trilogy (1930, 1932, 1936), the Citizen speaks in a dramatization of Robinson's authorial voice; he is helpfully omniscient, filling in important details about Robinson's world; his chapters are addressed directly to the reader in the second person; he is ironic and holds strong convictions, 'discriminating among and emphasizing certain values' in his own story.[19] Particularly amusing is his propensity to anticipate 'arguments with narratees who might form "erroneous" opinions', exclaiming, for example, 'Don't be naïve!' when the narratee is in danger of enjoying a moment of unadulterated hope, and elsewhere saying 'if you think you know how the world works, think again. You are deceived. You don't know; you can't see it, and the whole story has never been told to you. Sorry. Just the way it is.'[20] The ways in which the Citizen moulds and articulates an ideal reader are not simply referential play; it goes to the heart of Robinson's utopian project. As we shall see below, the Citizen's interventions in the final chapters of *New York 2140*, like Spahr's, subvert the fiction of sole authorship, welcoming the reader in to shape a utopia alongside the Citizen.

Even the novel's structure reveals its connection to past literary traditions: it is divided into eight parts named in humorous evocation of the sections of a historical or economic treatise ('The Tyranny of Sunk Costs', 'Liquidity Trap', 'The Comedy of the Commons', and so on). Each part is split into chapters which are named after, and comprise the first-person limited narrations of, individual characters in the cast the Citizen's chapters are the exception to this. This structure encourages a reading of the novel as an assemblage of a polyphony of voices which together reflect something of the otherwise inexpressible diversity and variety of the urban populace, a technique refined by Dos Passos in the *U.S.A.* trilogy. The epigraphs to each section of the novel, and the frequent intertextual asides made both by the novel's cast and the Citizen, are reminiscent of the journalistic collage technique from the 'Newsreel' sections of the *U.S.A.* novels, while the Citizen narrator and worldly cast resemble their 'Camera Eye' sections. Robinson has consciously worked with Dos Passos's polymedia, polyphonous method since the writing of *2312*, when he first encountered Dos Passos's work. Robinson describes the characters of the *U.S.A.* trilogy much like the cast of his own novel: 'like pinballs in a pinball machine, bouncing around America in the 1920s, trying to figure it out'; in adapting Dos Passos's format to tell his stories, including his most recent *Ministry of the Future*, Robinson indicates that he strives 'to convey an entire culture in more detail than any ordinary plot can provide'.[21] While the geographical and temporal scope of *New York 2140* is exactly as narrow as the title promises, its literary hauntings, generic play and the sense it conveys of a society glimpsed in the transition through monumental, traumatic histories offer a far richer and more verisimilitudinous world to its readers.

Sergeant goes so far as to argue that *New York 2140* should be read as a logical extension of the historical novel genre, whose represented historical moment has been steadily approaching its own present since its emergence as a form, finally 'pushed through the present and out into the other side'.[22] However, Sergeant's formalist structural critique of this novel fails to capture the generic fluidity of Robinson's commons poetics. Besides incorporating elements of the leading styles of past literature, *New York 2140* also plays irreverently with recent tropes of science fiction and climate change dystopias.

Leaving aside for the moment the novel's central structuring conceit of a fifty-foot sea level rise, the major differences between the Earth of 2140 and the Earth of the late 2010s – AI-controlled airships, skyfaring villages, extremely tall skyscrapers constructed using carbon building materials, laser-aided women's-only underwater sumo wrestling rings, and widespread blockchain currency – belong so glaringly to a generic 'future' aesthetic commonplace in late twentieth and early twenty-first-century media that they only serve to highlight the multitude of ways in which, despite ostensibly being a science fiction novel about the future, *New York 2140* is better apprehended as a realist historical novel set in an alternative present. This generic positioning aligns it, within Robinson's wider body of work, far more closely with *The Years of Rice and Salt* (2002), which imagines an alternate history in which the Black Death almost entirely eradicated the population of Europe, than with his canonically science fictional *Mars* trilogy.

In modern media, the stereotypically futuristic aesthetic of hyper-cities, technologically advanced airships, altered versions of regular sports, along with skintight costumes and neon lighting, all form part of a visual shorthand, valued by producers and audiences, for identifying a piece of media as set in the future. While some of these aesthetic tropes begin to appear in science fiction of the early twentieth century, most science fiction texts from the 1970s onwards have made use of this visual language. Influential works in this aesthetic include the early work of director Hayao Miyazaki, in particular *Laputa: Castle in the Sky* (1986), *Blade Runner* (1982, dir. Ridley Scott), *The Fifth Element* (1997, dir. Luc Besson), *Logan's Run* (1976, dir. Michael Anderson) and *Akira* (1988, dir. Katsuhiro Otomo). Where Robinson has previously used this visual shorthand at face value to evoke a future temporality (cf. the airships in *The Years of Rice and Salt* and *Red Mars*), in *New York 2140* it is deployed reflexively to remind the novel's readers that the very future they are encountering has been designed and imagined in the early twenty-first century and generated with extensive intertextual reference to the history of the nineteenth century. Even in its most futuristic aesthetics, *New York 2140* is politically and culturally a novel about our past and present. Bringing this relationship to the fore in an intra-chapter epigraph, Robinson recalls an illustration from a 1908 guidebook to New York depicting a future city of airships, skyscrapers and skybridges, titled 'The Cosmopolis of the Future'. American artist William Robinson Leigh's painting 'Visionary City' of the same year adopts a similarly grandiose, monolithic aesthetic.

To further underline this point, many science fictional elements in the novel are metaphorically related to past technologies. A 'small skyvillage of the Twenty-one Balloons type' is named after the 1940s children's book by William Pène du Bois. The character Amelia is an aviator, albeit more fortunate than Amelia Earhart. Her airship was built 'in Friedrichshafen' – the home of the original Zeppelin Company – 'right before the turn of the century', just like the original successful airship, the Zeppelin LZ 1, albeit 200 years later. Its long travelling career is described as reminiscent of 'the tramp steamers of the latter part of the nineteenth century'.[23] Here and at many other moments, while remaining a work of science fiction, *New York 2140* returns to a past which has occurred before our own present to help create its oddly familiar vision of the future.

The final significant generic tendency from which *New York 2140* borrows is the genre of cli-fi, a portmanteau of 'sci-fi' and 'climate fiction', which describes a recent wave of highly successful texts, set in the near present or near future,

Figure 1 Harry Pettit, 'The Cosmopolis of the Future' from *King's Views of New York* (New York: Moses King, 1908). Image courtesy of The Skyscraper Museum.

and concerned with climate disasters occurring on a planetary scale. Some notable examples of this growing corpus are the novella *The End We Start From* (Megan Hunter, 2017), the films *Snowpiercer* (2013, dir. Bong Joon-ho) and *Mad Max: Fury Road* (dir. George Miller, 2015), and the novels *Oryx and Crake* (Margaret Atwood, 2003), *The Island Will Sink* (Briohny Doyle, 2013), *California* (Edan Lepucki, 2014), *The Water Knife* (Paolo Bacigalupi, 2015), *Black Wave* (Michelle Tea, 2015), *Gold Fame Citrus* (Claire Vaye Watkins, 2015) and *American War* (Omar El Akkad, 2017). Unsurprisingly, the worlds of many of these novels revolve around water – either its deadly lack or its destructive surplus.[24] Like these texts, *New York 2140* offers a vision of the Earth and its systems on the road to '[t]he Anthropocide, the Hydrocatastrophe, the Georevolution', a human-engineered breakdown in the balance of the planet's systems.[25] Indeed, beating against the current of critical opinion on *New York 2140*, Ruth Levitas categorizes the book as 'a dystopia rather than a utopia' and justifies this position by writing that dystopias 'share with utopias the method of depicting an alternative society, but constitute a warning of what may happen if we go on as we are, rather than a projection of a desired future'.[26] Read in this way, *New York 2140* is an exemplary cli-fi text – a world inescapably and entirely modulated by a climate catastrophe centuries in the making.

New York 2140's relationship to dystopia is nonetheless more nuanced than Levitas makes out. Adeline Johns-Putra argues that since it is 'more accurate to identify climate change as a topic found in many genres', including dystopia, and because growing scientific consensus on the ongoing and emerging effects of climate change paints a distinctly un-rosy picture of the future, many texts in the recent groundswell of climate change fiction can be 'categorized as dystopian … or postapocalyptic'.[27] While critics including Baccolini, Lyman Tower Sargent and Moylan have identified a trajectory of 'critical dystopias' in speculative literature since the 1980s, Moylan goes to the heart of the distinction between (critical) dystopia as a genre on one hand and literature with dystopian elements on the other when he writes: 'Formally and politically, therefore, the dystopian text refuses a functionalist or reformist perspective. In its purview, no single policy or practice can be isolated as the root problem, no single aberration can be privileged as the one to be fixed so that life in the enclosed status quo can easily resume.'[28] From its didactic first pages, and then through the expostulations of the opinionated Citizen narrator, *New York 2140* repeatedly and consistently fails this litmus test: the root cause of all the ills of its fictional world is capitalism; the close association of the future world with our present world suggests that these ills can already be resisted now; and finally, a system-overthrowing revolution is the obvious and ultimately achievable cure.

The world of a dystopia must be depicted as measurably worse than the world of its author. *New York 2140* fails this test too, depicting instead a world which is both much worse and much better than ours. Although the socially liberal cast of characters may have something to do with it, New York in 2140 appears relatively free from racism, classism, sexism and other forms of overt discrimination; this point is underscored by the universal respect afforded to Gen Octaviasdottir, a Black female Inspector in the New York City Police Department.[29] Even the stockbroker Frank, by far the most bigoted member of the cast, quickly becomes more respectful and open-minded as he spends more time with the others, and eventually ends up falling in love with the radical leftist organizer 'Red' Charlotte Armstrong. Frank and Charlotte's relationship is political as much as it is intimate. Their union symbolizes the formation of a new, utopian unity between the social revolutionary tactics proposed by Charlotte which, in the end, involve her exposing the criminal activity of the chairman of the Federal Reserve and calling for a national rent strike, and Frank's intuitive understanding of neoliberal finance, which allows him to effectively manipulate the system from the inside, accelerating the effects of Charlotte's activity. Other utopian elements in Robinson's world highlight the importance of management, maintenance and 'staying with the trouble' of a damaged planet, such as the conversion of office towers to sustainable housing and high-rise farms; the planet's wholesale switch to renewable energy; and the widespread adoption of carbon sequestration technologies – necessary transitions to stave off an even more extreme sea level rise. Such tactics work together to reclaim the terrain of a drowned world from the jaws of dystopia, reminding the novel's audience that the material realities of disaster and crisis do not necessarily engender the affective responses of hopelessness and desolation.

These utopian elements emerge with particular force in the spatial production of lower Manhattan. In the years following the floods, abandoned by capital, the property left standing in the intertidal becomes practically free, opening the door for 'some kind of return of the commons'.[30] The intertidal becomes a fertile ground for the exploration of utopian tactics for communal life. With light touch and imaginative scope, Robinson conjures a fifty-year history for Lower Manhattan which has certainly never happened in our world, but comprises a dozen already existing alternatives to capitalism:

> a proliferation of cooperatives, neighborhood associations, communes, squats, barter, alternative currencies, gift economies, solar usufruct, fishing village cultures, mondragons, unions, Davy's locker freemasonries, anarchist blather, and submarine technoculture, including aeration and aquafarming. Also sky living in skyvillages that used the drowned cities as mooring towers and festival exchange points; containerclippers and townships as floating islands; art-not-work, the city regarded as a giant collaborative artwork; blue greens, amphibiguity, heterogeneticity, horizontalization, deoligarchification; also free open universities, free trade schools, and free art schools.[31]

This utopian vision, any aspect of which could easily fill a novel of its own, tactically combines cultural and social transformations in the lacunae of capitalism (the fantastic conjuration of 'skyvillages' as 'festival exchange points'; the radical simplicity of 'art-not-work'; the delightful portmanteau of 'amphibiguity' working against the horror narratives of climate catastrophe) with political and economic developments which defend, condition and extend their effects.

The spatialities of *New York 2140*

Neither science fiction nor historical novel nor dystopia, *New York 2140* is a novel of commons on many levels. The interplay of material, spatial commons; the highly intertextual narrative, which provides fertile ground for linking the past to the present and future; and the traumatic and utopian collusions which emerge as a result of this temporal liquidity are all contained in a commons poetics which is predicated on genre and structure. This commons poetics is grounded in the depiction of spatial tactics of inhabiting, occupying and resisting which allow the ongoing capitalist future of the centuries leading up to 2140 to be radically and profoundly overturned – and for an alternative utopian future to emerge in its place. The ways in which Robinson uses commons spatialities in *New York 2140* reveal a closely networked set of oppositional tactics and anti-capitalist politics which support the novel's contention that the future can be transformed in the present moment.

The Met Life Tower: an urban commons

The narrative of *New York 2140* is divided between the stories of a large and diverse host of characters who live in the Met Life Tower on Madison Square, completed in 1909 to serve as the headquarters of the Metropolitan Life Insurance Company and, by 2140, transformed into a partially submerged housing co-operative. The Met Life Tower occupies a central location not only in the narrative, but also on the novel's front cover, emerging between far taller buildings, and on the peninsula of Manhattan itself, sitting at the interchange point between the precarious, liminal zone at the very edge of the intertidal, where buildings regularly collapse into the oncoming tide, and the higher-altitude, drier streets to the north. As a result, the tower serves as the natural site of the novel's main commons, providing what Massimo De Angelis identifies as the three key aspects of a commons spatiality: shared resources (a large farm, a dining hall where residents work and eat, apartments, infrastructure and communal areas for relaxation); a community of people; and forms of 'doing in common, commoning', which are, however, put to the test when a significant percentage of the tower's residents consider dismantling the co-op management structure and selling up to a shadowy real estate speculator.[32]

The key reason for the Met Life Tower's prominence in the novel is, of course, the fact that its architects modelled it on the Campanile di San Marco in Venice, Italy – one of drowned New York's central aesthetic references. Another ironic resonance in the tower's centrality to the plot is the way in which it recalls the Metropolitan Life Insurance Company, an outfit which presumably fared quite badly in the decades leading up to 2140. In many ways, however, the Met Life Tower continues to provide insurance for its residents: its futuristic waterproof diamond coating and the ceaseless maintenance work of its superintendent Vlade protect the tower from flooding, while the co-operative executive committee, under the leadership of Charlotte, work in the tower's best interests as it navigates an uncertain future. It is in these

Figure 2 Front cover of *New York 2140* by Kim Stanley Robinson, copyright © 2017. Image reprinted by permission of Orbit, an imprint of Hachette Book Group, Inc.

dull, everyday activities – maintenance, upkeep, management, debate – that the 'doing in common' aspect of the Met Life commons emerges most clearly.

Berlant has characterized activities such as maintenance, defence and 'compromised endurance' as a form of fantasy which will only ever allow us to 'measure the impasse of living in the overwhelmingly present moment', not overcome it.[33] However, within the supporting structure – social, political, cultural and even ecological – of the Met Life tower commons, these activities take on a clearly oppositional flavour, aligning to engender a form of community-reinforcing, utopian activity. This provocation indexes a present and likely future where capitalism and the commons, ongoing apocalypse and oppositional utopia, are forced into coexistence by a world increasingly short on space and increasingly defined by catastrophe and devastation. From within this uncomfortable intermingling, however, commons can uncover paths to rewrite the dominant narratives of capitalism.

Recognizing this intermingling, which forces commons to emerge in the 'waste' and 'detritus' of a capitalist world, De Angelis searches for the 'communal constitution of struggles and the ability to reclaim and constitute commons in a condition of detritus'. His conclusion on how contemporary commons can work to escape these conditions could have easily been written about the antinomies of life lived on a flooded peninsula covered in the wreckage of the past three centuries:

> The rewards are not just individualised payoffs [...] commons also reward through their staying together and learning from one another, through the forming of affective links to replace the tenuous, formal or alienated connections that exist in the neoliberal city always on the run.[34]

Charlotte evokes this anti-capitalist, affective mode of communal life when she declares, angrily and idealistically, to her fellow co-operative members: 'Fuck money ... because everything is not fungible to everything else. Many things can't be bought. Money isn't time, it isn't security, it isn't health. You can't buy any of those things. You can't buy community or a sense of home.'[35]

Many of the novel's pivotal scenes, including a conference call between Frank, Charlotte and the ecological activist and 'cloud star' (reality TV show personality) Amelia Black, which emboldens Amelia to call upon her viewers to participate in a mass rent strike, occur in the tower's cooperatively worked dining hall. The spatiality of the hall emerges through the minor comforts and dramas of communal life. Amelia describes the 'hundreds of people in the serving lines and crowded side by side at long tables, talking and eating' as 'tadpoles in a pond', which suggests both the watery reality of life in New York, and the sense of the Met Life as incubating a larval utopian community. Charlotte's description is of a world of affable, functional chaos, harking back to Dos Passos's stream-of-consciousness style: 'dining hall jammed, very loud, people sitting on the floor against the walls with trays on their laps, glasses on the floor beside them'. Frank complains that with all the cast's newfound friends around one table, there are 'just a couple too many people to be able to have a single conversation easily, not least because there were a few hundred more people in the big dining hall, and it was therefore noisy'; his day is ruined further by 'a group in the corner … playing Reich's "Music for 18 Musicians" by clacking a set of variously sized spoons and singing wordlessly'.[36] While this performance annoys Frank, as background music for the dining hall commons, 'Music for 18 Musicians' is aptly chosen. Jesse Budel writes that the minimalist piece, with its complex, semi-improvised mixture of repeating, emerging and disappearing sounds creates 'a communal environment, where both individual decision making and organised ensemble activity determine the complex sonic result'. Robert Cowan highlights the indeterminate, open-ended nature of the piece; it is potentially utopian in the sense of endless, reflexive, communal possibility which emerges from its sparse original instructions.[37]

Enmeshed in countless other systems, urban and ecological, the commons of the Met Life simultaneously works to defend itself from enclosure by the grasping hands of capital, imagined as a powerful, shadowy 'octopus' of companies vying to buy out all the property in the intertidal made newly valuable by the care and maintenance activities of their anti-capitalist inhabitants, and to collectively build power and seek solidarity with other organizations who share its ethos. Vlade, the building's superintendent, is part of a 'kind of club' with the maintenance crews of the other buildings of lower Manhattan, 'all enmeshed with the mutual aid associations and cooperative groups that knitted together to make intertidal life its own society'. The metaphorical distinction between the web-like enmeshing and knitting together of these organizations and the singular, reaching tentacles of the octopus is telling, highlighting the difference between monolithic and distributed power. Charlotte, who has political sway in both the Lower Manhattan Mutual Aid Society, 'a kind of umbrella for all the rest of the organizations in the drowned zone' and the Householders' Union, 'some kind of public/private hybrid, a city agency or an NGO or something, there to help the renters, the paperless, the homeless, the water rats, the dispossessed', becomes pivotal to the rapid expansion of the Met Life's commoning power – the power to grow its own resources and members and become ever more common.[38]

Haiven identifies this power-to-grow, latent in any commons, as the 'commons horizon', the strategic, calculated 'conjecture of a future society based on our lived experience of the actuality of the commons and on the ethos of commoning'. Formed from venues where commons members can 'meet, debate, strategize, agree to disagree, make inter-collective decisions, trade or barter, and party or plot'; narratives, memories and histories which help unite members under a single story and build collective power; and finally, 'a vision, however hazy, of a future society', the commons horizon is the toolbox which inspires, focuses, engages and grows a commons. Through imagining a commons horizon and working towards it in daily life, a commons is able to transcend the material limitations of its existence embedded within capitalism, and 'make patient but urgent plans for revolutionary success'.[39] In *New York 2140*, the commons horizon hatched in the debates, victories, anxieties and activities of the residents of the Met Life Tower ultimately extends to inspiring a major national rent strike which, in turn, incapacitates the global economy and precipitates an economic crisis. One of the results of this crisis is the institution of what Robinson terms a 'Piketty Tax', named after the concept, espoused by Thomas Piketty, of a tax on wealth and capital gains to radically decrease financial inequality.[40] A wealth tax is not the only anti-capitalist transformation enacted at the novel's conclusion, where the Citizen lists '[u]niversal health care, free public education through college, a living wage, guaranteed full employment, a year of mandatory national service … and please feel free to add your own favorites'.[41] While each of these social and political changes are aspects of variously Left and anti-capitalist economic theories, from the welfare statist staples of universal health care and free public education to the more radical concept of universal conscription (proposed, among others, by Jameson), what is particularly utopian about this list is that the parameters of its evocation ('please feel free to add your own favorites') generates another commons horizon – one which expands to include the novel's audience.[42]

As in Robinson's earlier novels, utopia is a never-concluded project born of debate; unlike them, the reader of *New York 2140* is encouraged to make an active contribution to these debates, in deed as well as imagination. As the Citizen proclaims, 'people in this era did do it. Individuals make history, but it's also a collective thing, a wave that people ride in their time, a wave made of individual actions'.[43] Utopia for the intertidal co-operatives, then, is not simply a range of social changes directly opposed to the hegemony of capitalism, but one for which the ongoing critiques and contradictions of its publics are fundamental. As indicated earlier, it is the Citizen's evocation and construction of the novel's reader as an active narratee – a participant in the text, addressed in the second person and provided with space to form opinions and judgements – which allow this methodological, mutable, polyvalent utopianism to emerge so clearly at the novel's conclusion.[44] Like the Met Life, the novel's utopian imaginaries are themselves commons, bringing the reader into an active discourse with the possibility of alternative futures.

Farm, park, plaza: public spaces of disaster

At a critical turning point in the novel's narrative, New York is battered by a disaster born of capitalism's effect on the planet's climate – a huge hurricane, exponentially exacerbated by warmer oceans and the sheer quantity of water now available near the coast. 'Hurricane Fyodor' evokes Hurricane Katrina, which destroyed swathes of New Orleans in 2005, and Hurricane Sandy, which heavily damaged New York in 2012 and features in a number of other contemporary New York novels, including *10:04* by Ben Lerner (2014) and *MacArthur Park* by Andrew Durbin (2017). In both novels, as in *New York 2140*, the effects of the hurricane are not only material, but extend metaphorically, creating liminal subjectivities, generating new ways of life and undoing old systems. Tied to these processes of undoing and restructuring, and drawing upon its destructive physical power, the hurricane becomes an agent which permanently transforms spaces – both their physical form and the processes of inhabiting which have a crucial role in maintaining and generating them.

The political resonances of all these transformations are brought to the fore in *New York 2140*. The destruction wrought by a hurricane, although seemingly uniform, is always unequally distributed across the spatial plane, causing far greater damage to weaker structures, open areas and low-lying, flood-prone zones. More significantly still, this damage is unevenly distributed along social lines, particularly those of species, class and ethnicity. As was evident in the case of Hurricane Katrina, which haunts Robinson's novel through numerous references, these effects are conditioned overwhelmingly by the calculated deployment of state resources to protect the wealthy from the perceived threat of the poor. Ashley Dawson contends that the damage caused by recent hurricanes like Katrina and Sandy 'deepen the grooves of already-existing social inequality', noting that this is only one example of precarious life in the 'extreme city'. The 'consummate example' of the extreme city, for Robinson as well as Dawson, is New York: 'an urban space of stark economic inequality, the defining urban characteristic of our time, and one of the greatest threats to the sustainability of urban existence'. The 'natural vulnerabilities' of extreme cities to climate chaos – adjacency to the coast, inability to produce enough food and water to sustain their population, and precarious infrastructure – are always 'heightened by social injustice'. Dawson illustrates this point by noting that 'poor people (who are predominantly black) tend to live in low-lying, flood-prone areas, while the city's wealthy (and mainly white) residents live in the most elevated (and safe) areas'.[45] In *New York 2140*, this differential vulnerability to external crisis is critically underscored by the constant presence of fifty extra feet of water.

In *10:04*, a novel concerned with contemporary temporality, Ben Lerner's author/narrator watches as Hurricane Sandy swamps New York's suburbs in darkness while the skyscrapers of Manhattan remain lit, metaphorically pulling the financial district into the future and making it seem as if it is emerging from a 'different era'.[46] In Robinson's New York, the experiences of the residents of the Met Life Tower invert the effect of Lerner's spatially and temporally distancing narration, returning agency to individuals in the moment of disaster. Unlike the empty, alien Goldman Sachs tower, described by Lerner as 'like the eyeshine of some animal', the Met Life is home to hundreds of people who own it and rely on it for their survival, integrated with a large, open-ended network of humans, non-humans and infrastructures. The power grid of future

New York, we learn, is highly distributed and robust, with buildings generating much of their own electricity using photovoltaic paint. Before Hurricane Fyodor hits, Vlade joins 'a conference call with the local gridmaster', where the question is raised: 'Who had what if they were the sole generators? Did anyone have enough to shove some juice back to the local node at the Twenty-ninth and Park station, which would then spread it around to those in need?'[47] With electricity shared through social networks of co-operatives, as well as through physical infrastructures, getting through a disaster becomes less a matter of survival and more one of ingenuity, trust and patience.

But where the Met Life's natural strengths – a solid construction, good flood defences and an engaged superintendent – see it through the disaster practically unscathed, the same cannot be said for much of the rest of New York. In the aftermath of the hurricane, Robinson most clearly develops his utopian position on the behaviour of urban populations during disaster, and ultimately extends this position to argue that it is not natural disaster, but capitalism, which must be held responsible for the worst crises of the present and future.

New York's refugee crisis begins even before Hurricane Fyodor finishes passing the city. By nightfall, we learn that 'Central Park was being used as a refugee camp, that many people now homeless were taking refuge in their big park'. With the park's trees felled by the storm, and the newly barren space crowded with homeless, desperate people, makeshift shelters and campfires, the park reminds Charlotte of 'a giant piece of prairie expanding out of the space where the park had used to be … a sepia Hooverville photo'.[48] The connection with Hoovervilles is apposite – these shanty towns, named (ironically) after President Herbert Hoover, appeared across America in the 1930s as the Great Depression took its toll on working-class populations; one of New York's twenty Hoovervilles was built on a piece of land in Central Park which had been cleared for the construction of a lake, indefinitely delayed by the financial crisis. Roy Rosenzweig and Elizabeth Blackmar report that in the winter of 1932–3, 1.2 million Americans were homeless, with 2,000 of those living in New York's shanty towns.[49] On a wave of sympathetic public opinion, housed and homeless New Yorkers did their best to peacefully coexist. The New York Times quoted one Central Park resident as saying 'We work hard to keep it clean, because that is important', with the journalist adding: 'They repair in the morning to comfort stations to shave and make themselves look presentable and keep their shacks as clean as they can'. While the implication that these homeless people were morally deserving of support by dint of their good behaviour is unmistakable, this reportage allows a more radical reading, too: that commons of personal and social care emerge even in the worst of disaster conditions. On hearing the cases of some of these residents who had been arrested for vagrancy, a magistrate suspended their sentences and gave them each money from his own pocket; Rosenzweig and Blackmar write that he 'took an indulgent view of men who had treated the public park as if it were a "common" resource in the midst of an economic crisis deep enough to prompt many Americans to question the sanctity of private property rights'.[50] The commoning spatiality of the Central Park Hooverville was reinforced by a number of permanent structures, including a community hall called 'Rockside Inn' or 'The Manor', built by unemployed bricklayers and serving as a communal hub, recreation centre and location of the aforementioned 'comfort stations'.

Figure 3 The Hooverville in Central Park, New York City, 1930s. Image courtesy of the Everett Collection.

Central Park's irreparable spatial transformation in 2140 thus recalls its twentieth-century past while forcing the residents of the future New York to inhabit it in a mode born of their uncertain and precarious present. It is reconfigured through the destruction of the hurricane, offering a rare chance for New Yorkers to make use of this space to construct new, radical forms of inhabiting – albeit ones born of desperation and survival. This reconfiguration also harks back to a far more recent history writ large in *New York 2140* – that of urban protest occupations. Like the worldwide protest camps of the Occupy movement and allied occupations, especially those of Gezi Park in Turkey, Tahrir Square in Egypt and Euromaidan in Ukraine, the occupation of Central Park is a refiguring of space not only as a *post hoc* response to neoliberal disaster, but as an autonomous demand for greater recognition and authority by the masses of the 99 per cent. Occupation movements are a form of commoning, and the spatial enclosure realized in the New York City street grid 'limited the potentiality of the commons, bounding it to specific spaces like Central Park – rectangular, regulated, designed'.[51] The sea level rise and the hurricane create openings in this enclosure through which utopian forms of spatial production emerge.

As Bell indicates for utopian literature focused on the creation of place through intra-actions of inhabiting, the new residents of Central Park – just like their 1930s analogues – begin to create a utopian commons, not by fleeing from an enclosed space to a new world, but by filling an existing space, momentarily allowed to be metaphorically and literally 'open', with communal topographies, infrastructures and modes of inhabiting. Bell's description of the quality of place on the planet Annares in *The Dispossessed* as 'a dynamic form that plays an agential role in unfolding events' can also be applied to Central Park.[52] Rich in history, thereby generating metaphorical and political connections across temporal gulfs, Central Park is a generator of, and is generated by, forms of utopian inhabiting, giving a new power to Robinson's description of the space as '*their* big park'.[53]

The experiences of the homeless New Yorkers, both during the Great Depression and in 2140, are typical of the behaviour of urban populations during periods of crisis and disaster. Rather than turning to violence, disorder or selfishness, precarious publics in real-world crises tend to collaborate, build communal infrastructures, and help rebuild the places in which they are forced to live. The field of disaster studies has convincingly shown that it is precisely in moments of full-scale disaster such as these that people form the strongest commoning bonds. The belief that the aftermath of a natural disaster is defined by panic, violence, animalistic and lawless behaviour and destruction has been perpetuated by a variety of cultural forms ranging from disaster films (for example, *Aftershock* (2012, dir. Nicolás López) and *Don't Look Up* (2021, dir. Adam McKay)) to news media reports. The American essayist Rebecca Solnit, in her book *A Paradise Built in Hell* (2009), brings together a wide-ranging corpus of sociological case studies – including the 1985 Mexico City earthquake, the 1989 and 1906 San Francisco earthquakes, the 9/11 attacks and Hurricane Katrina – which strongly indicate that in the immediate wake of an unexpected disaster, survivors instead have an overriding tendency to behave altruistically and communally, rapidly self-organize and sometimes even enjoy themselves, 'if *enjoyment*', she writes, 'is the right word for that sense of immersion in the moment and solidarity with others caused by the rupture in everyday life'.[54] Disasters are objectively destructive occurrences, but the witnesses whose testimonies Solnit presents repeat the sentiment that the immediate aftermath of disaster is an unexpectedly happy, fulfilling and well-adjusted period for themselves and their communities.

Solnit draws extensively on the work of Charles Fritz, whose 1961 paper 'Disasters and Mental Health' was highly influential in the field of disaster studies. Fritz's own extensive case studies lead him to conclude that, while disasters are undoubtedly 'occasions for profound human misery', nonetheless 'most disasters produce a great increase in social solidarity among the stricken populace, and this newly created solidarity tends to reduce the incidence of most forms of personal and social pathology'.[55] When Charlotte walks around the park and sees a vision of the dispossessed and the homeless self-organizing into collectives, she cannot help but romanticize it:

> And the people. They were organized already into circles and groups, many into small bands of twenty or so, but there were quintets and couples and isolatoes too. Families, groups of friends, people from the same destroyed building. Thousands of them altogether, sitting on the ground or on concrete benches or on boxes, or the knobs of ancient stone sticking up out of the ground, the bones of the island offering seating now to its inhabitants. Lines of Walt Whitman's glanced off her mind

half-remembered, something about the streaming of faces across the Brooklyn Bridge, the suffering of the soldiers in the Civil War. The sense of Americans in trouble together.[56]

Charlotte appears to be misremembering the poem 'Crossing Brooklyn Ferry', which appears later in one of the novel's epigraphs; in these lines Whitman gazes upon 'the hundreds and hundreds that cross, returning home', feeling himself 'disintegrated yet part of the scheme' of a gathering of all humanity on the move, across a temporal commons of past, present and future:

> I am with you, you men and women of a generation, or ever so many
>   generations hence,
> Just as you feel when you look on the river and sky, so I felt,
> Just as any of you is one of a living crowd, I was one of a crowd[57]

Whitman's image of the crowd as both individual and collective is echoed not only by the crowds in Central Park, but by all the utopian multitudes in this book, in particular Spahr's protesting and rioting crowds in *That Winter the Wolf Came*.

Fritz and Solnit agree that the far more damaging disaster in twentieth- and twenty-first-century society, in terms of 'aggregate amount of death, destruction, pain, and privation' it has caused and continues to cause, is the disaster of '"normal" life', or as Solnit puts it, 'everyday life become a social disaster'. Although their studies are written almost five decades apart, the two argue in harmony that the primary cause of the anxiety and precariousness felt in everyday life is 'the very structure of our economy and society', defined by 'individualism, capitalism, and Social Darwinism', alongside the 'privatization of desire and imagination that tells us we are not each other's keeper'; Fritz similarly emphasizes 'social atomization and social alienation as the root causes of the social and psychological pathologies of everyday life'.[58] All are well-established consequences of what we now name neoliberalism, the economic rationality by which the profit of capitalist enterprise is maximized through the transformation of all social ties into economic relations. For Berlant, it is 'a scene of mass but not collective activity. It is a scene in which the lower you are on economic scales, and the less formal your relation to the economy, the more alone you are in the project of maintaining and reproducing life. Communities, when they exist, are at best fragile and contingent.'[59] Opposed to meaningful social and political formation, neoliberalism underpins the emergence of the ongoing present and is instrumental in preventing subjects from prefiguring utopian alternatives.

Work into disaster socialities clearly indexes the relationship between neoliberalism, sudden disaster and the subjects who are affected by both. When neoliberalism is ascendant, subjects are individualized and precarized, are thrust out of their communities and lack any sense of their own ability to enact meaningful political change.[60] When neoliberalism wanes, the same subjects are able to come together and act in ways which are social, communal, collaborative and productive. The repeated failures of capitalism to keep control in the face of a sufficiently disruptive disaster, however temporary, demonstrate the profound fragility of the neoliberal system – its very own precariousness – particularly in the sense of its inability to weather profound and unexpected shocks. However, awareness of neoliberalism's fragility coupled with the recognition that neoliberal strategies of control disrupt cohesive social life and that the absence of those strategies allows social life to rapidly develop again, do not translate to a set of coherent or productive tactics for opposing neoliberalism. Such tactics would, to adopt Graham Jones's phrase, be a 'shock doctrine of the left', helping anti-capitalist social and political movements to create 'disaster utopias' of communal survival beyond capitalist control.[61]

In a recent essay, the Out of the Woods collective take up Fritz and Solnit's formulation of disaster as generating temporary communal solidarities, quickly producing and distributing the necessary means for material survival in the absence of the 'normal' systems of capitalist society. Crucially, while Solnit does gesture at the political-economic underpinning to her case studies, Out of the Woods give this idea their full attention, arguing: 'we must go beyond Solnit's empirical focus on what happens in response to specific disaster-events and grasp the character of the capitalist disaster'.[62] Inspector Gen echoes these sentiments, contemplating that, while in the hurricane's immediate aftermath the situation in New York had seemed 'a true crisis', it was rapidly becoming 'just another fucking disaster'. Later, as if quoting Berlant, Gen worries that the situation in the park is unsustainable, 'yet there was no obvious next step, and meanwhile the impasse was something everyone could see and feel, something they were living moment to moment, day to day'.[63] All these terms index a sense of the present in which there is no perception of an alternative to the alienations, deprivations and precarities of what Jameson calls 'the seamless Moebius strip of late capitalism', in particular for populations who are already made precarious and exploitable along social lines including race, gender and citizenship.[64]

While those made precarious by neoliberal capitalism are always the ones most exposed to sudden disasters, it need not be neoliberal capitalism which always returns, seemingly stronger, in disaster's wake. What Out of the Woods christen 'disaster communism' and Solnit calls 'disaster utopia' is the transformation of the impasse of everyday, ongoing struggles against 'disaster-as-condition' into a new, oppositional, future-generating mode of social reproduction. The imaginary they evoke is a truly prefigurative utopianism, in modes both aspirational and realistic:

> The communism of disaster communism, then, is a transgressive and transformative mobilization without which the unfolding catastrophe of global warming cannot and will not be stopped. It is simultaneously an undoing of the manifold, structural injustices which perpetuate and draw strength from disaster, *and* an enactment of the widespread collective capacity to endure and flourish on a rapidly changing planet. This is an operation *within* that is pitched *against* and opens up space *beyond*. It is hugely ambitious, requiring redistribution of resources at several scales, reparations for colonialism and slavery; expropriation of landed private property for Indigenous peoples, the abolition of fossil fuels, and other monumental projects. We are clearly not there yet. But as Ernst Bloch noted in *The Principle of Hope*, that 'not-yet' is also in our present: in the collective responses to disaster, we find that many of the tools for constructing that new world already exist.[65]

Out of the Woods see disaster communism as emerging from abundance. Rather than a material abundance of commodities or security, this term gestures at a 'collective abundance' of social relations – a commons – which is able to continue generating itself against and beyond neoliberalism, producing future forms of communal resistance and emancipation to meet and survive future disasters. This is not, to be clear, a celebration of disaster or an exhortation to perpetuate its effects, but a political recognition that, at a time of climate crisis, when sudden and unstoppable disaster becomes commonplace, better forms of communal existence than capitalism must emerge to support the largest possible planetary population.

Robinson has reached a similar conclusion in his political work, writing: '[a]n adequate life provided for all living beings is something the planet can still do ... It won't be easy to arrange, obviously, because it would be a total civilizational project, involving technologies, systems, and power dynamics; but it is possible'.[66] Robinson applies this utopian possibility firmly to our real world, rather than a future time, drawing on and describing specific, already-existing tactics for collective opposition to capitalism and for a life lived beyond it. While in *New York 2140*, where he does much the same thing, such tactics might seem to be reserved for future populations dealing with a world on the brink of apocalypse, Robinson's commons poetics demand that we read them as instructions, manifestos and diktats meant for use by contemporary readers. Although the novel is written as a warning of a violent future, these tactics, suggests Robinson, can just as easily transform the world of the present into a commons which *need not* survive planetary catastrophe before it begins to build a planetary anti-capitalist utopia. As readers, we can make sense of the strategies required to build concrete utopias in the present through the prefigurative vision provided to us in the shape of diverse commons of *New York 2140*.

The initial tactics of the police, emergency workers and homeless residents of Central Park are straightforward tools for ensuring survival – building shelters, removing dead bodies from the water supply, documenting and housing the homeless. But these activities are soon eclipsed by far more active and oppositional tactics. Angered by the New York City mayor's refusal to divert more of the city's resources to the refugees, the residents of Central Park riot and march to the dry zone uptown, where more than half of the apartments of the futuristic skyscrapers of the 'Cloister Cluster' stand empty 'because they're owned by rich people from somewhere else'.[67] Before the riots, Charlotte had recommended that the mayor 'declare an emergency and use all those rooms as refugee centers', but is rebuffed; like *Exit West*, *New York 2140* came out in the aftermath of the Grenfell Tower fire, and Charlotte's demand is reminiscent of arguments from Labour party leader Jeremy Corbyn and others to house the refugees of Grenfell in the many 'land banking' mansions in the borough of Kensington and Chelsea.

The aesthetics of the riot scenes are reminiscent of depictions of the 2011 UK riots and the 2014 Ferguson protests. As in these images, the crowds in *New York 2140* are distinguished by the timeless aesthetics of riot: bonfires, burning brands, Molotov cocktails and the light of the full moon. In comparison, the skyscrapers towards which the rioters are moving are described in futuristic terms which pull them ever further into a seemingly inaccessible future: constructed from 'new composite building materials ... invented for not-yet-happening space elevator cables', they are 'a purplish velvet black' in the moonlight, 'possibly an effect of their photovoltaics'.[68] Robinson prevents mutual comprehension between the rioters and those protecting the skyscrapers through a well-worn literary technique, combining the individual rioters into a bestial mass subject and denying them the power of speech: 'Faces white-eyed, openmouthed. People who didn't appear to speak English or any other language. The noise incredible, a hair-raising roar punctuated by shrieks, but the noise wasn't what was causing the furor, because no one was listening anyway'.[69] The playwright Gillian Slovo, commenting on her verbatim theatre play about the 2011 UK riots, describes the riots as 'an incoherent and destructive cry, an anti-political cry of rage'; this politically dismissive sentiment is echoed by philosopher Alain Badiou, who sees the riots as 'violent, anarchic and ultimately without enduring truth', making it impossible to clearly distinguish 'between what pertains to a partially universalizable intention' of the rioters, 'and what remains confined to a rage with no purpose other than the satisfaction of being able to crystallize and find hateful objects to destroy or consume'. Slavoj Žižek takes these conclusions even further, arguing that it is impossible to conceive of the rioters as 'an emerging revolutionary subject', and concluding that the riots are far better understood as 'a consumerist carnival of destruction, an expression of acquisitive desire violently enacted when unable to realize itself in the "proper" way (by shopping)'.[70] These conclusions are all motivated by a unified liberal philosophy: riots are inherently a social ill, but the rioters themselves cannot be held responsible: they are all held entirely in the sway of neoliberal capitalism, and merely struggle against its chains the only way they know how.

Contemporary Marxist theorists, in particular Juliana Spahr's fellow poet and critic Joshua Clover, have argued against this reading of riot, which does as much to dehumanize and depoliticize rioting subjects as do disaster films and conservative news media. In their readings, riot is comprehensible as a 'particular form of struggle' which illuminates the character of neoliberal crisis:

> These transformations are the material restructurings that respond to and constitute capitalist crisis, and which feature surpluses of both capital and population as core features. And it is these that propose riot as a necessary form of struggle.[71]

Although the Central Park rioters are rendered incomprehensible in the moment of the riot itself, the events of the concluding chapters of *New York 2140* are indebted to what is later called 'the battle for the towers', and the appearance of the rioters as a political subject worthy of commensurability emerges here. Inspector Gen and Charlotte, and thus metonymically the NYPD and the US Congress, act and speak in full support of their actions, beginning to form 'a government of, by, and for the people'.[72] This political position is given credibility and focus because a private security firm shoots into the crowd to defend the super-skyscrapers. This private security firm reflects the violence of neoliberalism, while Inspector Gen and the reformed, pro-public NYPD's defence of the crowd offers a vision of an urban commons working to actively defend itself, by any means necessary, from violent enclosure by capitalism. Although the rioters fail to immediately achieve their own goals and occupy the skyscrapers, their demands are not only comprehended and acted upon, but are specifically understood as an anti-capitalist, utopian yearning to escape the limitations of their precarious situation within the neoliberal city and permanently reinforce the communal forms of life they have begun to construct in Central Park.

At the end of the novel, we witness the consequences of combining the political tactics of riot and the occupation of public space with economic tactics including an absentee tax, a capital assets tax and mandatory conversion of the super-skyscrapers into low-income housing. As the refugees are moved out of the park and into the skyscrapers – where each floor is able to house 600 people – another spatial transformation occurs, this time of the skyscrapers themselves. As a solution to the need for increased sanitation infrastructure, the 'dreadful', 'clean' lines of the skyscrapers are encrusted with external pipes – a messy industrial aesthetic opposed to the clean, futurist aesthetic discussed above, which traces its origins to the 'used future' aesthetic of science fiction films including *Dark Star* (1974, dir. John Carpenter) and *Alien* (1979, dir. Ridley Scott).[73] Meanwhile, Frank oversees the building of communal low-income housing, constructed directly over the flooded ruins of the intertidal, using futuristic lightweight materials and floating platforms which move with the tides, 'like eelgrass'.[74] In these scenes, the destruction of capitalism's clean aesthetics and obsession with static upward growth heralds a social transformation. As with Central Park, these spatialities are reconfigured, becoming disaster utopias born of oppositional new forms of life in common. The chaotic, if responsive, aesthetics of the emergency shelter and occupied park begin to transform into permanent infrastructures which not only support communal survival in a time of climate crisis, but also work to oppose and subvert the monolithic enclosure practices of capitalism.

Mezzrow's: the prefiguration of utopia

The final key spatiality of *New York 2140* provides a glimpse of life in an accreting utopia-in-the-making which can never be complete and which always seeks to follow its commons horizon towards an even more utopian reality. This space, named Mezzrow's, presumably after New York jazz musician Mezz Mezzrow, is a venue built into the water-proofed ruins of the 33rd Street subway station, just blocks away from the Empire State Building. Located in the very depths of the intertidal, Mezzrow's is a space of liminality and 'amphibiguity', home to lifestyles which are prefigurations of a utopian way of life even when threatened by the return of capitalist enclosure to the intertidal. Visiting the club to watch an underwater sumo wrestling match, Gen notices that many in the crowd 'were of indeterminate gender, wearing flamboyant water dress or undress. Lots of intergender in the intertidal; inter as such was a big thing now, amphibiguity a definite style, which like all styles liked to see and be seen. The big low chamber, now lit entirely by the pool lights, was in fact turning into quite a delanyden'.[75] The reference is to the work of Samuel R. Delany, particularly his novel *Trouble on Triton* (1976), which imagines Neptune's moon Triton as a space of radical possibility for fluid gender and sexual self-expression. Like the 'unlicensed sectors' of Triton, where no laws apply and which have 'a definite and different feel', the spatial form of Mezzrow's reflects, and emerges out of, the forms of life which take place there.[76] A network of cosy tunnels, staircases, watery pools and chambers deep underground, Mezzrow's is an antidote to the wide canal streets and open spaces of the city above, permitting its inhabitants to engage in more private, experimental and intimate forms of life in relative safety.

In the final scene of the novel, the squatter hackers Mutt and Jeff and the reality TV star and airship pilot Amelia head to Mezzrow's to see a band who, in the form of their music and the diversity of their identities, represent and celebrate the very heterogeneity and fluidity which distinguishes this space:

> Finally the young reed man stands up and gives the sax mouthpiece a lick, joins right in with the song already going. Okay, this is the star of the band. Immediately he is zooming around in the tune like a maniac. The other horn players instantly get better, the guitar players even more precise and intricate. The vocalists are grinning and shouting duets in harmony. It's like they've all just plugged into an electrical jack through their shoes. The young reed man sounds like he is maybe a klezmer star in his other bands, and it might not have been obvious before that klezmer fits so well with West African pop, but now it's very clear. He swoops up and down the scale, screeches across the supersonic, jams in a perfect driving rhythm with the others. It don't mean a thing if it ain't got that swing, but it does.[77]

Excited by this raw musical energy, Mutt, Jeff and Amelia, along with the rest of the audience, cannot help but dance:

> Jeff is a dancing fool; there are so many rhythms in this music that he almost matches one. In fact it's pretty amazing he can miss all of them at once, but he can. And he is Nureyev compared to Amelia. Mutt can't stop laughing at the sight of his two friends' gyrations. Amelia is grinning at him. Very few gals dance so badly, she's got a knack. The guys can't help enjoying the sight of such a clumsy babe. Their friend, their dance partner![78]

I have described Mezzrow's as 'loosely' representing a utopian society in particular because the key scenes in these chapters, including this night of improvised musical performance and wild dancing, are minor, intimate moments of shared human connection, rather than large-scale political narratives of utopian social restructuring. This scene, however, is among the most politically utopian in the book, because it is written using a commons poetics, demanding an understanding of politics which comes not from large-scale governmental systems, but from a commons, the unexpected and rewarding connections between utopian bodies in their desire to create meaningful ways of living together better. In the moment of dance, the body 'folds the world into itself, and, in doing so, it makes the world otherwise ... This is what one might call utopian figuration: a mode of expression that transforms the body into the figure of another world.'[79] The dancing bodies of Amelia, Mutt and Jeff enact ways of living otherwise which are not only liberatory and energized with jouissance, but are dorky, foolish and fun – the kind of world a utopian activist might actually wish to live in.

The utopian potential of music has been attested by a number of utopian theorists. For Bloch, music was the most utopian of all cultural forms: 'no art has so much surplus over the respective time and ideology in which it exists', a surplus of what he evocatively calls 'hope-material'.[80] While this utopian attitude to music-making is welcome, Bloch found that the most utopian musical forms were classical European ones, especially ballet, and detested jazz and its associated dance forms, writing that '[n]othing coarser, nastier, more stupid has ever been seen than the jazz-dances ... with a corresponding howling which provides the so to speak musical accompaniment'.[81] The reflections of his contemporary Theodor Adorno suggest that both philosophers read 1930s jazz as a capitalistic, ideological consumer form bearing no connection to its roots in African American culture. Arguing that the improvisational elements of jazz were 'merely ornamental', Adorno concludes that it subverts and degrades the very utopian promise of liberation which improvisational modern music is able to contain.[82] While a number of critics have attempted to contextualize Adorno's comments, arguing that the jazz-style music Adorno would have heard was heavily filtered through a German milieu and was thus linked to the same musical traditions as fascist military and propaganda music, the critical consensus is that Adorno's opinion on jazz is at best ill-informed and at worst racist, and we can assume that Bloch's opinion emerges out of the same general tendency.[83]

Of more contemporary utopian critics, Levitas provides a welcome reading across the grain of Bloch's critique, noting that in his work, music is not just utopian in its anticipation of a utopian world to come, but is prefigurative, evoking the world in the here and now: 'through its capacity to communicate that which is not (yet) utterable, music is uniquely capable of conveying and *effecting* a better world; it invokes, as well as prefigures, that world'.[84] Among the handful of critics who explicitly link improvisational music to utopian social organization, Bell's work is particularly valuable, arguing that 'when people take part in collective musical improvisation they are practising an anarchist form of organization'.[85] Improvisation, in this reading, is a set of communal practices within and beyond musical performance, constructed in the social relations between performers. In his later book, Bell links processes of improvisation directly to the commons, writing that the 'intra-actions' of performing improvisational music are a form of commoning which generates a mutually beneficial *power-to* create something together (rather than the more traditional sense of *power-over* others in social relations).[86]

An empowering commons is evoked when the klezmer player joins the others in the band, integrating his playing into their tunes, and joining his own musical traditions with their West African cultural knowledge, rather than playing against or over them: 'The other horn players instantly get better, the guitar players even more precise and intricate'. Mutt, Jeff and Amelia become common in their absorption into the 'big world' of the sweaty, heaving, dancing crowd, which renders them anonymous and safe to do as they wish and dance how they can, yet allows them to hold on to their individual identities: 'Might be some of the people in the room recognize [Amelia], but no one lets on, and maybe they don't. It's a big world.'[87] On nights like these, the space of Mezzrow's generates, and is regenerated by, a brief yet vital utopian community of joy and movement, harking back to Spahr's 'moment of sweaty relation larger than the intimate'.[88] This community is both momentary and lasting: momentary because it must be regenerated anew every night, which keeps its utopian potential firmly anchored on a commons horizon always just out of reach; and lasting because this constant process of improvisational regeneration prevents it from being enclosed and subsumed by capitalism. Seen in this light, the final lines of the novel are particularly utopian, offering a vision of the city as a diffuse, almost invisible network of such momentary utopias, gathering their publics in an expanding commons of music and dance: '"And now, look at this, here we are right on top of the place, and it's like they're not even there!" ... "Heck, there's probably fifty bands like them playing tonight in this city. Dances like that going on right now, all over town".'[89]

This scene illustrates the important argument that sweatiness, joy and fun are just as important to the long-term survival of commons as material production and spatial security. As Out of the Woods remind us, the life of social reproduction in disaster commons 'isn't just mundane, either. Groups organize parties, dancing lessons, and collective cookery sessions so that communal horizons might open beyond despair.'[90] Sophie Lewis, a member of Out of the Woods, continues this refrain by arguing that 'while situations necessitating "disaster communism" are not exactly enviable, it is obvious that what people are producing in them is joy, rest, conviviality, art, eros; a life worth living against all odds'.[91] Turning, in its closing pages, to minor utopian acts of commoning and minor utopian spaces emerging from disaster, *New York 2140* argues that it is collective assemblies of individual subjects and their surprising capacity for hope against the odds which are best positioned to dance into a world beyond capitalism.

New York 2140 is a novel about the possibility of achieving a fundamental and radical change in the form of the planet's governing economic and political system. It achieves this admirable goal by undermining the futurity of its own seemingly futuristic setting, underlining the fact that under the auspices of late capitalism, the future will remain economically, politically and even culturally almost identical to our present – with the only real transformation being in how much more precarious and deadly the climate crisis will become, notwithstanding serious and wholesale global intervention. In *New York 2140*, this long overdue intervention comes in the shape of various tactics and spatial practices for living life outside capitalism, including the construction of housing co-operatives and commons; a rent and debt strike; unionization; the occupation and repossession of empty apartments to provide emergency housing; riots whose political aims are taken up, rather than suppressed, by governments and the police; and the sweaty joy of listening to music and dancing together.

Robinson's most significant achievement here is his commitment to representing such tactics as wholly realizable and achievable in the present, a process which constantly re-situates the utopia created by the novel back within the contemporary moment. *New York 2140*'s sense of the future thus operates in two directions simultaneously. On the one hand, through its extension of the present into the future, it highlights the extreme and differentially experienced precarity which capitalist-generated climate crisis promises to the planet's population. On the other hand, by returning a revolutionary future of disaster and necessary collective survival back to the present, it highlights the possibility of enacting these oppositional tactics before the worst of the climate crisis takes place – in effect exhorting its readers to start prefiguratively building common infrastructures and utopian forms of social reproduction today.

Notes

1 Kim Stanley Robinson, *New York 2140* (London: Orbit, 2017), 279.
2 Joshua Rothman, 'Kim Stanley Robinson's Latest Novel Imagines Life in an Underwater New York', 2017, https://www.newyorker.com/books/page-turner/kim-stanley-robinsons-latest-novel-imagines-life-in-an-underwater-new-york; Brent Ryan Bellamy, 'Science Fiction and the Climate Crisis', *Science Fiction Studies* 45, no. 3 (2018): 417–19; Gerry Canavan, 'Utopia in the Time of Trump', *Los Angeles Review of Books*, 2017, https://lareviewofbooks.org/article/utopia-in-the-time-of-trump/.
3 Robinson describes himself as America's 'last utopian' here: Adam Rogers, 'The Sci-Fi Novelist Who Writes Like the Past to Warn of the Future', *Wired*, 2018, https://www.wired.com/story/kim-stanley-robinson-red-moon/.
4 Kim Stanley Robinson, *Green Mars* (London: Voyager, 2009), 269.
5 Jameson, *Archaeologies of the Future*, 216–17.
6 Jameson, *Archaeologies of the Future*, 232.
7 Jameson, *Archaeologies of the Future*, 416.
8 Spahr, 'The '90s', 181.
9 Canavan, 'Utopia in the Time of Trump'.
10 Haiven, 'Are Your Children Old Enough to Learn about May '68?', 83.
11 David Sergeant, 'The Genre of the Near Future: Kim Stanley Robinson's *New York 2140*', *Genre* 52, no. 1 (2019): 3.
12 Canavan, 'Utopia in the Time of Trump'.
13 Robinson, *New York 2140*, 207.
14 Robinson, *New York 2140*, 4–5.
15 Robinson, *New York 2140*, 6.
16 Sergeant, 'The Genre of the Near Future', 5.
17 Robinson, *New York 2140*, 5.
18 Robinson, *New York 2140*, 424.

19 Chatman, *Story and Discourse*, 241.
20 Chatman, *Story and Discourse*, 241; Robinson, *New York 2140*, 604, 318–19.
21 Kim Stanley Robinson, 'Kim Stanley Robinson on "The U.S.A. Trilogy"', To the Best of Our Knowledge, 2018, https://www.ttbook.org/interview/kim-stanley-robinson-usa-trilogy; D. Douglas Fratz, 'An Interview with Kim Stanley Robinson', *The SF Site*, 2012, https://www.sfsite.com/06a/ksr369.htm.
22 Sergeant, 'The Genre of the Near Future', 7; see also, quoted in Sergeant, Jameson on the historical novel: 'only our imaginary futures are adequate to do justice to our present … our history, our historical past and our historical novels, must now also include our historical futures as well'. Not for nothing does Jameson dedicate *The Antinomies of Realism* to Robinson. See: Fredric Jameson, *The Antinomies of Realism* (London: Verso, 2015).
23 Robinson, *New York 2140*, 285, 98.
24 A large critical field has already developed around climate change and ecological disaster fiction. The term 'cli-fi' was coined in 2008 by Dan Bloom. For wide-ranging reviews of the genre, see: Rebecca Tuhus-Dubrow, 'Cli-Fi: Birth of a Genre', *Dissent* 60, no. 3 (2013): 58–61; Adam Trexler, *Anthropocene Fictions: The Novel in a Time of Climate Change*, Under the Sign of Nature: Explorations in Ecocriticism (Charlottesville: University of Virginia Press, 2015); Adeline Johns-Putra, *Climate Change and the Contemporary Novel* (Cambridge, UK: Cambridge University Press, 2019).
25 Robinson, *New York 2140*, 34.
26 Ruth Levitas, 'Where There Is No Vision, the People Perish: A Utopian Ethic for a Transformed Future', *CUSP* 5 (2017): 4.
27 Adeline Johns-Putra, 'Climate Change in Literature and Literary Studies: From Cli-Fi, Climate Change Theater and Ecopoetry to Ecocriticism and Climate Change Criticism', *Wiley Interdisciplinary Reviews: Climate Change* 7, no. 2 (2016): 267.
28 Moylan, *Scraps of the Untainted Sky*, xii; for an overview of the history of both contemporary dystopian literature and of the term 'critical dystopia', see: Moylan and Baccolini, 'Dystopia and Histories'. See also: Lyman Tower Sargent, 'The Three Faces of Utopianism Revisited', *Utopian Studies* 5, no. 1 (1994): 1–37.
29 Gen's surname, 'Octaviasdottir' (or 'Octavia's daughter', a standard Icelandic surname form), is likely a reference to Octavia E. Butler, a radical and utopian African American science fiction writer, known for the *Parable* series (1993, 1998).
30 'Who Owns the Beach?' *On the Commons*, 2005, http://www.onthecommons.org/who-owns-beach.
31 Robinson, *New York 2140*, 209.

32 See: De Angelis, *Omnia Sunt Communia*, 10.
33 Berlant, *Cruel Optimism*, 48–9.
34 De Angelis, *Omnia Sunt Communia*, 235.
35 Robinson, *New York 2140*, 331.
36 Robinson, *New York 2140*, 43, 50, 133.
37 Robert Cowan, 'Reich and Wittgenstein: Notes towards a Synthesis', *Tempo*, no. 157 (1986): 2–7, cf. https://www.jstor.org/journal/tempo; Jesse Budel, 'Steve Reich's "Music for 18 Musicians" as a Soundscape Composition', *Directions of New Music*, 1, no. 2 (2018): 10.
38 Robinson, *New York 2140*, 27, 51.
39 Haiven, 'Commons as Actuality, Ethos, and Horizon', 30–2.
40 See: Thomas Piketty, *Capital in the Twenty-First Century*, trans. Arthur Goldhammer (Cambridge: The Belknap Press of Harvard University Press, 2014).
41 Robinson, *New York 2140*, 603–4.
42 For Jameson on universal conscription, see: Fredric Jameson, *An American Utopia: Dual Power and the Universal Army* (London: Verso, 2016); this book also features a short story by Robinson called 'Mutt and Jeff Push the Button', which would become, in expanded form, the first chapter of *New York 2140*.
43 Robinson, *New York 2140*, 603.
44 The textual strategy whereby the utopian text evokes its own addressee is a feature of utopian literature from More's *Utopia* onwards, particularly Edward Bellamy's *Looking Backward*, Russ's *The Female Man* and Ursula Le Guin's short story 'The Ones Who Walk away from Omelas' (1973).
45 Ashley Dawson, *Extreme Cities: The Peril and Promise of Urban Life in the Age of Climate Change* (London: Verso, 2017), 235, 6, 5, 10.
46 Ben Lerner, *10:04* (New York: Faber and Faber, 2014), 238.
47 Robinson, *New York 2140*, 465, 456.
48 Robinson, *New York 2140*, 474, 499.
49 Roy Rosenzweig and Elizabeth Blackmar, *The Park and the People: A History of Central Park* (Ithaca, NY: Cornell University Press, 1992), 442.
50 Rosenzweig and Blackmar, *The Park and the People*, 440.
51 Matthew Bolton, Stephen Froese, and Alex Jeffrey, 'This Space Is Occupied!: The Politics of Occupy Wall Street's Expeditionary Architecture and De-Gentrifying Urbanism', in *Occupying Political Science*, ed. Emily Welty et al. (New York: Palgrave Macmillan, 2013), 139.
52 Bell, *Rethinking Utopia*, 106.

53 Robinson, *New York 2140*, 474, emphasis added.
54 Rebecca Solnit, *A Paradise Built in Hell: The Extraordinary Communities That Arise in Disaster* (New York: Viking, 2009), 5.
55 Charles E. Fritz, *Disasters and Mental Health: Therapeutic Principles Drawn from Disaster Studies* (Newark: Disaster Research Center, University of Delaware, 1996), 10.
56 Robinson, *New York 2140*, 500.
57 Walt Whitman, *Leaves of Grass: Comprehensive Reader's Edition* (New York: New York University Press, 1965), 160.
58 Fritz, *Disasters and Mental Health*, 23, 24; Solnit, *A Paradise Built in Hell*, 3, 7, 9.
59 Berlant, *Cruel Optimism*, 165.
60 For a detailed theorization of the modes by which neoliberalism precarizes its subjects, see: Isabell Lorey, *State of Insecurity: Government of the Precarious* (London: Verso, 2015).
61 Solnit, *A Paradise Built in Hell*, 16. Jones's adaptation of Klein's concept of the 'shock doctrine' within a Leftist social movement framework offers a powerful set of tactics for responding to crises in embodied, reactive and emancipatory ways which can generate lasting social change. See: Graham Jones, *The Shock Doctrine of the Left* (Cambridge: Polity, 2018).
62 Out of the Woods Collective, 'Disaster Communism: The Uses of Disaster', in *Hope against Hope: Writings on Ecological Crisis* (Brooklyn: Common Notions, 2020), 230.
63 Robinson, *New York 2140*, 483, 509.
64 Jameson, 'Future City', 76.
65 Out of the Woods Collective, 'Disaster Communism: The Uses of Disaster', 240.
66 Kim Stanley Robinson, 'Dystopias Now', *Commune*, 2018, https://communemag.com/dystopias-now/.
67 Robinson, *New York 2140*, 500–1.
68 Robinson, *New York 2140*, 35, 513.
69 Robinson, *New York 2140*, 512.
70 Matt Trueman, 'Gillian Slovo: The Riots Act', *The Stage*, 2011, https://www.thestage.co.uk/features/2011/gillian-slovo-the-riots-act/; Alain Badiou and Gregory Elliott, *The Rebirth of History: Times of Riots and Uprisings* (London: Verso, 2012), 25; Slavoj Žižek, *The Year of Dreaming Dangerously* (London: Verso, 2012), 59–60.
71 Clover, *Riot. Strike. Riot.*, 1–3.
72 Robinson, *New York 2140*, 597, 503.

73 Robinson, *New York 2140*, 596. On the aesthetics of 'used future' worlds, see: Artur Skweres, *McLuhan's Galaxies: Science Fiction Film Aesthetics in Light of Marshall McLuhan's Thought* (Cham: Springer, 2019).
74 Robinson, *New York 2140*, 557.
75 Robinson, *New York 2140*, 183.
76 Samuel R. Delany, *Trouble on Triton: An Ambiguous Heterotopia* (Middletown: Wesleyan University Press, 1996), 8.
77 Robinson, *New York 2140*, 612.
78 Robinson, *New York 2140*, 612.
79 Haines, *A Desire Called America*, 14.
80 Bloch, *Principle of Hope*, 3:1063.
81 Bloch, *The Principle of Hope*, 1:394.
82 Theodor W. Adorno, 'Farewell to Jazz', in *Essays on Music*, ed. Richard D. Leppert, trans. Susan H. Gillespie (Berkeley: University of California Press, 2002), 497; Theodor W. Adorno, 'On Jazz', in *Essays on Music*, ed. Richard D. Leppert, trans. Susan H. Gillespie (Berkeley: University of California Press, 2002), 477.
83 Theodore A. Gracyk, 'Adorno, Jazz, and the Aesthetics of Popular Music', *The Musical Quarterly* 76, no. 4 (1992): 526–42; J. Bradford Robinson, 'The Jazz Essays of Theodor Adorno: Some Thoughts on Jazz Reception in Weimar Germany', *Popular Music* 13, no. 1 (1994): 1–25; Robert W. Witkin, 'Why Did Adorno "Hate" Jazz?' *Sociological Theory* 18, no. 1 (2000): 145–70.
84 Levitas, *Utopia as Method*, 41–2.
85 David M. Bell, 'Improvisation as Anarchist Organization', *Ephemera* 14, no. 4 (2014): 1012.
86 Bell, *Rethinking Utopia*, 107, 108. For a development of the distinction between power-over and power-to, see: John Holloway, *Change the World without Taking Power: The Meaning of Revolution Today* (London: Pluto Press, 2019).
87 Robinson, *New York 2140*, 612.
88 Spahr, *That Winter the Wolf Came*, 14.
89 Robinson, *New York 2140*, 613.
90 Out of the Woods Collective, 'Disaster Communism: The Uses of Disaster', 237.
91 Sophie Lewis, *Full Surrogacy Now: Feminism against Family* (London: Verso, 2019), 151.

4

Utopias beyond death: *Walkaway* and *The Book of Joan*

This chapter turns to commons which work against capitalism's final, and most insidious, hold over human nature – its control of life and death via precarization, the maintenance of surplus populations and biopolitical management. Where the previous chapters examined utopian forms of collective being beyond petrocapitalism (*That Winter the Wolf Came*), beyond the border regime (*Exit West*) and beyond the uneven distribution of disaster (*New York 2140*), this chapter examines two 2017 texts – *Walkaway* by Cory Doctorow and *The Book of Joan* by Lidia Yuknavitch – which depict humanity in the process of building commons which work against death itself.

Few classical utopian texts place immortality at the centre of their utopias, perhaps because the dream of immortality is so remote as to be beyond even the most anticipatory of illuminations. The inhabitants of More's island of Utopia avoid innovations on the issue by subscribing to religious beliefs which would have been very familiar to More: 'That the soul of man is immortal, and that God of His goodness has designed that it should be happy; and that He has, therefore, appointed rewards for good and virtuous actions, and punishments for vice, to be distributed after this life'.[1] Satirical play with the desire for everlasting life, and its consequences, appears in the shape of the Struldbruggs of Jonathan Swift's *Gulliver's Travels* (1726). They cannot die but continue ageing; they are declared legally dead at the age of eighty and henceforth prohibited from owning property, to prevent them from eventually acquiring all the world's land for themselves.[2] George Bernard Shaw's four-part play cycle *Back to Methuselah* (premièred in 1922) charts humanity's quest for longevity from the Garden of Eden to a disembodied, spacebound state some 30,000 years into our future, and is one of the earliest science fictional treatments of the subject, borrowing from contemporaneous scientific understandings of genetics and evolution. In the twentieth century, immortality in literature was primarily science fictional: cloning, mind uploads, artificial and cyborg bodies, distributed consciousnesses, cryonics and longevity-inducing cocktails of drugs and chemicals.[3]

Recent science fiction treatments of immortality have overwhelmingly highlighted the dangers of this gift falling into the hands of neoliberal capitalists. Notable among these are Doctorow's own first novel *Down and Out in the Magic Kingdom* (2003), Paolo Bacigalupi's short story 'The People of Sand and Slag' (2004), and the films *Iron Man* (dir. Jon Favreau, 2008), *Lucy* (dir. Luc Besson, 2014) and *Jupiter Ascending* (dir. The Wachowskis, 2015), which all represent the relationship between immortality and capitalism as inextricable, mutually violent, destructive, pessimistic and, at times, dystopian. *Walkaway* and *The Book of Joan* work against this trend, rendering the quest for immortality in explicitly anti-capitalist terms and depicting it through a commons poetics. At the same time, they refuse a nostalgic return to a normatively reproductive pre-capitalist pastoralism akin to the prelapsarian immortality of Adam and Eve; rather, their immortalities are born of futuristic technologies, non-human ecologies and virtual worlds.[4] The characters who become immortal in these novels are able to escape the capitalist system through their newfound ability to transcend the normative human condition and become what Donna Haraway has labelled 'cyborg', and what Cary Wolfe and Rosi Braidotti would describe as 'posthuman' or 'post-anthropocentric': they become 'creatures simultaneously animal and machine, who populate worlds ambiguously natural and crafted ... resolutely committed to partiality, irony, intimacy, and perversity ... oppositional, utopian, and completely without innocence'.[5] In becoming immortal, these characters become post-human.

Post-human theory and queer theory have had a long and fruitful coupling, and in these novels, post-human immortality is rendered as a queer way of life, experienced by a cast of queer subjects, alive to queer apprehensions of space and time, and situated in queer commons. Doctorow and Yuknavitch make use of immortality, post-human ontologies and queerness together to depict utopian spaces where capitalism has no home, and where even capitalism's agents are eventually swept away into a utopia of immortality. While the apocalyptic settings, wild ontological transformations and political revolutions of *Walkaway* and *The Book of Joan* seem to pose a significant challenge to the argument of this book – that utopian literature need not escape our present to create a better future – they remain, in a multitude of ways, extrapolations of the contemporary capitalist moment. In the conclusions of both novels, their characters make determined returns back into the core spaces of capitalism to challenge its systems from within. In *Walkaway*, the upper classes meet their final downfall when their prison guards and private armies join forces with the anarchist revolutionaries; in *The Book of Joan*, the capitalist antagonist himself – a Donald Trumpesque media personality-cum-dictator – reveals potential paths towards a queer post-human utopianism even as his space station falls into the sun.

Queer immortalities

Commons utopias reflect their authors' interest in specific crises of the capitalist present, and each offers a different depiction of a commons, complete with a cast of commoners and a commonwealth of shared resources, which opposes and eventually expands beyond the capitalist systems surrounding it. Importantly, each of these utopias is written for a key collective subject of the present, celebrating their achievements and powers, equipping them, within the world of the text, with particular technologies, and encouraging their brethren outside the text to have hope in their ability to themselves enact similar changes. Spahr's focus is the alienated, precariously unemployed millennials who were the genesis of the Occupy movement; Hamid writes of and for migrants fleeing natural and anthropogenic disasters; the union organizers and passionate commoners of *New York 2140* find new ways to survive climate disaster. In *The Book of Joan* and *Walkaway*, it is queer subjects who discover, defend and embrace the utopian potential of immortality.

My examination of queerness in the novels indexes the term both in the narrow sense of non-cisgender and non-heterosexual identity, and in the far broader sense articulated by a wide body of contemporary queer theorists – what Jack Halberstam, in particular, describes as a 'queer "way of life"'. As Halberstam writes, this phrase denotes queerness 'as an outcome of strange temporalities, imaginative life schedules, and eccentric economic practices' detached from sexual identity. While often joyous and liberating, queer ways of life are frequently enmeshed deeply with the precarizing methodologies of capitalism. Neoliberal logics separates queer subjects into those who willingly participate in the economic sphere, and can therefore be usefully absorbed into the market, and those who wholly or partially refuse to exist within capitalism. Opting, or being forced to, live and work 'outside of reproductive and familial time' and 'on the edges of logics of labour and production' also positions these queer subjects beyond the safety net of capital accumulation, surplus to the needs of capitalism and exposed to constant endangerment and precarity.[6] In response, queers take it upon themselves to create socialities and communities distinct from those of 'family, inheritance, and child rearing'. In this way, Elizabeth Freeman reads queer life as a form of 'becoming-collective-across-time'.[7]

Queer forms of life are not merely predicated on survival, however. In its refusal to submit to the constrictive logics of heteronormative life, queer temporality is a commoning: it blurs past and future, transforms and organizes bodies, and reveals glimmers of anticipatory utopias. In his luminous text on queerness and utopia, José Esteban Muñoz stakes out the claim that queerness 'is essentially about the rejection of a here and now and an insistence on potentiality or concrete possibility for another world'.[8] Analogously to the way in which the multitude in Spahr's poetry opposes post-Fordist segmentation, migrancy opposes border regimes and commoned urban infrastructure weathers neoliberal predation, queerness, in its relationship with time, holds the potential to rewrite the ways in which its subjects live, love and work, gesturing at a utopian horizon of existence beyond capitalism. At the far end of this horizon lies the possibility of immortality for queers – a refiguring of life itself and the ultimate insurance against a precarious ongoing present. As Bonnie Ruberg attests in an exploration of immortality in independent queer video games, '[f]or queer subjects today ... permanent living represents a particularly potent trope for expressing both hopes and concerns about contemporary queer life in the face of an uncertain future'.[9]

Queer ways of life and immortality are powerfully combined in 'San Junipero' (2016), an unexpectedly utopian episode of Charlie Brooker's anthology television show *Black Mirror*. In this episode, the virtual-reality resort town of San Junipero is a space where the characters Yorkie and Kelly can pursue a 'non-reproductive and queer immortality' contrasted with the heteronormative 'mortality, homophobia, and racial prejudice' of the real world.[10] The terminally ill Kelly and quadriplegic, permanently hospitalized Yorkie find love, fulfilment and escapist joy while their minds are plugged into San Junipero's data banks; in the time-travelling technicolour resort they become young, fit, and able-bodied and can fully express and explore their sexualities for the first time. But the utopianism of 'San Junipero' lies in the episode's final scenes, when the lovers decide to undergo euthanasia and are uploaded into San Junipero permanently, driving into the sunset to the tune of Belinda Carlisle's pop masterpiece 'Heaven Is a Place on Earth'.

As in 'San Junipero', the immortality effected by the characters of *Walkaway* and *The Book of Joan* is linked to their separation from the 'straight time' of capitalist heteropatriarchy.[11] 'Straight' here signifies not only the linear time of normative heterosexual life (the drive to colonize the future by repeating oneself in one's own children, and the economic and political logics which support this drive), but also highlights the distinction between queer futures and ongoing capitalist time as described by Berlant and others. Muñoz evokes a 'queer hermeneutics' in opposition to straight time, which undoes its oppressive logics: 'to live inside straight time and ask for, desire, and imagine another time and place is to represent and perform a desire that is both utopian and queer … to participate in a hermeneutic that wishes to describe a collective futurity'.[12] This repudiation of the primacy of the linear historicity of straight time allows us to read queer time as an alternative strategy of knowledge-making and a utopian future horizon. Where Muñoz describes a queer hermeneutics, I argue for a queer commons poetics – the textual representation of collective, collaborative spatialities and socialities which safeguard and empower queer lives.

Utopian world-making

Doctorow and Yuknavitch's fictional worlds in *Walkaway* and *The Book of Joan*, like those of *New York 2140* and *Exit West*, extrapolate contemporary realities rather than being wholly divorced from them. Comparing *The Book of Joan* with another recent dystopia, Dave Egger's *The Circle* (2013), Seeger and

Davison-Vecchione argue that in these novels, familiar social phenomena are taken as starting points 'for extrapolations to future or near-future scenarios which are both remote from our own moment yet unnervingly close to it at the same time'.[13] Doctorow has argued that *Walkaway* is a book depicting an advanced, utopian reconfiguration of modes of social and political organization and coordination, finding the same tendencies 'reflected in things like Occupy [and] the rise of far-right movements'. *The Book of Joan* was written partly in response to the election of US President Donald Trump, the climate crisis and stagnation in the utopian hopes of feminist movements.[14] The futures of these novels are not simply familiar, but bear a powerful anticipatory illumination of alternatives to this present. In his work on dystopian literature, Moylan cautions, via a reading of Suvin's work, that although 'many compelling and powerful sf works' have generated futures 'that expose current problems and warn of the dire consequences if such problems are not properly addressed', such fictions can 'be caught up in a narrowly technological accommodation with the status quo and back away from challenges to the fundamental premises or logics of a society'.[15] Despite being extrapolative and at times dystopian, the worlds of *Walkaway* and *The Book of Joan* avoid the dangers of uncritical world-building through their utopian conclusions, which depict a technological, corporeal and ontological transition beyond anything suggested by their initial dystopian settings.

The two authors are also similar in that their writing emerges from, and in turn generates, its own engaged readership. For Doctorow, this is a consequence of the social contract of popular fiction, which creates 'a "place to belong"' for its readers, generating in comfortingly recognizable narrative 'the utopian pull of a secure identity in an insecure world'; Yuknavitch's work is often directly addressed to her readers as a collective subject: 'I multiplied voices and mammalian bodies. Now it's us. We are the rest of you, reader'.[16] Both are active online and have built up dedicated Internet cult followings which distinguish them as natives of a contemporary, networked moment: while Doctorow has widespread recognition among science fiction fans, technology bloggers and web activists, Yuknavitch has an equally dedicated following among the readers, podcasters and bloggers of autofiction, memoir and feminist literary fiction. As a reviewer of *The Chronology of Water* writes, four years after the book's release, '"Viral" is a good meme for a memoir about the body, and seems appropriate for a small book published in 2011 [that] keeps popping up on blogs and social media feeds'.[17] Doctorow, in recognition of his large community of readers, has written on the reciprocal relationship between science fiction writers and fan communities. In an article on his decision to release many of his novels under a permissive Creative Commons license, which allows free access and encourages adaptation, he writes that science fiction is 'perhaps the most social of all literary genres', whose success is indebted to 'organized fandom'. He credits the science fiction genre's continuing success to the online nature of science fiction readership communities: 'online norms of idle chatter, fannish organizing, publishing and leisure'.[18] For both authors, the collective, the plural and the common are vital resources for the development of their writing practice.

The two novels deploy their prefigurative times and spaces using the instruments of a commons poetics. They exhibit narrative techniques, such as analepsis, which unsettle temporal boundaries, depictions of commons spaces, large casts of characters and multiple narratorial viewpoints, and the presentation of storytelling and broadcasting themselves as material tools of collective opposition. *The Book of Joan* is characterized by 'structural complexity [and] use of multiple temporalities, along with stylistic choices that often interweave graphically violent imagery and language with a corporeal poetics of queer/ed desires and posthuman subjectivities'; via these and other textual strategies, Yuknavitch deploys a utopian message of belief in 'the profound materiality of stories and their ability, for better or worse, to transform the world'.[19] Doctorow echoes the premise of Solnit's *A Paradise Built In Hell*, one of the primary inspirations for *Walkaway*, in setting out the ideological basis of his novel: '[o]ur disaster recovery is always fastest and smoothest when we work together ... the best science fiction does something much more interesting than prediction: It inspires. That science fiction tells us better nations are ours to build and lets us dream vividly of what it might be like to live in those nations'.[20] Key in Doctorow's commons poetics, as the numerous blog posts and thinkpieces quoted in this chapter reveal, is the paratextual gambit wherein the text is positioned not as the end of the discourse between author and reader, but as its beginning. In authorial commentary on his own novel – in particular on the platforms where readers can, and do, leave comments and hold discussions – Doctorow creates an immaterial, paratextual commons which can in turn change and influence the meaning of the novel, for those readers who choose to engage with this ongoing discourse.[21]

Walkaway

Throughout *Walkaway*, Doctorow represents the ongoing present as a time of crisis and precarity for surplus populations under late capitalism, and imagines the emergence of commons-based utopian spaces out of the same. The novel is an unusual blend of an action-packed near-future science fiction pulp thriller and a series of dialogues on philosophical, economic and sociological themes, charting the lives (and lengthy conversations) of a central cast of characters. These 'walkaways' imagine and prefiguratively build alternative oppositional futures through acts of civil disobedience, refusal, occupation, migration and riot. The narrative spans a number of decades, as the walkaways become tied up in a deadlier and increasingly hotter war with the hyper-rich capitalist overlords of their near-future world, until the novel's denouement sees Doctorow sketch the beginnings of a post-scarcity, post-capitalist utopia. *Walkaway* is an unusual utopian novel, but not an unusual commons utopia, in that it shows its readers not the utopia for which its author wishes, but the paths taken to reach that utopia.

As a number of critics have argued, *Walkaway* does not excel on the grounds of stylistic nuance, characterization and plotting – the main characters all speak in the same high-level technical register, as if the only people to escape capitalism are computer science graduates; they tend to exhibit little in the way of personality beyond a mechanical devotion to their revolutionary cause; and, as Jason Sheehan quips, the novel 'sometimes reads like a series of philosophical set-pieces stitched together with drone fights and lots of sex'.[22] *Walkaway* makes up for these shortcomings in its cohesive depiction of the role utopia and the commons could play for surplus populations under late capitalism, and in the originality of the anti-capitalist visions Doctorow dreams up.

Doctorow's association with anti-capitalist politics is well-attested: he is recognized as an activist and commentator on digital commons, open source software, copyright law and the rights of government whistle-blowers and pro-privacy hackers including Aaron Schwartz, Edward Snowden and Chelsea Manning. The concerns of Doctorow's science fiction writing closely parallel his activism – *Walkaway*, his tenth novel, returns to themes raised in his previous books, including opposition to government surveillance, the benefits of sharing technologies and ideas, and alternative social structures, often derived from the politics of the Burner (participatory attendees of the Burning Man festival and its global offshoots) and FOSS (Free and Open Source Software) communities. Doctorow's best-known novel, *Little Brother* (2008), depicts an alternate present in which a high school hacker experiences the full force of the repressive US secret services in the aftermath of a terrorist attack, and joins forces with other teenagers to change the system from within.

As many critics of *Walkaway* have noted, the near-future Canada in which the novel's narrative is set, like the New York of *New York 2140* and the world cities of *Exit West* is, at times, barely distinguishable from our own realist present. This temporally ambiguous world, named 'default' by the novel's anti-capitalist protagonists, is depicted in the wake of a re-consolidation of power and prestige by the 1 per cent – the extremely wealthy classes, now named the 'zottarich' or 'zottas' – after a period of climatological, economic and social crises. As the novel opens, we are introduced to a world where 'the climate spins out of control, the middle class diminishes to an infinitesimal speck, the very rich grab all the wealth and resources, traditional employment disappears, factories sit empty and hundreds of thousands opt out of society altogether'.[23] Despite these profound planetary transformations, default is less an original post-apocalyptic imaginary than the transition of the previously liberal and economically stable nations of the Global North into a political and economic reality which is closer to that of the extreme neoliberalism, precarious inequality and political disenfranchisement of oil- and mineral-rich Middle East and African nations, where '[t]he masses are left to hustle for the dregs of what's left in the ultimate dystopian version of the "gig" economy'.[24]

Given the precarious bleakness of this world, it should come as little surprise that the utopian hope which inspires and focuses the oppositional and prefigurative work of the walkaways – the aforementioned thousands who have opted to walk away from capitalism and build a better life in the industrial wastelands of its abandoned rural fringes – is the development of immortality. This attainment functions as a final and absolute victory against the precarity of life in the ongoing present. As *Walkaway*'s long narrative unfolds, the scientists and engineers of the planet's disparate walkaway communities come together to transform this dream into a material reality through the development of the science fictional technologies of mind uploading and body cloning. The search for immortality is spearheaded and readily embraced by the cast of queer characters who people Doctorow's novel.

The technologies and modalities of immortality in *Walkaway* emerge from the same early twenty-first-century cultural tendency we have been exploring in the preceding chapters. In *Walkaway* – the title of which, until Kim Stanley Robinson suggested that Doctorow change it, was *Utopia* – the technological basis of the immortality is the scanning and uploading of brains to a distributed online network.[25] Both the villainous, capitalistic zottas and the diverse, anarchic walkaways are, as the novel's first act closes, working on a cure for human death. Notably, where the zottas desire immortality for precisely the reason that the Struldbruggs are denied its full potential – absolute control derived from the perpetual ownership of all the world's wealth and labour power – the walkaways want to make immortality open source and freely available for all, thus setting up the violent conflict which comes as the zottas desperately attempt to prevent this democratization. For the walkaways, the geographically distributed, non-physical, informational immortality promised by the uploading of brains into BitTorrent-style peer-to-peer networks, 'as unkillably immortal as data could be', becomes not only a utopia, but a necessity: it is the only thing which can prevent their destruction at the hands of the zottas' private militias.[26]

The walkaways' drive for collective and accessible immortality emerges as the mirror image of the zottas' self-serving desire for immortality. Like Doctorow, the walkaways talk of commons, peer networks, radical equality and open access. The tragedy of the commons is evoked as '[a] fairy tale about giving public assets to rich people to run as personal empires'. The character Limpopo believes that '[i]f you build systems that make people focus on mastery, cooperation, and better work, we'll have a beautiful inn full of happy people'; later, she states the walkaways' utopian dream is 'making a world where greed is a perversion'. In contrast, the zottas – who, for the most part, are only represented in walkaway accounts – figure as an alienated group of 'sociopaths who clawed their way to the top of default's pyramid of skulls', each of whom is desperate to institute themselves and their family as 'pharaohs', 'godlike immortals', 'Olympian masters', and 'permanent god-emperors'. This argument, while hyperbolic, is also grounded in economic reality; as one character argues, as long as both a worker and a 'hereditary global powerbroker' have merely human lifespans, it is possible to convince the working classes that some modicum of equality exists in the capitalist system, but once immortality becomes universal, plentiful and accessible, this new and radical form of equality outstrips any of the rewards offered by capitalist ideology: 'When you think ... everyone you know might live forever – something happens'.[27]

The near-future world of *Walkaway* is home to two quite separate utopias. The anarchic, mobile, distributed community called Walkaway is a politically and ethically ideological material utopia, built upon and working to surpass the tyranny of practical concerns such as resource scarcity, division of labour, social structure and commons organization. On the other hand, the simulation of human minds inside Walkaway's distributed digital networks is a response to metaphysical concerns regarding human nature and post-human ethics. The two utopian worlds, crucially, are interdependent and cannot exist without each other. While the virtual world of informational immortality is, in some ways, akin to the world of 'San Junipero', its simulated minds do not enjoy an embodied virtual existence in an artificially generated physical space – rather, they exist in the real world, interacting with the still-living through screens, speakers and cameras, manipulating the simulations of their own minds in the way a programmer would manipulate a piece of code, and, in the beginning, acutely struggling with a sense of abject horror stemming from the absence of their bodies. In one of the novel's most disturbing passages, one such 'sim', with her consent, is kept running by fellow computer scientists for valuable data analysis even as she repeatedly loses her mind: '"It's such a terrible feeling. Everything I've just said, it's bullshit. There's no continuity. I'm not me. I'm just me enough to know that I'm not me [...]". [...] The computer made a noise Iceweasel had never heard. Weird. Unearthly. A scream'.[28]

Furthermore, unlike the high-tech, corporate 'data-cemetery' of TCKR Systems where Kelly and Yorkie's brains are uploaded in 'San Junipero', *Walkaway*'s virtual world is itself fully imbricated in material and physical issues: the brain scans, 'too bulky to fully mirror', have to be physically transported out of zones without network connectivity so they can be uploaded to the cloud; and the computers which run the simulations must themselves be packed down and set up whenever the walkaways need to move.[29] Doctorow does not shy away from tackling head-on the economic and material concerns which, as Eleanor Drage points out, are generally elided in 'San Junipero' and much other virtual reality media: 'would individuals trust a corporate giant with their ever-after? What kind of guarantee could TCKR systems offer that they would keep a person's soul for eternity? Could this ever be profitable for any enterprise, or has their society changed so completely that payment and profit are no longer a priority?'[30] Doctorow mocks the sleek aesthetics and improbable economics of other virtual reality texts when one of his characters contemplates that '[w]hether "real" data centers were neat, ranked terraces of aerodynamic hardware, that's not how walkaways did them'. The embodied reality of virtual immortality is underlined when word goes out to nearby communities 'for compute-power. People came with whatever horsepower they had ... the collection of motley devices, sprinkled around the tunnels, linked by tangles of fiber in pink rubber sheaths, delivered compute cycles that made Dis *leap* into consciousness.'[31]

Furthermore, where the bland facade of TCKR Systems stands in sharp contrast to the nostalgic, technicolour, queer world which its virtual simulations offer, the aesthetics of Doctorow's setting and the form of the metaphysical immortality which appears within it are closely linked, both emerging out of a sense of surplus. The economic position of the walkaways is the first mode of surplus in *Walkaway*: 'Default has no use for us except as a competition for other non-zottas ... We are surplus to default's requirements.'[32] This is a textbook Marxist reading of the walkaways as 'relative surplus population'. This section of the population under capitalism encompasses all those workers who are unemployed, under-employed and unable to be employed – those who are surplus to the requirements of capitalism. While an unemployed surplus population may appear to be the enemy of a functioning capitalist system, Marx's insight was in revealing that it is capitalism itself which generates, conditions and maintains this surplus.[33] The fundamental operation of capitalism is to drive the cost of labour down (by fostering the conditions which would create more workers), while driving the amount of profit gleaned from labour up (by forcing workers to work more for less pay, thereby making their existences more precarious); it does so via 'the structural maintenance of a certain level of unemployment' which keeps wages in line 'with the needs of accumulation'. Furthermore, as the collective Endnotes argues, 'this surplus population need not find itself completely "outside" capitalist social relations.

Capital may not need these workers, but they still need to work. They are thus forced to offer themselves up for the most abject forms of wage slavery in the form of petty-production and services.'[34] In other words, to be able to keep its labour costs down and its surplus value high, capitalism keeps a sector of the population unemployed, and thus willing to work for very low wages, which also prevents more secure and better-paid workers from exerting bargaining power in a wage context. The integration of precariously surviving surplus populations into expanding service and circulation economies, along with the shrinking of the manual and industrial labour market in the Global North, signals that surplus populations are not only a condition of, but themselves condition the form of, contemporary capitalism.

The second form of surplus in *Walkaway* is the surplus material waste of capitalism, which permits the walkaways to live a life of what contemporary radical leftist thinkers have described as 'fully automated luxury communism' in the wilderness beyond urban spaces. The *onsen* baths; waste-recycling breweries; 3D printers for medicine, clothing, and food; drones; zeppelins; and spatially distributed, high-bandwidth wireless networks which define walkaway communities, as well as the futuristic technologies which allow them to effortlessly pack up and move to new locations to avoid discovery or attack, are all predicated on the 'endless surplus of sacrifice zones, superfund sites, no-man's-lands and dead cities' which default has produced.[35] The third and final mode of surplus is linked to this sense of material limitlessness, and returns us to Muñoz's queer utopianism via his conception of a queer surplus, which itself draws on Bloch's concept of cultural surplus. As Muñoz writes, the utopian function of queerness – particularly queer art – is 'enacted by a certain surplus in the work that promises a futurity, something that is not quite here'. This surplus is aesthetic, camp or ornamental, gaudy, chaotic, unpredictable, a 'distortion' which is not simply an addition to the core of the work, but a vital part of it, a 'stuttering particularity that shoves one off course, out of straight time'. The 'not quite here', represented in queer aesthetic surplus, is a future-oriented source of hope, vitality and opposition to the 'hopeless heteronormative maps of the present'; furthermore, it 'exceeds the functionalism of capitalist flows' and 'conveys other modes of being that do not conform to capitalist maps of the world'.[36]

The aesthetic surplus of *Walkaway* is incompatible with the productive demands of capitalism in its ornamentation, its queer communal luxury and the sense of joy it engenders. It is defined by an aesthetics of what Doctorow's characters describe as 'refu-luxury', which throws together the utilitarian technologies and practical aesthetics of UNHCR-derived communal habitations with the impractical, the imaginative and the luxurious. One of the community's zeppelins, named *Better Nation*, is adorned on its underside with 'cargo hooks, sensor packages, and gay illustrations of androgynous space-people dancing against a backdrop of cosmic pocket-litter: ringed saturnesques and glittering nebulae'. Walkaway is, at its core, a distributed network of refugee communities, but the aesthetic differences between the original UNHCR camps and those of Walkaway are important to the walkaways, hence the tone of pride in Limpopo's description of the Belt & Braces: 'there was a world of difference between dishing up M.R.E.s to climate refus and serving fancy dry-ice cocktails made from wet-printers and powdered alcohol. No refugee camp ever went through quite so many cocktail parasols and perfect-knot swizzle sticks'. As a result of this politics of luxury, walkaway communities enjoy a life that the surplus populations of default could not imagine: 'power, water, fresh hydroponics, and soft beds. Took about three hours a day each to keep the whole place running. Spent the rest of the time re-creating a Greek open-air school, teaching each other music and physics and realtime poetry.'[37] As in the work of Thomas Pynchon, the 'oddballs and misfits' of Walkaway are dedicated to living time against the capitalist demands of the working day, making sloth 'a creative practice – an art of revolt, as well as an art of time.'[38]

Through this aesthetic commitment, Doctorow's novel can be understood to obscure the hardships and traumas faced by refugees in the present, portraying an unsettled and homeless life as a fun adventure in living otherwise, in much the same way as *New York 2140* never fully commits to representing the true horror of flooding the planet's coastlines fifty feet deep. However, like *Exit West*, Doctorow's novel is utopian in its construction of a mobile commons, refusing to commit to describing the migrant condition as one constituted purely of suffering and, like Hamid's novel, is fuelled by a sense that the human of the future might just be – and should be – a human forever on the move. At the culmination of a conflict between the core group of walkaways and a new group who take over their community and institute a reputation economy,

Limpopo simply calls on her friends to leave and build a new community elsewhere. To the incredulous coup leader, she says:

> We're called walkaways because we *walk away*. [...] We can live like it's the first days of a better world, not like it's the first pages of an Ayn Rand novel. Have this place, but you can't have us. We withdraw our company.[39]

Gesturing well beyond Hamid's near-present utopia, however, *Walkaway* contends that the human of the future will travel beyond death itself.

This move beyond death – the fundamental utopian horizon of *Walkaway*'s commons poetics – is queer firstly in terms of the sexual and gender identities of those who become the original immortals of the novel. The walkaways are an anti-normative, anti-straight collective whose association with the end of death is both a repudiation of a lived history of queer death, and a precondition of this immortality emerging in the first place. The central group of walkaways includes Natalie, a bisexual woman who has relationships with two women, Gretyl and Nadie; Seth, a Black man in a relationship with Tam, a trans woman; and Limpopo, a Latina woman in a relationship with a white man.[40] By way of contrast, the zotta characters we meet in the novel are white, heterosexual, upper-class men and their normative families, obsessed not only with holding on to wealth but also with the allegorical figure of the Child as the insurance for this wealth's future existence. Indeed, the book's narrative revolves around the relationship between the character Natalie/Iceweasel and her zotta father, who pursues her and the walkaways who, in his understanding, have kidnapped and brainwashed her. In Natalie's father's eyes, the core ideological conflict of the novel is reduced to a familial one predicated on inheritance – he assumes that the walkaways want to gain access to his inherited wealth and social power, when in reality they seek to live in a world where comfort, joy and security are divorced entirely from familial and genetic ties. It is only through the development of immortality that the power of inherited wealth, and the family structures which uphold it, can be overcome.

Doctorow's novel puts forward the laudable claim that these queer characters, in their oppositional diversity, require nothing less than immortality to survive and escape the violence, repression, apocalypse and trauma of straight time: precariousness, homelessness, climate crisis and AI-targeted drone bombing. As Drage argues of the queer immortality utopia of 'San Junipero', 'Kelly and Yorkie's queer romance was not the coincidental winner of Black Mirror's happy ending, but the condition for the appearance of that hopeful future: their queerness is the horizon for their second chance at life'.[41] Immortality in *Walkaway* is likewise not just a scientific breakthrough or an elegant solution to a complex programming puzzle, but also materially, metaphysically and aesthetically an evocation of a queer surplus, and is thus the utopian promise of a safe, secure, communal and queer world beyond capitalist realism.

Evidence for the surplus nature of *Walkaway*'s immortality is plentiful. After Dis, the original simulated mind, learns to keep herself in an 'envelope' of parameters which prevent her from having an existential crisis at the reality of her physical death, she engages with another form of surplus: 'Being liberated from the vagaries of the flesh and being able to adjust her mind's parameters so she stayed in an optimal working state turned Dis into a powerhouse researcher'. This paradoxical combination of moderation ('the numbness, that's the sim, it's trying to keep you from going nonlinear. It's damping your reactions') and excess ('I'm going to knock the compute-time to execute a sim down by *two orders of magnitude*. We're about to get a fuck-load more bots. As in, no one will ever have to die again'), leads, by the end of the novel, to a world whose inhabitants are on the way towards vanquishing not only death, precarity and need, but also the limitations of the human body and physical brain, becoming post-human in the process.[42]

The final, most decidedly utopian chapter of Doctorow's novel portrays a more distantly future world wherein some of these simulated minds are then downloaded back into artificially created human bodies, while others eschew bodies entirely and exist only in virtual space ('[t]hey're offworld, most of the time. They entangle a lot, with each other and others'). This is a brief glimpse of a world where bodies themselves are a kind of surplus, interchangeable, modifiable, transformable and tweakable at will. In these final transformations of the human, Doctorow combines two classic tropes – the brain upload and the clone body – to create a form of immortality based on futuristic technological advances. *Walkaway* also engages directly with the concept of 'strong AI' which has become inescapable in science media in the last decade. Strong AI, also known as artificial general intelligence, is the final, utopian form of artificial intelligence. It stands in contrast with 'weak AI' minds which can only solve specific, narrowly defined problems, while general AI minds could be indistinguishable from human minds in their ability to learn new information and make decisions. As in *Walkaway*, the development of such futuristic forms of intelligence ushers in a technological singularity, an explosion in computational power where artificial minds rapidly learn how to augment themselves beyond the capabilities of human minds.[43]

The post-human and the queer are natural bedfellows – both ontological modes are premised on the argument that the human, and life more broadly, must be constituted beyond the dominant humanist conception of the white cisgender man as the measure of humanity. In the critical work of Muñoz, Halberstam, Sara Ahmed, Mel Y. Chen and others, the subjects centred by the intersection of post-human and queer theory include women, people of colour, queers, monsters, cyborgs, machines and animals. More generally, queer theory and post-human theory reject individual experience as a framework for identity construction, placing the common, the collective and the multitude at the focal point of such constructions.[44] Queerness is about the production and experience of identity through desire, and as Patricia MacCormack argues, the 'creations of connections – life as relation not dividuation – is posthuman living. Desire is, put most simply, the need to create connections with other things, not to have or know but collapse the self with other(s). In this sense posthumanism is a form of queer desire, or queer "life"'.[45] Throughout the novel, when the walkaways are isolated, undergoing existential and moral crises, or feel hatred towards the people working to kill them, they remind each other as a kind of mantra that 'our identities exist in combination with other people', or that '[e]very human was a hyper-dense node of intense emotional and material investment'.[46]

This wording is reminiscent of the way in which Isabel Lorey, via Judith Butler, casts precariousness as 'co-extensive' with life from the moment of birth, 'since survival depends from the beginning on social networks, on sociality and the work of others'.[47] For Butler and Lorey, precariousness – injurability, vulnerability, exposure – is never an individual condition, but is always shared. The two philosophers distinguish between this existential and social condition, which is neither good nor bad, and the 'category of order' termed *precarity*.[48] While precariousness brings living beings closer together in their apprehension of one another by highlighting the *interrelations* that their differences make, precarity highlights the *distinctions* between living beings by applying external hierarchies and determinations to these interrelations. Precarity assesses, hierarchizes and classifies lives (individual instances of precariousness), by dominating the relations which compose them (the conditions of those lives, the experience of 'being-with others'). Capitalism – neoliberal capitalism in particular, with its strategies of atomization and alienation – is the key precarizing force of our lifetimes.

To employ Lorey's model here, I argue that, when embedded in the socialities of Walkaway, the walkaways oppose and throw off the governmental precarization through which the zottas manage their surplus populations, and instead construct a new commons within which intrinsic, existential precariousness is collectively managed. To illustrate this point with a plot twist worthy of the best didactic utopia, near the novel's conclusion, the walkaways take in the same coup leader from whom they had chosen to walk away, as a result of which Limpopo offers the following pearl of wisdom:

> 'I came back to help you because helping people is what you do, whether or not they're in your thing, because that's the best world to live in.'
> 'First days of a better nation,' he said, with a little sarcasm.[49]

In its final chapters, *Walkaway* depicts the stage of oppositional, anti-capitalist action which Lorey describes as 'the exodus of the many, a constituting, an organizing, of the manifold singularities', an exodus that emerges specifically 'in order to "return" and fundamentally change the existing social relations'. In the world of the novel this 'return' is depicted through the normalization of walkaway as a form of political and social organization. This return is profoundly utopian in the sense I have been discussing throughout this book of making space, rather than escaping from it, and of creating better forms of life in the imperfect, difficult world which is accessible and available to us today, rather than waiting on a transformational event which may never occur to usher us into an ideal future. Lorey writes that such an exodus can emerge through the 'invention of common notions', and *Walkaway*'s common notion, immortality, is one which renders even existential precariousness, the fact of human death, only one problem among the many solved in its utopia.[50] Moreover, this commonness is derived from, and re-inscribes, a queer collectivity. Through their gradual transition into a community of queer post-human immortals, the characters of *Walkaway* find ways to live and thrive beyond precarized straight time and the capitalist systems which maintain it, and transition into a post-precarious utopian horizon which only queerness can produce.

The Book of Joan

Walkaway and *The Book of Joan* share a portrayal of the inequality, alienation and violence of an extreme version of late capitalism which, nevertheless, bears close parallels to the real-world present, a vision of imaginary spaces of collective anti-capitalist opposition, an interest in the role queerness plays in utopia and a particular focus on the consequences of immortality for the quest of human liberation. *The Book of Joan* may appear to be an unusual turn from Yuknavitch, who is best known as the author of the acclaimed memoir *The Chronology of Water* (2011), has written extensively on queer sexuality, mental health, misfit corporeality and war, and is part of a loose collective of contemporary experimental literary writers including Kathy Acker, Chuck Palahnuik and Cheryl Strayed. *The Book of Joan* is preoccupied with different concerns from those of *Walkaway*. It employs an eloquent and visceral style; there are only two central characters, the upper-class artist Christine and the rough-spoken ex-child soldier Joan, and both are characterized as more multifaceted and complex than the loveable nerds of *Walkaway*. Yuknavitch's world-building, on the other hand, is delivered in broad strokes and pays less attention than *Walkaway* to systems-scale issues of politics and economics. Rather, *The Book of Joan* is a science fiction text committed not to narrative conflict and wide genre appeal, but to exploring issues of female bodily autonomy, queerness, patriarchal power, the role of narrative in oppositional action and the place of the human in wider planetary ecological systems.

By far the most apocalyptic text examined in this book, *The Book of Joan* offers its readers a vision of an Earth well beyond the point of no return: 'a spotted apocalyptic terrain … [a] lifeless ball of dirt'.[51] This barren wasteland is the result of a long climatological crisis and a phenomenally violent near-future war between Joan's armies of eco-revolutionaries and the despotic, eugenicist capitalist Jean de Men, which only concludes when Joan summons a super-human 'apocalyptic body song' in an attempt to end the conflict once and for all: 'the sky lit with fire, half from the weapons of his attack, half from her summoning of the earth and all its calderas'.[52] Even in the aftermath of this apocalypse, life continues to cling on in underground caves and on board de Men's orbital space station, CIEL, where the last remnants of humanity's upper classes are slowly living their way to species extinction after Joan's 'geocatastrophe' precipitated a rapid mutation in which they lost their sexual and reproductive organs, hair and skin coloration. With the population no longer able to conceive children or even have sex, de Men has embarked on a horrific programme of enforced insemination of female prisoners, which at the novel's outset has proven fruitless.

In contrast with the technologically abetted immortality of *Walkaway*, the immortality of *The Book of Joan* is primarily genetic and ecological. The central immortal character is Joan of Dirt – a reborn Joan of Arc – who holds unique powers over the arbitration of life and death. She comes back to life when she is burnt at the stake, can heal the injured and bring the dead briefly back to life and almost destroys all life on Earth in a bid to stop her nemesis, de Men. The moment in the novel tied explicitly to immortality occurs in the finale, where Joan merges, at a genetic level, with the planet itself. She is absorbed into the Earth's soil, creating a 'mega catalyst of sorts' which restarts life on the planet in an entirely new biological 'language':

> the cradle of my pelvis disintegrating and rebecoming in new DNA strands, my femur, tibia, fibula, the phalanges of my feet and hands. [...] A different story, leading whoever is left toward something we've not yet imagined.[53]

In this absorption and molecular reconfiguration of Joan's life-giving energy, her life, as it becomes eternal, also becomes irreversibly post-human, merging and broadening into a 'relationship with all matter' which is impossible to quantify in relation to human life and death. Indeed, Joan decries the description of this act as 'suicide', describing it instead as 'a new way to travel'. Joan's transformation is the natural culmination of Yuknavitch's discursive stance throughout the novel – mostly delivered through the narration of the artist Christine – that the anthropocentric obsession with human life and death, embodied by avaricious eugenicist de Men, is fundamentally at odds with a more-than-human understanding of all matter as part of ongoing articulations of energy in incredible forms: 'You have to let go of the idea that you are a singular savior or destroyer. Everything is matter. Everything is moved by and through energy. Bodies are miniature renditions of the entire universe.'[54]

A commons poetics of escape from and resistance to straight time is particularly evident in *The Book of Joan*, which overflows with queer forms of relationality. Joan and her companion Leone are in love, though neither acts on their mutual desire until the very end of the novel; only in a posthumous letter does Joan write their love beyond the human, into the fabric of life on the planet and into the shape of the universe: 'You deserve the word "love", spoken over and over again and untethered from prior lexicons, an erotic and unbound universe, the dead light of stars yet aching to stitch your name across the night sky, the ocean waters singing your body hymn to shore day into night into day.'[55] This love is queer not only because Joan and Leone are queer, but because it embodies a queering of language, space and time. Joan's immortality is evinced through the absorption of her human body into the genetic codes of the post-apocalyptic planet, triggering a new start for life. In portraying this transformation, Yuknavitch 'figures the (post)human body as heterogenous and always already entangled with other materially agentic organisms and environments'.[56] Joan's love for Leone – who is also post-human, owing to the pig heart with which her defective heart has been replaced – is another such entanglement; as Jennings argues, these post-human bodies also function 'as a discursive site for resisting and contesting oppressive bio-practices by queering the very "nature" of desire in order to destabilize heteronormative investments in reproductive futurity'.[57] Yuknavitch develops the oppositional power of these queer desires through the temporally fluid, interwoven structure of her novel, through forms of queer collective narration, and through the post-human, common spaces of underground caves in which a number of the novel's pivotal scenes occur.

The first two of these aspects – a queer mode of temporal fluidity and the foregrounding of storytelling and narration as collective acts – are particularly apparent in those sections of the novel narrated by Christine, an artist onboard CIEL named after the proto-feminist Medieval author Christine de Pizan, and the author of the novel's own 'Book of Joan'. Like the rest of CIEL's population, Christine has lost her sexual and reproductive organs, alongside her skin pigmentation and hair. One of the results of this '[d]evolution' of the human species is the development of an art of laser-aided body scarification – the writing of literal, tactile stories on human skin. The skin stories written by de Men are misogynistic romances of 'egregious gender nostalgia' in which 'for his women, happily ever after meant rape, death, insanity, prison, or marriage'. At the same time, de Men bans all sexual expression onboard CIEL, in particular the sort of queered sexual activity – aided by fantastic mechanical devices and bawdy, hypersexual Shakespearean wordplay and poetry ('Christ! Come here this instant, you reeling-ripe dove-egg. Get here and lay me a kiss … You tickle-brained harlot!') – which Christine engages in with her gay friend and lover Trinculo. With no sexual organs to make use of, Christine and Trinculo queer the idea of sexual play itself by engaging in a cerebral, non-reproductive narration of liberatory sexual pleasure – 'Mount the table and spread your legs, Christine. I'll bore a new hole into your luscious otherworldly flesh'– which opposes de Men's obsessive desire to control all human bodies and their expressions.[58]

It is in one of these sexual performances that Trinculo reveals to Christine that Joan is still alive – a linguistic orgasm which shatters the line between physical and mental erogenous pleasure, and begins the novel's central narrative:

> He does not penetrate me, but as I clasp my legs around him, bear-hugging his torso and burying my face in the folds of his grafts, he whispers into my ear, raising every hair and fast-devolving erogenous cell to the surface of my body. 'She's alive. Your dead icon? She's alive.'[59]

Consequently, in opposition to de Men's anti-feminist narratives, Christine begins to write a new kind of scarified story, different in two ways: firstly, it tells the story of Joan's struggle against him and reveals that she still lives; secondly, it is not contained by a single body, but is spread across a collective of queer bodies who join Christine's revolution. 'Young. Smooth-skinned. Sexless, but filled with an astonishingly repressed agency they have no idea what to do with', they form a queer commons:

> I will collect, fragment, and displace individual lines from my epic body poem onto the bodies of others until we become an army of sorts [...] a resistance movement of flesh. The action will culminate in plural acts of physical violence so profound during our performance no one will ever forget the fact of flesh.[60]

As can be seen in these lines, the sections of the novel narrated by Christine evoke a queer time. They leap analeptically forward in time to describe and prefiguratively anticipate Christine's utopian dreams of victory over de Men as well as proleptically returning from Christine's present into a retelling – sometimes in Christine's narrative voice, sometimes in Joan's and sometimes in transcripts from Joan's interrogation – of Joan's childhood, the War and her apparent death. As the novel unfolds, chapters centred on Joan herself – also narrated in the third person but in a diction far rougher and more practical than Christine's effusive 'body poem' – reveal her life in the present on the surface of the Earth, until these multiple timelines and narrative strands collapse in the novel's violent dénouement. These textual strategies queer and fragment not only the internal temporality of the novel, in which de Men presents a singular, cohesive narrative of his rise to power as a mighty military leader and saviour of humanity, despite the best efforts of the genocidal eco-terrorist Joan, but also work 'on a metaliterary level to disrupt readers' expectations of the novel as a straightforward apocalypse'.[61] *The Book of Joan*'s queer post-apocalypticism is a radical demand for the recognition that some stories, such as the end of humanity's repeated attempts to control the planet, its species and each other's bodies, hopes and desires, require an apocalypse to be properly told.

While Christine and Trinculo wage their narrative and representational revolution against de Men on board CIEL, Joan and Leone hide from their enemies in a series of caves. The sexual and reproductive symbolism of caves and caverns is plentiful and productive, as is the queer interplay between cave and closet; Virginia Woolf articulated one of the finest examples of the latter when she wrote, in *A Room of One's Own* (1929): 'For if Chloe likes Olivia and Mary Carmichael knows how to express it she will light a torch in that vast chamber where nobody has yet been. It is all half lights and profound shadows like those serpentine caves where one goes with a candle peering up and down, not knowing where one is stepping.'[62] *The Book of Joan* rediscovers, revives and reworks these serpentine caves in a textual mode which is as post-human as it is queer. In Yuknavitch's post-apocalyptic world, caves are the last functioning ecosystems, containing all the planet's remaining species, including human beings, and the novel goes to considerable lengths to describe the complexity of life they contain. The Son Doong cave, a real-world cave in Vietnam, is described as a complete and intricate microcosm of the planet which once existed above it:

> Here, beyond their little cave's entryway, stretched five miles of underground life thriving beyond imagination [...] a biodiversity so rich and secret it was nearly its own world. A jungle, a river, a lake; countless old and new species of plant and animal life; even some things in between that Joan was still studying. Fields of algae as large as foothills. Stalagmites as tall as old-growth redwoods. A whole verdant underworld defying the decay of the world above it. There were times Joan half expected a mammal to emerge from its waters, blinking and dripping, the new species taking its first steps onto land.[63]

The last lines foreshadow Joan's eventual subsumption into the planet in order to create a world of 'new species', an act which also happens in a cave complex – the Sarawak Caves in Malaysia, which open out onto the sea. Joan chooses these caves as the site of her genetic transfer because of their biodiversity – just as humans onboard CIEL have lost the ability to reproduce and change, cave life has rapidly evolved, creating a post-human, multi-species, symbiotic commons of 'fungi. Amoebas. Multicellular life-forms adapting and evolving at fantastic rates ... Sound. Light. Energy. ... Living energy'. Yuknavitch's description of this new cave life as 'living energy' allies it, even before Joan has performed her rebirthing act, to Joan herself, who is described by another character with the neologism 'engenderine', a mythological being 'closer to matter and elements than to human'.[64]

The caves are not only the site of a new, fantastic rebirth of life, which queers the boundaries between human, non-human and a wider universe of energy and matter, but are also a space of queer time. Joan and Leone are the products of a childhood and young adulthood of unimaginable trauma, and the caves – spaces of relative safety, comfort and intimacy – act as repositories for the vital memories and histories of their relationship:

> Joan's heart beats up in her chest for a long minute. She remembers: a month's respite from war she'd spent with Leone, near Australia. The neon blue and yellow backs and bellies of ribbon eels, sliding through ocean water, alongside them in an underwater cave pool. The two of them laughing.[65]

The ribbon eels, like Woolf's candlelit caverns, encode a cryptic queerness which is explicated for us by Yuknavitch, who seemingly interrupts her own novel in a direct, apostrophic address to the reader set in the historical present tense:

In the subterranean caves of Christmas Island, a variety of hermaphroditic and protandric species thrives. The ribbon eel is one of them [...] As they mature, they would swap genders. Eels that were born male grew into females that changed color and laid eggs. They could live twenty years this way, their gender entirely fluid.[66]

The memories of better pasts which the caves allow Joan to inhabit extend not only to Leone, but to her brother, with whom she shares a close bond: 'If she feels anything about the word *brother*, it is here, in this space that smells of water and dirt and living things. Her memory remains loyal to all the times they played in the woods together as children. His death, then, should bring life back into the walls and ground and water.'[67] These lines – their narration in the third person, their omniscient yet intimate style and their concern with memory and language – read like those parts of Joan's history which, earlier in the novel, had been narrated by Christine on her skin; this stylistic play highlights the commoning of temporality and memory which Yuknavitch deploys at this late stage in the novel.

On CIEL, queer subjectivity is developed further in the character of de Men himself, who, at the climax of the narrative, is revealed as a trans man. His grotesque history of violence against women, and the narration of this section of the novel – in an omniscient mode but delimited by Christine's narratorial authority – means that his literal exposure as transgender is described in a hostile, unsympathetic, even transphobic light. A number of textual tactics, including the switch of pronouns used to describe de Men from masculine to feminine, and the descriptions of him as 'what is left of a woman', 'the horrid corporeal truth of her', and '[w]rong mother. Woman destroyed', all make it difficult to read this revelation as anything other than a ciphered insinuation that de Men's violence against female bodies is a consequence of a sense of dysphoric shame or anger at the failures of his body.[68] This stance, like the transphobic characterization of Buffalo Bill in *Silence of the Lambs* (dir. Jonathan Demme, 1991), equates transgender identity with extreme violence and psychopathy, promotes a reactionary and conservative gender essentialism, and prevents a critical interrogation of the sources and consequences of gendered violence under patriarchy.

This crypto-transphobic direction in *The Book of Joan* makes it necessary to examine de Men's character further if the novel can truly function as a queer text. In particular, the eponymic and narrative association of Jean and Joan means that with de Men described as a failed woman and yet not a real man ('a bulbous sagging gash sutured over and over where ... where life had perhaps happened in the past, or not, and worse, several dangling attempts at half-formed penises, sewn and abandoned, distended and limp'), Joan's otherwise post-human, utopian characterization is brought disappointingly down to the human level through the concomitant association of her virgin, cisgender body with a 'proper', pure, untainted femininity.[69] Indeed, while Joan is the immortal character of the novel, and the catalyst for the utopian transformation of life at its end, de Men's twisted biopolitical experiments and necropolitical reign also gesture at a (failed) queer utopia – one which is, perhaps, more relational, more understandable and more human than Joan's post-human absorption.

The ending of the novel, in particular, owes much to the anti-relational thesis in queer theory, stated comprehensively by Lee Edelman in *No Future* (2004). For Edelman, a queer politics must distance itself completely from what he terms 'reproductive futurity', a regulation of political discourse fully in service to the allegorical 'image of the Child' which abjects queer subjects from politics as a consequence of their non-generative sexual practices. Edelman polemically calls for queer theory to embrace the absolute negativity of rejecting reproductive futurity, demanding 'a queer oppositionality that would oppose itself to the structural determinants of politics as such'.[70] Muñoz describes Edelman's project thus:

> Political hope fails queers because, like signification, it was not originally made for us. It resonates only on the level of reproductive futurity. Instead, Edelman recommends that queers give up hope and embrace a certain negation endemic to our abjection within the symbolic. What we get, in exchange for giving up on futurity, abandoning politics and hope, is a certain jouissance that at once defines and negates us.[71]

In its final chapters, *The Book of Joan* engages with this anti-relational position, generating its utopia not only out of the jouissance of new life, but out of a negation of humanity and its achievements. In her letter to Leone, Joan writes:

> I've wondered hundreds of times, since we lost humanity as we knew it: Is this what animals feel? Plants? Before we colonize and brutalize them away from their relationship to all matter? Think about it: What need is there for

scientific discovery, or intellectual or cultural apex, if humanity is gone? See? That's not something to say aloud. There is no longer any reason to further a philosophy. There is only being.[72]

In the sense that it refuses the snuffing out of all life on Earth, the conclusion of *The Book of Joan* is relatively hopeful. However, under the auspices of Joan as queer destroyer/creator, this conclusion is not just post-human, but anti-human, forging a future which is entirely absent of the figure of the Child. In this reading, the brief consummation of Joan and Leone's mutual desire is polemically, rather than simply factually, non-generative: 'Desire blooms between us, my ravaged body, hers. We will not conceive this way. Reproduction will become another kind of story.'[73]

Jean de Men's attempt at moulding and generating futurity, however, does not mirror Joan's anti-human futurity. His numerous failed attempts at generating life, which range from the controlled breeding of plants and animals to artificial insemination, cloning and the manufacture of artificial wombs, are likewise attempts to create a world beyond straight time and outside of normative reproductive futurity. Moreover, de Men's abiogenesis refuses to give up on relationality and connection, however twisted his aims may be; as Muñoz writes, a utopian queer futurity works against anti-relationality 'by insisting on the essential need for an understanding of queerness as collectivity'.[74] De Men's unforgivable crime is his inability to distinguish living humans – however changed they have become aboard CIEL – from machines and non-human technologies, and his refusal to elicit consent for the procedures he performs. His crime is not – though it is coded this way in the novel – his desire to create life with the aid of technology. Seen in this light, de Men's Hieronymus Bosch-esque final moments can be read not as the ironic deliverance of his *hamartia*, but as a brief moment of queer relational utopianism at the end of the world:

> Slowly at first and then with increasing velocity and form, at de Men's feet, children begin to materialize from nothingness and rise. First just a few, then many, a hundred or more. Naked children. The wail that emerges from Jean de Men reverbs my jaw; her head rocks back; some as-yet unnamed emotion beyond measure. The children of all colors and ages swarm from the ground up, devouring, consuming, like a swarm of bees at a honeycomb, until I see nothing left of Jean de Men beneath the multitudinous wave.[75]

In this scene, the singular, allegorical image of the Child is replaced with a multitude of children who spring literally from CIEL's metal ground, defying the limitations of biology and technology. It is notable that these surreal, post-human children are both diverse in ways that CIEL's inhabitants are no longer ('all colors and ages'), and cross over into the non-human ('like a swarm of bees at a honeycomb'). They are the realization of de Men's dream of reproduction, and like Buffalo Bill's trademark – leaving the cocoon of a death's head moth lodged in his victims' throats, a symbol of death and birth – become insect almost as soon as they are born. The tragedy of de Men, in his final moments, has commonality with that of Joan and Leone – he can briefly realize his desire to people the world with a diverse, post-human version of humanity only when it is far too late. I am sympathetic to Halberstam's reading of Buffalo Bill, and by extension of the monstrous, psychopathic character of de Men as well:

> What he constructs is a posthuman gender, a gender beyond the body, beyond the human, and a veritable carnage of identity [...] the cause for Buffalo Bill's extreme violence against women lies not in his gender confusion or his sexual orientation but in his humanist presumption that his sex and his gender and his orientation must all match-up to a mythic norm of white heterosexual masculinity.[76]

Just like Buffalo Bill, de Men ('of men') is crushed and twisted by the straight time of heteropatriarchal capitalism until he believes that only in the normative representation of himself – on the battlefield, on the screen, in the operating room – can he forge an immortal identity to survive Joan's queering of the universe. Just as Buffalo Bill 'emblematizes the ways in which gender is always posthuman, always a sewing job which stitches identity into a body bag', de Men eventually, if briefly, is able to do the same with the tactics of reproduction, queering them and giving them a post-human, collective form.[77]

For those readers opening *The Book of Joan* hoping for a relational, queerly collective human-centred utopia after the end of patriarchy, the concluding experiences of the novel's protagonist and antagonist may be a bitter pill to swallow. There is hope left over in the narrative, albeit unrealized, for a queer, utopian immortality to be formed from the unification of these two queer strategies – a relational queerness which embraces the complexities of gender and species. Such a queerness does not reject the future of the human species outright but does reject the allegorical image of the Child, understanding children instead as utopian cyborgs: diverse and multitudinous, not limited to the biological, the gendered or even the corporeal, and transforming into post-human forms from the moment they spring from the floor of an orbital space colony. Such cyborg strategies of reproduction must, as Sophie Lewis demands, include 'not only abortion, miscarriage, menstruation and pregnancy ... but also other life-enabling forms of holding and letting go that do not involve anatomical uteri, such as trans mothering, end-of-life care, adoption, foster care and other practices that provide for births, better deaths or survival'.[78] In relation to *The Book of Joan*, I would add immortality to these. *The Book of Joan* is, after all, full of a queer poetics of care. Grown-up child soldiers hold space for each other's traumas; desexed queers stripped of corporeal identity create new sexualities in language; humans keep watch over the return of a startling non-human biodiversity. In the novel, immortality can function as a mode of care for all living creatures and their ongoing survival which surpasses itself – the absorption of the human, and its profound ability for care, into networks beyond the human.

The utopian immortalities of *Walkaway* and *The Book of Joan* are relational and collective as queerness demands them to be. These visions are especially powerful when they break through a straight, capitalist form of time which threatens to normalize, atomize and individuate its subjects, and instead represent new ways of 'becoming-collective-across-time'. Muñoz describes this form of relationality in a particularly captivating mode in one of his final pieces of writing before his death:

> Queer thought is, in large part, about casting a picture of arduous modes of relationality that persist in the world despite stratifying demarcations and taxonomies of being, classifications that are bent on the siloing of particularity and on the denigrating of any expansive idea of the common and commonism. [...] The incommensurable thought project of inhumanity is the active self-attunement to life as varied and unsorted correspondences, collisions, intermeshings, and accords between people and nonhuman objects, things, formations, and clusterings.[79]

Unambiguously linking queerness to post-humanism, Muñoz here offers a template for a new way of understanding life in excess of the human. In

Walkaway and *The Book of Joan*, an actively anti-capitalist immortality, born out of revolutionary struggle and a demand for the recognition of immortality as a queer form of life, is figured as one of these 'arduous modes of relationality that persist in the world'. Diverse to the end, the immortality of Joan and the walkaways – and briefly, corruptedly, even of de Men – is an immortality predicated upon 'the common and commonism' in all its multiplicities.

These two novels are among the most explicit and ultimately totalizing utopias I have examined in this book. Where Hamid's and Robinson's novels and Spahr's poetry offer partial glimpses and hopeful, shining articulations of better worlds, Doctorow's and Yuknavitch's worlds are populated by recognizably human beings, alongside and often in collaboration with non-human ones. Spahr's occupiers, Hamid's migrants and Robinson's New Yorkers make use of technologies, tactics and *dispositifs* which allow them to cross borders, travel through time, survive both natural and engineered disasters, and most importantly of all, imagine and create utopian commons in the lacunae of their capitalist totalities. For all this they remain merely, if rewardingly, human: always exposed to precariousness and needing the commons and collectivities they create all the more for this biological and ontological fragility. In *Walkaway* and *The Book of Joan*, this system is turned gloriously on its head – suddenly, it is the utopian dreamers, organizers and creators who are immortal, and the previously total and unbroachable structure of capitalism itself seems shaky, precarious, and on the wane. What places these two novels firmly within the corpus of commons poetics texts that have emerged since 2008 is their unequivocal concern with utopia as a never-finished process, as a collective mode of being, and as a space which emerges from within capitalism to oppose it. To highlight this final point, at the conclusion of *The Book of Joan*, the previously atomized and disempowered inhabitants of CIEL pilot the space station into the sun, ending capitalism for good; near the end of *Walkaway*, the walkaways are joined by members of the private police forces who had once worked to destroy them at the behest of default. It is these climactic transitions in political power, as much as the ontological revolution of immortality, which decide the fates of the old systems. In these novels, utopia does not happen outside capitalism – revolutionary action is at last able to tear capitalism asunder from within.

Notes

1. Thomas More, *Utopia*, ed. Stephen Duncombe (Wivenhoe: Minor Compositions, 2012), 121.
2. Jonathan Swift, *Gulliver's Travels*, Oxford World's Classics (Oxford: Oxford University Press, 2005), 198–200.
3. A comprehensive overview of immortality in science fiction literature is presented in: George Edgar Slusser, Gary Westfahl, and Eric S. Rabkin, eds., *Immortal Engines: Life Extension and Immortality in Science Fiction and Fantasy* (Athens: University of Georgia Press, 1996). For a recent review, see: Victor E. Grech, Clare Vassallo, and Ivan Callus, 'Immortality and Infertility in Science Fiction: Who Wants to Live Forever?' *SFRA Review* 299 (2012): 5–10.
4. On these features of Genesis, see: Carolyn Merchant, *Reinventing Eden: The Fate of Nature in Western Culture* (New York: Routledge, 2003).
5. Donna J. Haraway, 'A Cyborg Manifesto', in *Manifestly Haraway* (Minneapolis: University of Minnesota Press, 2016), 9.
6. Jack Halberstam, *In a Queer Time and Place: Transgender Bodies, Subcultural Lives* (New York: New York University Press, 2005), 1, 10.
7. Carolyn Dinshaw et al., 'Theorizing Queer Temporalities: A Roundtable Discussion', *GLQ: A Journal of Lesbian and Gay Studies* 13, no. 2 (2007): 177–95.
8. Muñoz, *Cruising Utopia*, 1.
9. Bonnie Ruberg, 'Permalife: Video Games and the Queerness of Living', *Journal of Gaming & Virtual Worlds* 9, no. 2 (2017): 161.
10. Eleanor Drage, 'A Virtual Ever-After: Utopia, Race and Gender in Black Mirror's "San Junipero"', in *Black Mirror and Critical Media Theory*, ed. Angela M. Cirucci and Barry Vacker (London: Lexington Books, 2018), 32, 33.
11. Muñoz, *Cruising Utopia*, 22.
12. Muñoz, *Cruising Utopia*, 26.
13. Sean Seeger and Daniel Davison-Vecchione, 'Dystopian Literature and the Sociological Imagination', *Thesis Eleven* 155, no. 1 (2019): 12.
14. Samuel Montgomery-Blinn, 'Interview: Cory Doctorow's *Walkaway* Puts an Optimistic Spin on the Disaster Novel', *INDY Week*, 2017, https://indyweek.com/api/content/3685cf90-f513-5397-836e-cec801702fe8/; Kelly Thompson, 'Breaking The Binaries: A Conversation With Lidia Yuknavitch', *The Rumpus*, 2017, https://therumpus.net/2017/04/breaking-the-binaries-a-conversation-with-lidia-yuknavitch/.
15. Moylan, *Scraps of the Untainted Sky*, 44.

16   Scott McCracken, *Pulp: Reading Popular Fiction* (Manchester: Manchester University Press, 1998), 10; Yvonne Conza, 'I Will Never Tire of Swimming Inside Language: The Millions Interviews Lidia Yuknavitch', *The Millions*, 2017, https://themillions.com/2017/06/will-never-tire-swimming-inside-language-millions-interviews-lidia-yuknavitch.html.

17   Valerie Stivers-Isakova, 'Review: Lidia Yuknavitch's *The Chronology of Water* - A Body Memoir Gone Viral', *HuffPost*, 2013, https://www.huffpost.com/entry/the-chronology-of-water_b_2681133.

18   Cory Doctorow, 'Giving It away', *Forbes*, 2006, http://forbes.com/2006/11/30/cory-doctorow-copyright-tech-media_cz_cd_books06_1201doctorow.

19   Hope Jennings, "Anthropocene Storytelling: Extinction, D/Evolution, and Posthuman Ethics in Lidia Yuknavitch's *The Book of Joan*", *Lit: Literature Interpretation Theory* 30, no. 3 (2019): 191–210.

20   Cory Doctorow, 'Coase's Spectre', *Crooked Timber*, 2017, http://crookedtimber.org/2017/05/10/coases-spectre/. On the influence of Solnit's work on *Walkaway*, see: Mary Woodbury, 'Interview with Cory Doctorow, *Walkaway*', Dragonfly: An Exploration of Eco-fiction, 2017, https://dragonfly.eco/interview-cory-doctorow-walkaway/.

21   See, for instance, this series of responses: Henry Farrell, 'Cory Doctorow Seminar', Crooked Timber, 2017, https://crookedtimber.org/2017/05/10/cory-doctorow-seminar/.

22   Jason Sheehan, 'In "Walkaway," A Blueprint For A New, Weird (But Better) World', *NPR.org*, 2017, http://www.npr.org/2017/04/27/523587179/in-walkaway-a-blueprint-for-a-new-weird-but-better-world; Redfern Jon Barrett, '*Walkaway* by Cory Doctorow', *Strange Horizons*, 2017, http://strangehorizons.com/non-fiction/reviews/walkaway-by-cory-doctorow/.

23   Scott Timberg, 'Leave It to Cory Doctorow to Imagine a Post-Apocalyptic Utopia', *Los Angeles Times*, 2017, https://www.latimes.com/books/jacketcopy/la-ca-jc-cory-doctorow-20170525-htmlstory.html.

24   Sean Gallagher, 'Cory Doctorow's *Walkaway*: Hardware Hackers Face the Climate Apocalypse', *Ars Technica*, 2017, https://arstechnica.co.uk/gaming/2017/04/cory-doctorow-walkaway-book-review/.

25   Robinson also suggested the final title, and on Doctorow's part at least, it is (disappointingly!) not an homage to Le Guin's utopian short story 'The Ones Who Walk away from Omelas'; see: Cory Doctorow, 'Tweet', Twitter, 2019, https://twitter.com/doctorow/status/1112455367428980736.

26   Cory Doctorow, *Walkaway* (London: Head of Zeus, 2017), 171.

27 Doctorow, *Walkaway*, 50, 108–9, 498, 140–1.
28 Doctorow, *Walkaway*, 148.
29 Doctorow, *Walkaway*, 167.
30 Drage, 'A Virtual Ever-After', 31.
31 Doctorow, *Walkaway*, 143.
32 Doctorow, *Walkaway*, 286.
33 Karl Marx, *Capital: A Critique of Political Economy*, trans. Ben Fowkes, vol. 1 (London and New York: Penguin Books in association with New Left Review, 1981), 798.
34 Endnotes, 'Misery and Debt: On the Logic and History of Surplus Populations and Surplus Capital', *Endnotes* 2 (2010): 29, 30.
35 Doctorow, *Walkaway*, 316. Kristin Ross powerfully depicts the Paris Commune of 1871, politically and aesthetically, as a utopian form of 'communal luxury'. See: Kristin Ross, *Communal Luxury: The Political Imaginary of the Paris Commune* (London: Verso, 2016); Aaron Bastani, *Fully Automated Luxury Communism: A Manifesto* (London: Verso, 2019).
36 Muñoz, *Cruising Utopia*, 147.
37 Doctorow, *Walkaway*, 90, 59, 76.
38 Haines, *A Desire Called America*, 160.
39 Doctorow, *Walkaway*, 118.
40 Despite the diversity of its cast, *Walkaway* is far from an unproblematically queer novel, and I side fully with Julia Powles in her assessment that the depictions of these characters in *Walkaway* is laden with a 'weirdly conservative heteronormativity', apparent, for instance, in the fact that Tam is 'rarely mentioned without anatomical commentary' and that Natalie and Gretyl's love, 'though compelling, fails to resist elaboration through the prism of a dysfunctional maternal relationship'. See: Julia Powles, 'Walking Away from Hard Problems', *Crooked Timber*, 2017, http://crookedtimber.org/2017/05/04/walking-away-from-hard-problems/.
41 Drage, 'A Virtual Ever-After', 35.
42 Doctorow, *Walkaway*, 143, 392, 158.
43 Doctorow, *Walkaway*, 503. For notable science fiction treatments of cloning and consciousness upload, see: *Do Androids Dream of Electric Sheep?* (Philip K. Dick, 1968); *Never Let Me Go* (Kazuo Ishiguro, 2005); *To Live Forever* (Jack Vance, 1956); *Lord of Light* (Roger Zelazny, 1967); *Ancillary Justice* (Ann Leckie, 2013); and *Avatar* (dir. James Cameron, 2009). Strong AI memorably appears in *2001: A Space Odyssey* (dir. Stanley Kubrick, 1968), *Neuromancer* (William Gibson, 1984), and the *Culture* series (Iain M. Banks, 1987–2012).

44 For key interventions, see: Jack Halberstam and Ira Livingston, *Posthuman Bodies* (Bloomington: Indiana University Press, 1995); Sara Ahmed, *Queer Phenomenology: Orientations, Objects, Others* (Durham: Duke University Press, 2006); Mel Y. Chen, *Animacies: Biopolitics, Racial Mattering, and Queer Affect* (Durham: Duke University Press, 2012).
45 Patricia MacCormack, 'Queer Posthumanism: Cyborgs, Animals, Monsters, Perverts', in *The Ashgate Research Companion to Queer Theory*, ed. Noreen Giffney and Michael O'Rourke (London: Routledge, 2009), 113.
46 Doctorow, *Walkaway*, 396, 161.
47 Lorey, *State of Insecurity*, 19. For the precedents of Lorey's argument, see: Judith Butler, *Precarious Life: The Powers of Mourning and Violence* (London: Verso, 2004); Judith Butler, *Frames of War: When Is Life Grievable?* (London: Verso, 2009). Lorey's thinking is also influenced by Jean-Luc Nancy's discourse on the political and social condition of 'being-with' as a form of 'mutual exposure': Jean-Luc Nancy, *Being Singular Plural* (Stanford: Stanford University Press, 2000).
48 Lorey, *State of Insecurity*, 11.
49 Doctorow, *Walkaway*, 351.
50 Lorey, *State of Insecurity*, 102.
51 Lidia Yuknavitch, *The Book of Joan* (New York: Harper, 2017), 115.
52 Yuknavitch, *The Book of Joan*, 112.
53 Yuknavitch, *The Book of Joan*, 260.
54 Yuknavitch, *The Book of Joan*, 260, 258, 222.
55 Yuknavitch, *The Book of Joan*, 265.
56 Jennings, 'Anthropocene Storytelling', 201.
57 Jennings, 'Anthropocene Storytelling', 201.
58 Yuknavitch, *The Book of Joan*, 105, 150, 21, 25, 31, 32.
59 Yuknavitch, *The Book of Joan*, 32.
60 Yuknavitch, *The Book of Joan*, 91.
61 Jennings, 'Anthropocene Storytelling', 199–200.
62 Virginia Woolf, *A Room of One's Own* (Chichester: John Wiley & Sons, 2015), 61.
63 Yuknavitch, *The Book of Joan*, 140–1.
64 Yuknavitch, *The Book of Joan*, 148–9.
65 Yuknavitch, *The Book of Joan*, 155–6.
66 Yuknavitch, *The Book of Joan*, 156.
67 Yuknavitch, *The Book of Joan*, 166.
68 Yuknavitch, *The Book of Joan*, 250.

69 Yuknavitch, *The Book of Joan*, 245–6.
70 Lee Edelman, *No Future: Queer Theory and the Death Drive* (Durham: Duke University Press, 2004), 11, 4.
71 Muñoz, *Cruising Utopia*, 91.
72 Yuknavitch, *The Book of Joan*, 263.
73 Yuknavitch, *The Book of Joan*, 259.
74 Muñoz, *Cruising Utopia*, 11.
75 Yuknavitch, *The Book of Joan*, 252.
76 Jack Halberstam, *Skin Shows: Gothic Horror and the Technology of Monsters* (Durham: Duke University Press, 1995), 164.
77 Halberstam, *Skin Shows*, 176.
78 Sophie Lewis, 'Cyborg Uterine Geography: Complicating "Care" and Social Reproduction', *Dialogues in Human Geography* 8, no. 3 (2018): 302.
79 José Esteban Muñoz et al., 'Theorizing Queer Inhumanisms', *GLQ: A Journal of Lesbian and Gay Studies* 21, nos. 2–3 (2015): 209–10.

Epilogue

This study has examined a set of post-2008 texts which challenge the logics and power of contemporary capitalism through the imagining of alternative social, political and economic spaces for collective flourishing – a literary tendency I have described as commons utopias.

Literary utopias have been, and remain, crucial tools for helping readers and audiences to learn from the oppositional energies of past struggles, to understand what is missing from the present, and to imagine concrete alternatives which make this missing element a reality. Like many utopian texts which have opposed the dominant powers of their time, and in particular like the critical utopias of the 1960s and 1970s which are their direct precursors in the utopian literary genre, these texts 'have added to the ways in which we perceive the dissatisfaction of the present and tune into the pull of future possibilities', and take their place in the 'oppositional dialogue that informs contemporary radical politics'.[1] In this historical moment, the return of utopian figurations – even if that return is still piecemeal and uncoordinated – signals an irrepressible social desire to build a better society from within the shell of the old. The group of texts I have examined in this book is small, predominantly owing to the specific combination of features for which I was searching: demonstrable commitment to anti-capitalist politics; a reading of the present not as foreclosed, but as engaged in an imaginative, prefigurative conversation with a utopian future; and the use of commons not only at the level of narrative and theme, but also as a formal and aesthetic strategy. However, the wider genres and literary movements within which these texts circulate are repositories for other utopian and quasi-utopian imaginings: political, anticipatory and innovative in their own valuable ways. Like the utopian worlds of Whileaway, Anarres, Mattapoisett and Triton examined by Moylan in *Demand the Impossible*; like Robinson's Mars and Octavia Butler's

Acorn; the worlds imagined in these novels and poems 'help sustain us after long meetings and political defeats', 'provoke our imaginations as we work out new strategies to meet our needs and desires' and 'challenge us to play with alternatives and thereby break out of the ideological chains that have restricted our socialized imaginations'.[2]

Two key innovations distinguish the commons utopias I have been analysing in this book from the utopian literature which has served as precursor and inspiration for them, and from other contemporary writing which is political, speculative or both. Firstly, they locate oppositional and revolutionary energy specifically in commons predicated on equality, sharing, accessibility, oppositional energy and future dreaming, rather than any other organizational structure such as the state, representative democracy, the vanguard party or exilic intentional communities. The works do so through the use of a commons poetics, an aesthetic, formal and thematic toolkit which evokes and depicts commons at a number of textual levels.

If we can broadly describe this first innovation as *spatial* – based on the argument that utopias and commons should be recognized primarily as spatial forms produced by a multitude of collective processes of inhabiting – the second innovation which distinguishes commons utopias is fundamentally *temporal*. In many of the preceding chapters, I have addressed the claim that under late capitalism, in what Berlant calls the ongoing present, the future does not have an unfamiliar, alternative, distinctive quality, but is simply missing, replaced with loops, glitches and modes of continual survival born of precarity under late capitalism. In a dialogue with Adorno, Bloch evokes the profound utopianism of a line by playwright Bertold Brecht: 'something's missing'.[3] The utopian element missing from the present is nothing less than its future – the possibility that tomorrow will be different. As the protagonist Phil, played by Bill Murray, says in the 1993 film *Groundhog Day* (dir. Harold Ramis): 'Well what if there is no tomorrow? There wasn't one today.'

In this sense, the task of contemporary oppositional social movements and of the cultural works which emerge alongside them is to challenge the all-consuming spatial and temporal hegemony of capitalism by demanding, imagining and engaging with alternative futures, and to do so prefiguratively, by pulling those futures back to do their radical work on the present, and to return to it the sense of the future as an open space of potential and possibility once more. As Rebecca Solnit argues:

These other versions of what revolution means suggest that the goal is not so much to go on and create the world as to live in that time of creation, and with this the emphasis shifts from institutional power to the power of consciousness and the enactments of daily life, toward a revolution that does not institute its idea of perfection but opens up the freedom for each to participate in inventing the world. [...] The revolutionary days I have been outlining are days in which hope is no longer fixed on the future: it becomes an electrifying force in the present.[4]

The work of activists in the real world and of oppositional utopian literature is similar in that both work to electrify the present through representation, discourse and imagination, as well as the labour of material social reproduction and resistance to dominant power in which activist movements engage. Commons utopias are a new, valuable, though not unexpected voice in this conversation, as new forms of predatory, precarizing capitalism emerge in the wake of the GFC and the ascent of neoliberalism to increasing global dominance.

The vision I have painted here is certainly inspiring and evocative, suggestive of a cultural sense that the new utopian texts of the last decade hold a renewed focus on the 'process of willed transformation' and 'activism required for social revolution' which was last apparent in the critical utopias, signalling a return to the engaged, militant, passionately anti-hegemonic utopian discourses of the 1960s and 1970s, after decades spent in the wilderness of political disillusionment, structural stagnation and postmodernist hesitation.[5] And indeed, if this were the whole story, there would be no real need for this book; a simple updated critical bibliography would suffice to highlight new developments in the utopian literary field. However, while activist movements work ceaselessly to bring about more just and more equal worlds accessible to all, the global situation is not nearly so hopeful; crucially, daily life for global human and non-human populations is more precarious now than it was in the 1960s and 1970s. One of the key arguments I have made in this study is that late capitalism has damaged not only our ability to imagine the future otherwise, but has gravely endangered the potential for the flourishing – and perhaps even survival – of the planet's many interlinked species in the decades and centuries to come.

The state to which anthropogenic climate change – precipitated by successive advances in industrial and post-industrial capitalism over the last 200 years –

will bring the planet's climate, water cycle and ecological systems in the future is extremely difficult to predict. Nevertheless, as a number of recent studies show, current rates of carbon dioxide emissions will undoubtedly have a catastrophic effect on the planet in the next century and beyond if not curbed. Recent investigative analysis has shown that a small number of corporations are responsible for the majority of these emissions.[6] The same tendencies are borne out in other areas, such as social equality and wealth distribution: while the effects of the GFC continue to be felt by low-income populations, the wealthiest individuals continue to amass ever greater percentages of the world's wealth. Likewise, while citizens of nations in the Global North are able to cross borders with ease, millions of others cannot escape the precarious conditions of their existences. The effects of climate change, inequality, environmental destruction and austerity are felt more acutely – as dangers to life rather than precarities to be survived – by surplus populations, women, impoverished people, labourers in the Global South, people of colour and disabled people; these effects are intersectional and mutually reinforcing. The worldwide rise of populist leaders, the resurgence of nationalist and fascist ideologies, and the emergence of threats to liberal institutions including democracy, the right to protest and freedom of expression should be seen as concomitant responses, by those who hold power, to instability, precarity and anxiety in the face of an increasingly uncertain future. Time to change the balance of forces in the world is running out, in a multitude of ways which had not been considered possible even thirty years ago.

The crisis of the Covid-19 pandemic, too, is not a standalone event, but merely a new salvo in the biopolitical modulation of precariousness by the state. In many countries, capitalist governments have responded to the pandemic in ways which have exacerbated, extended and promulgated existing and ongoing crises, twisting them into new shapes and opening new fissures of profound potentiality in the shell of the present through which the future can escape. None of the books I have explored in this study deal with a global pandemic directly, but many of the concerns, solutions and hopeful dreams they reveal will be very familiar to us from the last few years. *New York 2140* explores financial crisis, grassroots mutual aid societies and the possibility of a transition to ecological sustainability in the aftermath of a profound planetary shock. In the wake of the vast profits reaped in the last few years by those multi-billionaires who have capitalized on the crisis, in part as a result of the readiness with which governments offload vital medical services to the private sector, Doctorow's call in *Walkaway* to break free from the entrapping cycle of capitalism feels ever more salient. *The Book of Joan* deals with human bodies in the aftermath of a biological crisis so fundamental that the word 'pandemic' does not do it justice. Yuknavitch, too, asks us to consider what sort of crises open the doors to utopia, and what sort of beings should be allowed to inherit the worlds which come next.

In response to these precarities of the contemporary moment, this book has argued that, if anti-capitalist movements are to pose a serious and committed challenge to the forces of capitalism, the stories they tell about themselves and the better worlds they seek to create must be motivated by three factors: a commitment to realistically depict the present, a belief that the future can be different, and most importantly, a militant and radical hope. Hope, as Bloch reminds us, is a source both of radical energy and of vulnerability: 'Hope is the opposite of security. It is the opposite of naive optimism. The category of danger is always within it.'[7] Moylan echoes this sentiment when he contends, in his response to Piercy's *Woman on the Edge of Time*, that '[t]he future is never certain. Utopia is never fixed once and for all.'[8] Hope underscores commons utopias because, like the utopianism they portray, it is a reflexive and mutable process, a utopian act, which connects activist energy in the present to its consequences and possibilities in the future. The precariousness of life lived in hope demands the construction of resilient, caring institutions of mutual aid and collective solidarity. To return to the reflections of the Occupy Oakland activists I introduced alongside Spahr, hope serves as a hermeneutic for living in the world anticipated by all anti-capitalist struggles:

> But the questions still remain: what would it mean to actually take care of each other and to collectively sustain and nurture an unstoppable insurrectionary struggle? How can we dismantle and negate the oppressive power relationships and toxic interpersonal dynamics we carry with us into liberated spaces? How can we make room for the myriad of revolts within the revolt that are necessary to upend all forms of domination?[9]

In the reading of Sean Grattan, what activist movements like Occupy are occupying in working to answer these questions is, precisely, 'the hope that the everyday can become bearable'. In his estimation, the danger of the present 'only increases the need to search for fragments of hope and string those fragments together, to see, test, feel, and weigh the ways we survive'.[10] It is the suggestion of this study that a critical, oppositional hope is crucial for transforming these utopian anticipations into concrete realities. In the past years, such fragments of hope have been taken up in a variety of activist movements including but certainly not limited to Black Lives Matter and the George Floyd protests, the Dakota Access Pipeline protests, the school strikes against climate change inaction; anti-government protests in Belarus, Hong Kong and across the Middle East; the anti-austerity work of feminist direct action group Sisters Uncut; and actions against the US-Mexico border regime. Future texts will necessarily adopt the energies of these oppositional moments and weave stories out of and beyond them, because, as US politician Alexandria Ocasio-Cortez recently stated in conversation with climate activist Greta Thunberg:

> I learned that hope is not something that you have. Hope is something that you create, with your actions. Hope is something you have to manifest into the world, and once one person has hope, it can be contagious. Other people start acting in a way that has more hope.[11]

Hope is manifested in Robinson's flooded, defiant New York, in Doctorow's beautifully chaotic wilderness communes, in Yuknavitch's caves crawling with unimaginable new species, in Hamid's indefatigable migrant cities, and in Spahr's riotous barricades. These imaginary worlds offer us, as readers and activists, the material, spatial and utopian manifestations of hope.

Notes

1   Moylan, *Demand the Impossible*, 188, 190.
2   Moylan, *Demand the Impossible*, 194.
3   Ernst Bloch, *The Utopian Function of Art and Literature: Selected Essays* (Cambridge: MIT Press, 1988), 15.
4   Rebecca Solnit, *Hope in the Dark: Untold Histories, Wild Possibilities* (Edinburgh: Canongate, 2016), 95.
5   Moylan, *Demand the Impossible*, 195.

6 Rajendra K. Pachauri et al., *Climate Change 2014: Synthesis Report. Contribution of Working Groups I, II and III to the Fifth Assessment Report of the Intergovernmental Panel on Climate Change* (Geneva: IPCC, 2014), https://www.ipcc.ch/pdf/assessment-report/ar5/syr/AR5_SYR_FINAL_SPM.pdf; Valérie Masson-Delmotte et al., *Global Warming of 1.5°C: An IPCC Special Report on the Impacts of Global Warming of 1.5°C Above Pre-Industrial Levels and Related Global Greenhouse Gas Emission Pathways, in the Context of Strengthening the Global Response to the Threat of Climate Change, Sustainable Development, and Efforts to Eradicate Poverty* (Geneva: IPCC, 2018), https://www.ipcc.ch/sr15/; Paul Griffin, *CDP Carbon Majors Report 2017* (London: CDP, 2017), https://www.cdp.net/en/reports/downloads/2327.
7 Bloch, *The Utopian Function of Art and Literature*, 16.
8 Moylan, *Demand the Impossible*, 140.
9 Some Oakland Antagonists, 'CrimethInc.'
10 Grattan, *Hope Isn't Stupid*, 153.
11 Emma Brockes, 'When Alexandria Ocasio-Cortez Met Greta Thunberg: "Hope Is Contagious"', *The Guardian*, 2019, https://www.theguardian.com/environment/2019/jun/29/alexandria-ocasio-cortez-met-greta-thunberg-hope-contagious-climate.

Bibliography

Abensour, Miguel. 'William Morris: The Politics of Romance'. In *Revolutionary Romanticism: A Drunken Boat Anthology*, edited by Max Blechman, 125–62. San Francisco: City Lights Books, 1999.

Adorno, Theodor W. 'Farewell to Jazz'. In *Essays on Music*, edited by Richard D. Leppert, translated by Susan H. Gillespie, 496–500. Berkeley: University of California Press, 2002.

Adorno, Theodor W. 'On Jazz'. In *Essays on Music*, edited by Richard D. Leppert, translated by Susan H. Gillespie, 470–95. Berkeley: University of California Press, 2002.

Agustín, Óscar García, and Martin Bak Jørgensen. *Solidarity and the 'Refugee Crisis' in Europe*. Cham: Springer International Publishing, 2019.

Ahmed, Sara. *Queer Phenomenology: Orientations, Objects, Others*. Durham: Duke University Press, 2006.

Al-Nakib, Mai. 'Finding Common Cause: A Planetary Ethics of "What Could Happen If"'. *Interventions*, 2019: 1–18.

Anam, Nasia. 'The Migrant as Colonist: Dystopia and Apocalypse in the Literature of Mass Migration'. *ASAP/Journal* 3, no. 3 (2018): 653–77.

Badiou, Alain, and Gregory Elliott. *The Rebirth of History: Times of Riots and Uprisings*. London: Verso, 2012.

Barrett, Redfern Jon. '*Walkaway* by Cory Doctorow'. *Strange Horizons*, 2017. http://strangehorizons.com/non-fiction/reviews/walkaway-by-cory-doctorow/.

Barrett, Ross, and Daniel Worden, eds. *Oil Culture*. Minneapolis: University of Minnesota Press, 2014.

Bastani, Aaron. *Fully Automated Luxury Communism: A Manifesto*. London: Verso, 2019.

Bell, David M. 'Improvisation as Anarchist Organization'. *Ephemera* 14, no. 4 (2014): 1009–30.

Bell, David M. *Rethinking Utopia: Place, Power, Affect*. New York: Routledge, 2017.

Bellamy, Brent Ryan. 'Science Fiction and the Climate Crisis'. *Science Fiction Studies* 45, no. 3 (2018): 417–19.

Berlant, Lauren. *Cruel Optimism*. Durham: Duke University Press, 2011.

Bernes, Jasper, Joshua Clover, and Juliana Spahr. 'Book Notes – Joshua Clover, Jasper Bernes, and Juliana Spahr (Commune Editions)'. *Largehearted Boy*, 2015. http://www.largeheartedboy.com/blog/archive/2015/09/book_notes_josh_28.html.

Bernes, Jasper, Joshua Clover, and Juliana Spahr. 'Self-Abolition of the Poet (Part 3)'. *Jacket2*, 2014. http://jacket2.org/commentary/self-abolition-poet-part-3.

Bernes, Jasper, Joshua Clover, and Juliana Spahr. 'Spring and All, Farewell to Jackets'. *Jacket2*, 2014. http://jacket2.org/commentary/spring-and-all-farewell-jackets.

Bloch, Ernst. *Principle of Hope*. Vol. 1. Cambridge: MIT Press, 1986.

Bloch, Ernst. *Principle of Hope*. Vol. 3. Cambridge: MIT Press, 1986.

Bloch, Ernst. *The Utopian Function of Art and Literature: Selected Essays*. Cambridge: MIT Press, 1988.

Bolton, Matthew, Stephen Froese, and Alex Jeffrey. 'This Space Is Occupied!: The Politics of Occupy Wall Street's Expeditionary Architecture and De-Gentrifying Urbanism'. In *Occupying Political Science*, edited by Emily Welty, Matthew Bolton, Meghana Nayak, and Christopher Malone, 135–61. New York: Palgrave Macmillan, 2013.

Bookchin, Murray. *Urbanization without Cities: The Rise and Decline of Citizenship*. Montreal: Black Rose Books, 1992.

Brigstocke, Julian. 'Occupy the Future'. In *Space, Power and the Commons: The Struggle for Alternative Futures*, edited by Leila Dawney, Samuel Kirwan, and Julian Brigstocke, 150–65. London: Routledge, 2016.

Brockes, Emma. 'When Alexandria Ocasio-Cortez Met Greta Thunberg: "Hope Is Contagious"'. *The Guardian*, 2019. https://www.theguardian.com/environment/2019/jun/29/alexandria-ocasio-cortez-met-greta-thunberg-hope-contagious-climate.

Budel, Jesse. 'Steve Reich's "Music for 18 Musicians" as a Soundscape Composition'. *Directions of New Music*, no. 2 (2018): 1–15.

Buikema, Rosemarie. 'A Poetics of Home: On Narrative Voice and the Deconstruction of Home in Migrant Literature'. In *Migrant Cartographies: New Cultural and Literary Spaces in Post-Colonial Europe*, edited by Sandra Ponzanesi and Daniela Merolla, 177–87. Oxford: Lexington Books, 2005.

Butler, Judith. *Frames of War: When Is Life Grievable?* London: Verso, 2009.

Butler, Judith. *Precarious Life: The Powers of Mourning and Violence*. London: Verso, 2004.

Caffentzis, George, and Silvia Federici. 'Commons against and beyond Capitalism'. *Community Development Journal* 49, no. S1 (2014): i92–i105.

Calhoun, Craig J., and Georgi M. Derluguian, eds. *Business as Usual: The Roots of the Global Financial Meltdown*. New York: New York University Press, 2011.

Canavan, Gerry. 'Utopia in the Time of Trump'. *Los Angeles Review of Books*, 2017. https://lareviewofbooks.org/article/utopia-in-the-time-of-trump/.

Chambers, Claire. *Making Sense of Contemporary British Muslim Novels*. New York: Palgrave Macmillan, 2019.

Chambers, Iain. *Migrancy, Culture, Identity*. London: Routledge, 1994.

Chatman, Seymour. *Story and Discourse: Narrative Structure in Fiction and Film*. Ithaca: Cornell University Press, 1993.

Chen, Mel Y. *Animacies: Biopolitics, Racial Mattering, and Queer Affect*. Durham: Duke University Press, 2012.

Chisholm, Dianne. 'Juliana Spahr's Ecopoetics: Ecologies and Politics of the Refrain'. *Contemporary Literature* 55, no. 1 (2014): 118–47.

Clover, Joshua. *Riot. Strike. Riot.: The New Era of Uprisings*. London: Verso, 2016.

Collis, Stephen. 'Of Blackberries and the Poetic Commons'. Forum on Public Domain, 2014. https://www.yumpu.com/s/GaMgC9QgHE9Qvofj.

Collis, Stephen. 'Of Blackberries and the Poetic Commons'. In *The Commons*, 127–36. Vancouver: Talonbooks, 2014.

Conrad, Joseph. *Heart of Darkness*. London: Penguin Books, 2007.

Conza, Yvonne. 'I Will Never Tire of Swimming Inside Language: The Millions Interviews Lidia Yuknavitch'. *The Millions*, 2017. https://themillions.com/2017/06/will-never-tire-swimming-inside-language-millions-interviews-lidia-yuknavitch.html.

Cooper, Brittney C. 'An Ontology of CRUNK: Theorizing (the) Turn Up'. *Crunk Feminist Collective*, 2014. http://www.crunkfeministcollective.com/2014/04/29/an-ontology-of-crunk-theorizing-the-turn-up/.

Cooper, Davina. *Everyday Utopias: The Conceptual Life of Promising Spaces*. Durham: Duke University Press, 2014.

Cowan, Robert. 'Reich and Wittgenstein: Notes towards a Synthesis'. *Tempo*, no. 157 (1986): 2–7.

Cross, Hannah. *Migrants, Borders and Global Capitalism: West African Labour Mobility and EU Borders*. London: Routledge, 2013.

Daniel, Jamie Owen. 'Reclaiming the "Terrain of Fantasy": Speculations on Ernst Bloch, Memory, and the Resurgence of Nationalism'. In *Not Yet: Reconsidering Ernst Bloch*, edited by Jamie Owen Daniel, and Tom Moylan, 53–62. London: Verso, 1997.

Dawney, Leila, Samuel Kirwan, and Julian Brigstocke. 'Introduction: The Promise of the Commons'. In *Space, Power and the Commons: The Struggle for Alternative Futures*, edited by Leila Dawney, Samuel Kirwan, and Julian Brigstocke, 1–27. London: Routledge, 2016.

Dawson, Ashley. *Extreme Cities: The Peril and Promise of Urban Life in the Age of Climate Change*. London: Verso, 2017.

De Angelis, Massimo. *Omnia Sunt Communia: On the Commons and the Transformation to Postcapitalism*. London: Zed Books, 2017.

Delany, Samuel R. *Trouble on Triton: An Ambiguous Heterotopia*. Middletown: Wesleyan University Press. 1996.

Deleuze, Gilles, and Félix Guattari. *A Thousand Plateaus: Capitalism and Schizophrenia*. Minneapolis: University of Minnesota Press, 1987.

Dick, Kirby, and Amy Ziering Kofman, directors. *Derrida*. Zeitgeist Films, 2002.

Dinshaw, Carolyn, Lee Edelman, Roderick A. Ferguson, Carla Freccero, Elizabeth Freeman, Jack Halberstam, Annamarie Jagose, Christopher S. Nealon, and Tan Hoang Nguyen. 'Theorizing Queer Temporalities: A Roundtable Discussion'. *GLQ: A Journal of Lesbian and Gay Studies* 13, no. 2 (2007): 177–95.

Doctorow, Cory. 'Be the First One to Not Do Something That No One Else Has Ever Not Thought of Doing Before'. *Locus Online*, 2017. https://locusmag.com/2017/07/cory-doctorow-be-the-first-one-to-not-do-something-that-no-one-else-has-ever-not-thought-of-doing-before/.

Doctorow, Cory. 'Coase's Spectre'. *Crooked Timber*, 2017. http://crookedtimber.org/2017/05/10/coases-spectre/.

Doctorow, Cory. 'Giving It Away'. *Forbes*, 2006. http://forbes.com/2006/11/30/cory-doctorow-copyright-tech-media_cz_cd_books06_1201doctorow.

Doctorow, Cory. 'Tweet'. Twitter, 31 March 2019. https://twitter.com/doctorow/status/1112455367428980736.

Doctorow, Cory. *Walkaway*. London: Head of Zeus, 2017.

Drage, Eleanor. 'A Virtual Ever-After: Utopia, Race and Gender in Black Mirror's "San Junipero"'. In *Black Mirror and Critical Media Theory*, edited by Angela M. Cirucci and Barry Vacker, 27–39. London: Lexington Books, 2018.

Duthely, Regina. 'Black Feminist Hip-Hop Rhetorics and the Digital Public Sphere'. *Changing English* 24, no. 2 (2017): 202–12.

Edelman, Lee. *No Future: Queer Theory and the Death Drive*. Durham: Duke University Press, 2004.

Eigler, Friederike. *Heimat, Space, Narrative: Toward a Transnational Approach to Flight and Expulsion*. Rochester: Camden House, 2014.

Elson, Anthony. *The Global Financial Crisis in Retrospect*. New York: Palgrave Macmillan, 2017.

Endnotes. 'Afterword: The Idea of the Workers' Movement'. *Endnotes* 4 (2015): 168–92.

Endnotes. 'Communisation and Value-Form Theory'. *Endnotes* 2 (2010): 68–105.

Endnotes. 'Misery and Debt: On the Logic and History of Surplus Populations and Surplus Capital'. *Endnotes* 2 (2010): 20–51.

Ergin, Meliz. 'Intimate Multitudes: Juliana Spahr's Ecopoetics'. In *The Ecopoetics of Entanglement in Contemporary Turkish and American Literatures*, 85–125. New York: Palgrave Macmillan, 2017.

Farrell, Henry. 'Cory Doctorow Seminar'. *Crooked Timber*, 2017. https://crookedtimber.org/2017/05/10/cory-doctorow-seminar/.

Fisher, Mark. *Capitalist Realism: Is There No Alternative?* Winchester: Zero Books, 2009.

Fratz, D. Douglas. 'An Interview with Kim Stanley Robinson'. *The SF Site*, 2012. https://www.sfsite.com/06a/ksr369.htm.

Freccero, C. 'Queer Times'. *South Atlantic Quarterly* 106, no. 3 (2007): 485–94.

Freeman, Elizabeth. *Time Binds: Queer Temporalities, Queer Histories*. Durham: Duke University Press, 2010.

Friedman, Thomas L. 'Global Weirding Is Here'. *The New York Times*, 2010. https://www.nytimes.com/2010/02/17/opinion/17friedman.html.

Fritz, Charles E. *Disasters and Mental Health: Therapeutic Principles Drawn from Disaster Studies*. Newark: Disaster Research Centre, University of Delaware, 1996.

Gallagher, Sean. 'Cory Doctorow's *Walkaway*: Hardware Hackers Face the Climate Apocalypse'. *Ars Technica*, 2017. https://arstechnica.co.uk/gaming/2017/04/cory-doctorow-walkaway-book-review/.

George, Rosemary Marangoly. *The Politics of Home: Postcolonial Relocations and Twentieth-Century Fiction*. Berkeley: University of California Press, 1999.

Gilroy, Paul. *Postcolonial Melancholia*. New York: Columbia University Press, 2004.

Gracyk, Theodore A. 'Adorno, Jazz, and the Aesthetics of Popular Music'. *The Musical Quarterly* 76, no. 4 (1992): 526–42.

Grattan, Sean Austin. *Hope Isn't Stupid: Utopian Affects in Contemporary American Literature*. Iowa City: University of Iowa Press, 2017.

Grech, Victor E., Clare Vassallo, and Ivan Callus. 'Immortality and Infertility in Science Fiction: Who Wants to Live Forever?' *SFRA Review* 299 (2012): 5–10.

Gregory, Julia. '8 Grenfell Families Are Still Living in Temporary Homes 27 Months On'. *My London*, 2019. https://www.mylondon.news/news/west-london-news/8-grenfell-families-still-living-17131649.

Griffin, Paul. 'CDP Carbon Majors Report 2017'. London: CDP, 2017. https://www.cdp.net/en/reports/downloads/2327.

Haines, Christian P. *A Desire Called America: Biopolitics, Utopia, and the Literary Commons*. New York: Fordham University Press, 2019.

Haiven, Max. 'Are Your Children Old Enough to Learn about May '68?: Recalling the Radical Event, Refracting Utopia, and Commoning Memory'. *Cultural Critique* 78, no. 1 (2011): 60–87.

Haiven, Max. 'Commons as Actuality, Ethos, and Horizon'. In *Educational Commons in Theory and Practice: Global Pedagogy and Politics*, edited by Alexander J. Means, Derek Ford, and Graham B. Slater, 23–38. New York: Palgrave Macmillan, 2017.

Haiven, Max, and Alex Khasnabish. *The Radical Imagination: Social Movement Research in the Age of Austerity*. London: Zed Books, 2014.

Halberstam, Jack. *In a Queer Time and Place: Transgender Bodies, Subcultural Lives*. New York: New York University Press, 2005.

Halberstam, Jack. *Skin Shows: Gothic Horror and the Technology of Monsters*. Duke University Press, 1995.

Halberstam, Jack, and Ira Livingston. *Posthuman Bodies*. Bloomington: Indiana University Press, 1995.

Hamid, Mohsin. *Exit West*. London: Penguin Books, 2018.

Haraway, Donna J. 'A Cyborg Manifesto'. In *Manifestly Haraway*, 3–90. Minneapolis: University of Minnesota Press, 2016.

Haraway, Donna J. *Staying with the Trouble: Making Kin in the Chthulucene*. Durham: Duke University Press, 2016.

Hardin, Garrett. 'The Tragedy of the Commons'. *Science* 162, no. 3859 (1968): 1243–8.

Hardt, Michael, and Antonio Negri. *Multitude: War and Democracy in the Age of Empire*. New York: Penguin, 2004.

Hart, David. 'Supreme Court – the Right to Be on the Beach'. UK Human Rights Blog, 2015. https://ukhumanrightsblog.com/2015/02/25/supreme-court-the-right-to-be-on-the-beach/.

Harvey, David. *The Condition of Postmodernity: An Enquiry into the Origins of Cultural Change*. Oxford: Blackwell, 1989.

Harvey, David. 'From Space to Place and Back Again: Reflections on the Condition of Postmodernity'. In *Mapping the Futures: Local Cultures, Global Change*, edited by John Bird, Barry Curtis, Tim Putnam, Lisa Tickner, and George Robertson, 2–29. Hoboken: Taylor and Francis, 2012.

Harvey, David. *Spaces of Hope*. Edinburgh: Edinburgh University Press, 2000.

Higgins, Parker. '"We Will Need Writers Who Can Remember Freedom": Ursula K Le Guin at the National Book Awards'. Parker Higgins Dot Net, 2014. https://parkerhiggins.net/2014/11/will-need-writers-can-remember-freedom-ursula-k-le-guin-national-book-awards/.

Holloway, John. *Change the World Without Taking Power: The Meaning of Revolution Today*. London: Pluto Press, 2019.

Honeywell, Carissa. 'Utopianism and Anarchism'. *Journal of Political Ideologies* 12, no. 3 (2007): 239–54.

The Invisible Committee. *The Coming Insurrection*. Los Angeles: Semiotext(e), 2009.

Jameson, Fredric. *An American Utopia: Dual Power and the Universal Army*. London: Verso, 2016.

Jameson, Fredric. *The Antinomies of Realism*. London: Verso, 2015.

Jameson, Fredric. *Archaeologies of the Future: The Desire Called Utopia and Other Science Fictions*. London: Verso, 2005.

Jameson, Fredric. 'Future City'. *New Left Review* 21 (2003): 65–79.

Jameson, Fredric. 'The Politics of Utopia'. *New Left Review* 25 (2004): 35–54.

Jennings, Hope. 'Anthropocene Storytelling: Extinction, D/ Evolution, and Posthuman Ethics in Lidia Yuknavitch's *The Book of Joan*'. *Lit: Literature Interpretation Theory* 30, no. 3 (2019): 191–210.

Johns-Putra, Adeline. *Climate Change and the Contemporary Novel*. Cambridge: Cambridge University Press, 2019.

Johns-Putra, Adeline. 'Climate Change in Literature and Literary Studies: From Cli-Fi, Climate Change Theater and Ecopoetry to Ecocriticism and Climate Change Criticism'. *Wiley Interdisciplinary Reviews: Climate Change* 7, no. 2 (2016): 266–82.

Jones, Graham. *The Shock Doctrine of the Left*. Cambridge: Polity, 2018.

Kabo, Raphael. 'Towards a Taxonomy of Edgelands Literature'. *Alluvium*, 2015. https://www.alluvium-journal.org/2015/06/26/towards-a-taxonomy-of-edgelands-literature/.

Kaes, Anton. *From Hitler to Heimat: The Return of History as Film*. Cambridge: Harvard University Press, 1989.

Kaplan, Caren. *Questions of Travel: Postmodern Discourses of Displacement*. Durham: Duke University Press, 1996.

Keller, Lynn. '"Post-Language Lyric": The Example of Juliana Spahr'. *Chicago Review* 55, no. 3/4 (2010): 74–83.

Kim, Myung Mi. *Commons*. Berkeley: University of California Press, 2002.

King, Natasha. *No Borders: The Politics of Immigration Control and Resistance*. London: Zed Books, 2016.

Laboria Cuboniks. 'Xenofeminism: A Politics for Alienation'. 2015. http://www.laboriacuboniks.net/.

Lamm, Kimberly. 'All Together/Now: Writing the Space of Collectivities in the Poetry of Juliana Spahr'. In *American Poets in the 21st Century: The New Poetics*, edited by Claudia Rankine, and Lisa Sewell, 133–50. Middletown: Wesleyan University Press, 2007.

Lefebvre, Henri. *The Production of Space*. Translated by Donald Nicholson-Smith. Oxford: Blackwell, 1991.

Lerner, Ben. *10:04*. New York: Faber and Faber, 2014.

Levitas, Ruth. *Utopia as Method: The Imaginary Reconstitution of Society*. New York: Palgrave Macmillan, 2013.

Levitas, Ruth. 'Where There Is No Vision, the People Perish: A Utopian Ethic for a Transformed Future'. *CUSP* 5 (2017): 3–15.

Lewis, Sophie. 'Cyborg Uterine Geography: Complicating "Care" and Social Reproduction'. *Dialogues in Human Geography* 8, no. 3 (2018): 300–16.
Lewis, Sophie. *Full Surrogacy Now: Feminism Against Family*. London: Verso, 2019.
Leyshon, Cressida. 'Mohsin Hamid on the Migrants in All of Us'. *The New Yorker*, 2016. https://www.newyorker.com/books/page-turner/this-week-in-fiction-mohsin-hamid-2016-11-14.
Lo, Andrew W. 'Reading about the Financial Crisis: A Twenty-One-Book Review'. *Journal of Economic Literature* 50, no. 1 (2012): 151–78.
Lorey, Isabell. *State of Insecurity: Government of the Precarious*. London: Verso, 2015.
Lotringer, Sylvère. 'Foreword: We, the Multitude'. In Paolo Virno, *A Grammar of the Multitude*, 16–7. Los Angeles: Semiotext(e), 2004.
MacCormack, Patricia. 'Queer Posthumanism: Cyborgs, Animals, Monsters, Perverts'. In *The Ashgate Research Companion to Queer Theory*, edited by Noreen Giffney and Michael O'Rourke, 111–26. London: Routledge, 2009.
Marx, Karl. *Capital: A Critique of Political Economy*. Translated by Ben Fowkes. Vol. 1. London and New York: Penguin Books in association with New Left Review, 1981.
Marx, Karl. *Economic and Philosophic Manuscripts of 1844*. Translated by Martin Milligan. Amherst: Prometheus Books, 1988.
Marx, Karl. *Grundrisse: Foundations of the Critique of Political Economy*. Translated by Martin Nicolaus. London: Penguin Books, 1993.
Massey, Doreen. *For Space*. London: Sage, 2005.
Masson-Delmotte, Valérie, Panmao Zhai, Hans-Otto Pörtner, Debra Roberts, Jim Skea, and Priyadarshi R. Shukla. *Global Warming of 1.5°C: An IPCC Special Report on the Impacts of Global Warming of 1.5°C Above Pre-Industrial Levels and Related Global Greenhouse Gas Emission Pathways, in the Context of Strengthening the Global Response to the Threat of Climate Change, Sustainable Development, and Efforts to Eradicate Poverty*. Geneva: IPCC, 2018. https://www.ipcc.ch/sr15/.
Mbembe, Achille. 'Necropolitics'. *Public Culture* 15, no. 1 (2003): 11–40.
McCracken, Scott. *Pulp: Reading Popular Fiction*. Manchester: Manchester University Press, 1998.
Mendlesohn, Farah. *Rhetorics of Fantasy*. Middletown: Wesleyan University Press, 2008.
Merchant, Carolyn. *Reinventing Eden: The Fate of Nature in Western Culture*. New York: Routledge, 2003.
Mezzadra, Sandro. 'The Gaze of Autonomy: Capitalism, Migration and Social Struggles'. In *The Contested Politics of Mobility: Borderzones and Irregularity*, edited by Vicki Squire. London: Routledge, 2010, 121–42.
Mignolo, Walter, and Catherine E. Walsh. *On Decoloniality: Concepts, Analytics, Praxis*. Durham: Duke University Press, 2018.

Miller, David. 'Border Regimes and Human Rights'. *The Law & Ethics of Human Rights* 7, no. 1 (2013): 1–23.

Milne, Heather. 'Dearly Beloveds: The Politics of Intimacy in Juliana Spahr's *This Connection of Everyone with Lungs*'. *Mosaic: A Journal for the Interdisciplinary Study of Literature* 47, no. 2 (2014): 203–18.

Montgomery-Blinn, Samuel. 'Interview: Cory Doctorow's *Walkaway* Puts an Optimistic Spin on the Disaster Novel'. *INDY Week*, 2017. https://indyweek.com/api/content/3685cf90-f513-5397-836e-cec801702fe8/.

More, Thomas. *Utopia*. Edited by Stephen Duncombe. Wivenhoe: Minor Compositions, 2012.

Moylan, Tom. *Becoming Utopian: The Culture and Politics of Radical Transformation*. London: Bloomsbury Academic, 2021.

Moylan, Tom. *Demand the Impossible: Science Fiction and the Utopian Imagination*. Edited by Raffaella Baccolini. Oxford: Peter Lang, 2014.

Moylan, Tom. *Scraps of the Untainted Sky: Science Fiction, Utopia, Dystopia*. Boulder: Westview Press, 2000.

Moylan, Tom, and Raffaella Baccolini. 'Dystopia and Histories'. In *Dark Horizons: Science Fiction and the Dystopian Imagination*, edited by Tom Moylan, and Raffaella Baccolini, 1–12. Routledge, 2013.

Mukherji, Subha. 'Introduction'. In *Thinking on Thresholds: The Poetics of Transitive Spaces*, edited by Subha Mukherji, xvii–xxviii. London: Anthem Press, 2011.

Muñoz, José Esteban. *Cruising Utopia: The Then and There of Queer Futurity*. New York: New York University Press, 2009.

Muñoz, José Esteban, J. Haritaworn, M. Hird, Z. I. Jackson, J. K. Puar, E. Joy, U. McMillan, et al., 'Theorizing Queer Inhumanisms'. *GLQ: A Journal of Lesbian and Gay Studies* 21, nos. 2–3 (2015): 209–48.

Nancy, Jean-Luc. *Being Singular Plural*. Stanford: Stanford University Press, 2000.

Nasta, Susheila. *Home Truths: Fictions of the South Asian Diaspora in Britain*. Basingstoke: Palgrave, 2002.

Nguyen, Viet Thanh. 'March's Book Club Pick: "Exit West," by Mohsin Hamid'. *The New York Times*, 2017. https://www.nytimes.com/2017/03/10/books/review/exit-west-mohsin-hamid.html.

On the Commons. 'Who Owns the Beach?' 2005. http://www.onthecommons.org/who-owns-beach.

Ostrom, Elinor. *Governing the Commons*. Cambridge: Cambridge University Press, 2015.

Out of the Woods Collective. 'Disaster Communism: The Uses of Disaster'. In *Hope Against Hope: Writings on Ecological Crisis*, 229–40. Brooklyn: Common Notions, 2020.

Pachauri, Rajendra K., Myles R. Allen, Vicente R. Barros, John Broome, Wolfgang Cramer, Renate Christ, John A. Church, Leon Clarke, Qin Dahe, and Purnamita

Dasgupta. *Climate Change 2014: Synthesis Report. Contribution of Working Groups I, II and III to the Fifth Assessment Report of the Intergovernmental Panel on Climate Change*. Geneva: IPCC, 2014.

Papadopoulos, Dimitris, and Vassilis S. Tsianos. 'After Citizenship: Autonomy of Migration, Organisational Ontology and Mobile Commons'. *Citizenship Studies* 17, no. 2 (2013): 178–96.

Perelman, Bob. 'Parataxis and Narrative: The New Sentence in Theory and Practice'. *American Literature* 65, no. 2 (1993): 313–24.

Phillips, Siobhan. 'A Catalogue of Us with All: Juliana Spahr's "Well Then There Now"'. *Los Angeles Review of Books*, 2011. https://lareviewofbooks.org/article/a-catalogue-of-us-with-all-juliana-spahrs-well-then-there-now/.

Piketty, Thomas. *Capital in the Twenty-First Century*. Translated by Arthur Goldhammer. Cambridge: The Belknap Press of Harvard University Press, 2014.

Powles, Julia. 'Walking away from Hard Problems'. *Crooked Timber*, 2017. http://crookedtimber.org/2017/05/04/walking-away-from-hard-problems/.

Pynchon, Thomas. 'A Journey into The Mind of Watts'. *The New York Times*, 1966. https://archive.nytimes.com/www.nytimes.com/books/97/05/18/reviews/pynchon-watts.html.

Rancière, Jacques. *Dissensus: On Politics and Aesthetics*. Translated by Steve Corcoran. London: Continuum, 2010.

Raver, Anne. 'Bananas in the Backyard'. *The New York Times*, 2002. https://www.nytimes.com/2002/11/07/garden/nature-bananas-in-the-backyard.html.

Ricoeur, Paul. 'Rhetoric - Poetics - Hermeneutics'. In *From Metaphysics to Rhetoric*, edited by Michel Meyer, 137–49. Dordrecht: Springer, 1989.

Rigby, Kate. 'Ecopoetics'. In *Keywords for Environmental Studies*, edited by Joni Adamson, William A. Gleason, and David N. Pellow, 79–81. New York: New York University Press, 2016.

Robinson, J. Bradford. 'The Jazz Essays of Theodor Adorno: Some Thoughts on Jazz Reception in Weimar Germany'. *Popular Music* 13, no. 1 (1994): 1–25.

Robinson, Kim Stanley. 'Dystopias Now'. *Commune*, 2018. https://communemag.com/dystopias-now/.

Robinson, Kim Stanley. *Green Mars*. London: Voyager, 2009.

Robinson, Kim Stanley. 'Kim Stanley Robinson on "The U.S.A. Trilogy"'. To The Best of Our Knowledge, 2018. https://www.ttbook.org/interview/kim-stanley-robinson-usa-trilogy.

Robinson, Kim Stanley. *New York 2140*. London: Orbit, 2017.

Rogers, Adam. 'The Sci-Fi Novelist Who Writes Like the Past to Warn of the Future'. *Wired*, 2018. https://www.wired.com/story/kim-stanley-robinson-red-moon/.

Ronda, Margaret. 'Anthropogenic Poetics'. *The Minnesota Review* 83 (2014): 102–11.

Ronda, Margaret. 'Mourning and Melancholia in the Anthropocene'. *Post45*, 2013. http://post45.research.yale.edu/2013/06/mourning-and-melancholia-in-the-anthropocene/.

Rosenzweig, Roy, and Elizabeth Blackmar. *The Park and the People: A History of Central Park*. Ithaca, NY: Cornell University Press, 1992.

Ross, Kristin. *Communal Luxury: The Political Imaginary of the Paris Commune*. London: Verso, 2016.

Rothman, Joshua. 'Kim Stanley Robinson's Latest Novel Imagines Life in an Underwater New York'. *The New Yorker*, 2017. https://www.newyorker.com/books/page-turner/kim-stanley-robinsons-latest-novel-imagines-life-in-an-underwater-new-york.

Ruberg, Bonnie. 'Permalife: Video Games and the Queerness of Living'. *Journal of Gaming & Virtual Worlds* 9, no. 2 (2017): 159–73.

Sargent, Lyman Tower. 'The Three Faces of Utopianism Revisited'. *Utopian Studies* 5, no. 1 (1994): 1–37.

Sargisson, Lucy. *Fool's Gold?: Utopianism in the Twenty-First Century*. London: Palgrave Macmillan, 2012.

Seeger, Sean, and Daniel Davison-Vecchione. 'Dystopian Literature and the Sociological Imagination'. *Thesis Eleven* 155, no. 1 (2019): 45–63.

Sergeant, David. 'The Genre of the Near Future: Kim Stanley Robinson's *New York 2140*'. *Genre* 52, no. 1 (2019): 1–23.

Sheehan, Jason. 'In "Walkaway", a Blueprint for a New, Weird (But Better) World'. *NPR.org*, 2017. http://www.npr.org/2017/04/27/523587179/in-walkaway-a-blueprint-for-a-new-weird-but-better-world.

Sheller, Mimi. *Mobility Justice: The Politics of Movement in the Age of Extremes*. London: Verso, 2018.

Shelley, Percy Bysshe. 'A Defence of Poetry'. In *Essays, Letters from Abroad, Translations and Fragments*, edited by Mary Shelley, 1–57. London: Edward Moxon, 1840.

Skinner, Jonathan. 'Editor's Statement'. *Ecopoetics* 1 (2001): 5–8.

Skweres, Artur. *McLuhan's Galaxies: Science Fiction Film Aesthetics in Light of Marshall McLuhan's Thought*. Cham: Springer International Publishing, 2019.

Slusser, George Edgar, Gary Westfahl, and Eric S. Rabkin, eds. *Immortal Engines: Life Extension and Immortality in Science Fiction and Fantasy*. Athens: University of Georgia Press, 1996.

Soja, Edward W. *Thirdspace: Journeys to Los Angeles and Other Real-and-Imagined Places*. Cambridge: Blackwell, 1996.

Solnit, Rebecca. *Hope in the Dark: Untold Histories, Wild Possibilities*. Edinburgh: Canongate, 2016.

Solnit, Rebecca. *A Paradise Built in Hell: The Extraordinary Communities that Arise in Disaster*. New York: Viking, 2009.

Some Oakland Antagonists. 'The Rise and Fall of the Oakland Commune'. *CrimethInc.*, 2013. https://crimethinc.com/2013/09/10/after-the-crest-part-ii-the-rise-and-fall-of-the-oakland-commune.

Spahr, Juliana. 'The '90s'. *Boundary 2* 36, no. 3 (2009): 159–82.

Spahr, Juliana. *Du Bois's Telegram: Literary Resistance and State Containment*. Cambridge: Harvard University Press, 2018.

Spahr, Juliana. *Everybody's Autonomy: Connective Reading and Collective Identity*. Tuscaloosa: University of Alabama Press, 2001.

Spahr, Juliana. 'Poetry in a Time of Crisis'. *Poetry Project Newsletter 189*, (2002).

Spahr, Juliana. *That Winter the Wolf Came*. Oakland: Commune Editions, 2015.

Spahr, Juliana. *This Connection of Everyone with Lungs*. Berkeley: University of California Press, 2005.

Spahr, Juliana. *The Transformation*. Berkeley: Atelos, 2007.

Spahr, Juliana. *Well Then There Now*. Boston: David R. Godine, 2011.

Srnicek, Nick, and Alex Williams. *Inventing the Future: Postcapitalism and a World Without Work*. London: Verso, 2016.

Stavrides, Stavros. 'Common Space as Threshold Space: Urban Commoning in Struggles to Re-Appropriate Public Space'. *Footprint*, 2015, 9–19.

Stivers-Isakova, Valerie. 'Review: Lidia Yuknavitch's *The Chronology of Water* - A Body Memoir Gone Viral'. *HuffPost*, 2013. https://www.huffpost.com/entry/the-chronology-of-water_b_2681133.

Suvin, Darko. *Metamorphoses of Science Fiction: On the Poetics and History of a Literary Genre*. Oxford: Peter Lang, 2016.

Sweeney, John. 'Signs of Postnormal Times'. *East-West Affairs: A Quarterly Journal of North-South Relations in Postnormal Times* 1, no. 3/4 (2013): 5–12.

Swift, Jonathan. *Gulliver's Travels*. Oxford: Oxford University Press, 2005.

Tally, Robert T., Jr. *Utopia in the Age of Globalization: Space, Representation, and the World-System*. New York: Palgrave Macmillan, 2013.

Thebault, Reis, Luis Velarde, and Abigail Hauslochner. 'The Father and Daughter Who Drowned at the Border Were Desperate for a Better Life, Family Says'. *Washington Post*, 2019. https://www.washingtonpost.com/world/2019/06/26/father-daughter-who-drowned-border-dove-into-river-desperation/.

Thompson, Kelly. 'Breaking the Binaries: A Conversation with Lidia Yuknavitch'. *The Rumpus*, 2017. https://therumpus.net/2017/04/breaking-the-binaries-a-conversation-with-lidia-yuknavitch/.

Timberg, Scott. 'Leave It to Cory Doctorow to Imagine a Post-Apocalyptic Utopia'. *Los Angeles Times*, 2017. https://www.latimes.com/books/jacketcopy/la-ca-jc-cory-doctorow-20170525-htmlstory.html.

Trexler, Adam. *Anthropocene Fictions: The Novel in a Time of Climate Change*. Charlottesville: University of Virginia Press, 2015.

Tronti, Mario. 'A New Type of Political Experiment: Lenin in England'. In *Workers and Capital*, 65–72. London: Verso, 2019.

Trueman, Matt. 'Gillian Slovo: The Riots Act'. *The Stage*, 2011. https://www.thestage.co.uk/features/2011/gillian-slovo-the-riots-act/.

Tuhus-Dubrow, Rebecca. 'Cli-Fi: Birth of a Genre'. *Dissent* 60, no. 3 (2013): 58–61.

Turner, Victor. *The Ritual Process: Structure and Anti-Structure*. Ithaca: Cornell University Press, 1977.

UNHCR. *Refugees & Migrants Arrivals to Europe in 2018 (Mediterranean)*. Geneva: UNHCR, 2018. https://data2.unhcr.org/en/documents/download/68006.

United Nations. *The Global Social Crisis: Report on the World Social Situation 2011*. New York: United Nations Publications, 2011. http://www.un.org/esa/socdev/rwss/docs/2011/rwss2011.pdf.

Vieira, Fátima. 'The Concept of Utopia'. In *The Cambridge Companion to Utopian Literature*, edited by Gregory Claeys, 3–27. Cambridge: Cambridge University Press, 2010.

Voyce, Stephen. '"Poetry and Other Antagonisms": An Interview with Commune Editions'. *The Iowa Review* 47, no. 1 (2017): 177–87.

Waldman, John. 'With Temperatures Rising, Here Comes "Global Weirding"'. *Yale Environment 360*, 2009. http://e360.yale.edu/features/with_temperatures_rising_here_comes_global_weirding.

Wegner, Phillip E. *Imaginary Communities: Utopia, the Nation, and the Spatial Histories of Modernity*. Berkeley: University of California Press, 2002.

Wegner, Phillip E. *Invoking Hope: Theory and Utopia in Dark Times*. Minneapolis: University of Minnesota, 2020.

Welch, Tana Jean. 'Entangled Species: The Inclusive Posthumanist Ecopoetics of Juliana Spahr'. *The Journal of Ecocriticism* 6, no. 1 (2014): 1–25.

Whitman, Walt. *Leaves of Grass: Comprehensive Reader's Edition*. New York: New York University Press, 1965.

Witkin, Robert W. 'Why Did Adorno "Hate" Jazz?' *Sociological Theory* 18, no. 1 (2000): 145–70.

Woodbury, Mary. 'Interview with Cory Doctorow, *Walkaway*'. *Dragonfly: An Exploration of Eco-fiction*, 2017. https://dragonfly.eco/interview-cory-doctorow-walkaway/.

Woolf, Virginia. *A Room of One's Own*. Chichester: John Wiley & Sons, 2015.

Yuknavitch, Lidia. *The Book of Joan*. New York: Harper, 2017.

Žižek, Slavoj. *The Year of Dreaming Dangerously*. London: Verso, 2012.

Index

Adorno, Theodor W. 30, 125, 170
anthropocentrism 29, 152–3
anti-capitalism *see* neoliberalism, Occupy Movement, oppositional movements, precarity
apocalypse
   capitalism 2
   in *Exit West* 68, 76–7, 80
   in *New York 2140* 97–8, 108, 120
   in *The Book of Joan* 151–2, 155
artificial intelligence 148–9

Baccolini, Raffaella 9, 103
Bacigalupi, Paolo 9, 103, 134
Barrett, Ross 37, 41
Bell, David M. 15, 16, 20 n.7, 115, 126
Berlant, Lauren 9, 10, 65, 108, 117, 118
Bernes, Jasper 25, 50
Blackmar, Elizabeth 113–14
Bloch, Ernst 3, 14, 47, 56, 80–2, 119, 125, 170, 173
Bookchin, Murray 78, 79
border regimes 55–7, 58, 65, 68, 84–6, 87 n.7
Brecht, Bertold 54 n.52, 170
Brigstocke, Julian 13–14
Butler, Judith 149
Butler, Octavia 6, 129 n.29

Canavan, Gerry 96, 97
capitalism *see* neoliberalism, petrocapitalism
Chambers, Claire 60, 63, 88 n.24, 90 n.61
Chambers, Iain 79
climate change fiction (cli-fi) *see* climate crisis, science fiction
climate crisis
   climate change fiction (cli-fi) 9
   contemporary 11, 171–2
   in *New York 2140* 93, 101–5, 111–13
   in *The Book of Joan* 151–2

Clover, Joshua 12, 25, 45, 50, 121–2
cognitive estrangement 49, 54 n.52
Collis, Stephen 31, 33, 50, 96
commons
   commoning 17–18, 33, 106–10, 115–16, 126, 136
   economic 36
   enclosure 17–18, 67, 109, 115, 123
   in *Exit West* 79–80
   history 2, 8, 36
   literary 3, 27–31, 96–9
   in *New York 2140* 105, 106–11, 113
commons poetics
   defined 3, 170
   and ecopoetics 27
   in *Exit West* 58–60, 86
   in *New York 2140* 105–6, 120
   in *That Winter the Wolf Came* 30–4, 35
   in *Walkaway* and *The Book of Joan* 137–9, 162
commons utopias (literary tendency)
   late capitalist setting 4, 7–10, 13, 50, 73, 96–8, 127–8, 135, 140–1
   readerships 8, 10, 99, 110–11, 135, 138–9
   spatiality 8, 14–18, 105–28, 143–4, 170
   temporality 10–14, 42–3, 45–6, 48–51, 96–7, 138, 170–1
   virtual 143–4, 148–9
Cooper, Brittney C. 47, 49
Covid-19 pandemic 7, 172–3
crisis 7, 28, 76, 115–20, 122; *see also* apocalypse

De Angelis, Massimo 17, 33, 106, 108
decoloniality 58–9, 64–5, 75–6, 87 n.13
Delany, Samuel R. 5, 123
Deleuze, Gilles, and Guattari, Felix 15
Dickens, Charles 98–9
disaster communism 119–20, 127
disaster studies 115–20

Doctorow, Cory 8, 9, 19, 21 n.21, 133–51, 161–2, 173, 174
Dos Passos, John 98–100, 109
Drage, Eleanor 144, 147–8
dystopia 5–6, 67, 103–4, 137–8

ecopoetics 26–7
ecosystems 35, 155–6
Edelman, Lee 158
Endnotes (collective author) 12, 144

Fielding, Harry 98, 99
Fritz, Charles E. 116–18

genre 9, 29–30, 61, 63, 73, 95–104, 139, 169
George, Rosemary Marangoly 63, 73
Global Financial Crisis (GFC) 6, 7, 97, 172
global warming *see* climate crisis
Grattan, Sean Austin 173
Grenfell Tower fire 75, 120

Haines, Christian 12, 14, 31, 45
Haiven, Max 8, 13, 17, 46, 96, 110
Halberstam, Jack 135–6, 149, 160
Hamid, Mohsin 8, 9, 18, 55–86, 93, 135, 146–7, 162, 174
Haraway, Donna J. 72, 134
Hardt, Michael, and Negri, Antonio 32–3, 45
Harvey, David 10, 15–16, 79
Heimat 56, 80–3
home 66–7, 73–5, 79–80
Hunter, Megan 9, 103

immortality
  in *The Book of Joan* 152, 160–2
  and capitalism 134
  in utopian literature 133–4
  in *Walkaway* 141–3, 147–51, 161–2
intimacy
  in *The Book of Joan* 153–4, 159
  in *Exit West* 82–3
  in *New York 2140* 104, 124–6
  in *That Winter the Wolf Came* 28–9, 34, 43, 48–9
  in *Walkaway* 149
Invisible Committee (collective author) 12, 38

Jameson, Fredric 1–2, 4, 6, 11, 94–5, 119

King, Natasha 65, 84–5

Lamm, Kimberly 32
Language poetry 26, 33, 35
Lefebvre, Henri 15–16
Le Guin, Ursula K. 1, 5, 130 n.42, 164 n.25
Lerner, Ben 111–12
Levitas, Ruth 15, 33, 82, 103, 125
Lewis, Sophie xi, 127, 161
liminality
  spatial 12–13, 68–71, 74–5, 77, 93, 106
  subjective 71–3, 75–6, 85, 111
Lorey, Isabel 149–50
Lotringer, Sylvère 45–6
love *see* intimacy
lyric 26, 33–4, 39, 43–4

Mars trilogy (Robinson) 6, 94–5
Marxism 10, 12, 15–16, 38, 45, 82, 121–2, 144–5
Massey, Doreen 16–17
migrancy
  migrant autonomy 55–6; *see also* mobile commons
  migrant camps 61, 70, 71, 74, 77–8, 113, 116–17, 146–7
  migrant literature 63, 73
  migration crises 56, 113–14, 122–3
  Syrian refugee crisis 7, 57
mobile commons 55–6, 83–6, 146
More, Thomas 4, 133
Moylan, Tom 3, 4–5, 9, 103, 138, 173
Muñoz, José Esteban 136, 137, 145, 149, 158, 159, 161
music 33–4, 47–8, 67, 109, 124–6

Nasta, Susheila 73–4, 75
necropolitics 57–8, 158
neoliberalism
  in *Exit West* 56, 84
  in *New York 2140* 108, 117–22
  queer subjects 136–7
  in *The Book of Joan* 151–2, 162
  in *That Winter the Wolf Came* 32, 39–40
  utopian literature 4, 6, 7, 9–11
  in *Walkaway* 141, 149–50, 162

Occupy movement 7, 26, 33, 42, 44–8, 50, 70, 115, 138, 173–4
ongoing present 2, 9–12, 97–8, 118–19, 170
oppositional movements 6–7, 13, 36–8, 70, 170–4
Out of the Woods (collective author) 118–19, 127

Papadopoulos, Dimitris 83–4
parataxis 3, 35, 39, 53 n.34, 59
petrocapitalism 29, 36–43
Piercy, Marge 5, 173
portal fantasy 61
posthumanism 32, 134–5, 148–9, 152–3, 159, 161
precarity
    anti-precarity movements 32
    capitalism 7, 117–19, 144–5, 149–51, 172
    in *Exit West* 76
    literature 9
    queer subjects 135–6
prefiguration
    commons utopias 13–14, 15, 18, 170–1
    commons 32–3
    disaster communism 119–20
    music 126
    in *That Winter the Wolf Came* 49
    in *Walkaway* 140–1
protest camps *see* Occupy movement
protest *see* oppositional movements
Pynchon, Thomas 47, 146

queerness
    queer identities 71–2, 123–4, 135–7, 147–8, 149, 150–1, 153, 157–62
    queer theory 134–6, 149, 158–9
    queer time 153, 155–7

refugees *see* migrancy
Rigby, Kate 27
riot 44–8, 117, 120–2
Robinson, Kim Stanley 6, 8, 18–19, 93–128, 142, 162

Rosenzweig, Roy 113–14
Russ, Joanna 5

San Junipero (*Black Mirror* episode) 136–7, 143, 148
Sargent, Lyman Tower 103
science fiction (sf) 9, 95–6, 100–3, 134, 138–9, 140, 151
Sergeant, David 97, 100
Sheller, Mimi 84–5
Skinner, Jonathan 26–7
Soja, Edward W. 16
Solnit, Rebecca 116–19, 139, 170–1
space
    inhabiting 17–18, 62–3, 70, 111, 115
    production of 8, 15–17, 115, 123, 150
Spahr, Juliana 8, 18, 25–51, 126, 135, 136, 162
speculative literature *see* science fiction
Stavrides, Stavros 17, 70
surplus 44–5, 120–1, 144–6, 148

technology
    in *Exit West* 66, 68, 77–9
    in *New York 2140* 101
    in *The Book of Joan* 159
    in *Walkaway* 141–2, 145–6, 148–9
Trump, Donald 57, 135, 138
Tsianos, Vassilis S. 83–4
Turner, Victor 69, 71–2

utopian literature
    educational function 3, 5, 8, 15, 169
    genre blurring 9–10
    periodization 4–6, 169

Wegner, Philip E. 16, 20 n.7
Whitman, Walt 97, 98, 116–17
Worden, Daniel 37, 41

Yuknavitch, Lidia 8, 19, 133, 134, 137–9, 151–7, 162, 173, 174

www.ingramcontent.com/pod-product-compliance
Lightning Source LLC
Chambersburg PA
CBHW052119300426
44116CB00010B/1727